Principles of Primary Education

This fully updated, third edition of *Principles of Primary Education* provides a solid foundation for student teachers on all types of initial teacher training courses – Postgraduate Certificate in Education (PGCE), BA Qualified Teacher Status (QTS), BEd and modular – and for those returning to teaching after a career break or considering moving from secondary to primary teaching. Based on tried-and-tested materials, each chapter provides an interactive overview to different aspects of education that trainee teachers require to pass the standards for QTS.

A friendly, supportive and interactive style enables the reader to take control of the learning process. There are planning sheets, proformas and reminders to develop effective classroom practice, and each chapter is linked to the QTS standards and sets out learning objectives, activities and references to further sources of guidance. The Every Child Matters (ECM) agenda is highlighted throughout the book, as is the changing role of teachers and other professionals in school, making *Principles of Primary Education* invaluable reading for all trainee teachers as well as students on courses such as Education Studies, Children's Studies and foundation degrees.

Pat Hughes is Senior Lecturer in Primary Education at Liverpool Hope University College and has taught extensively in early years, primary and further education settings. She has written numerous publications for teachers, students and children including the in-house version of this text, initially developed as the core text for PGCE courses at Liverpool Hope.

Principles of Primary Education
Third edition

Pat Hughes

Routledge
Taylor & Francis Group

LONDON AND NEW YORK

First published 2000
by David Fulton Publishers

This edition first published
by Routledge
2 Park Square, Milton Park, Abingdon, Oxon, OX14 4RN

Simultaneously published in the USA and Canada
by Routledge
270 Madison Ave, New York, NY10016

Routledge is an imprint of the Taylor & Francis Group, an informa business

© 2000, 2002, 2008 Pat Hughes

Typeset in Bembo by
Florence Production Ltd, Stoodleigh, Devon
Printed and bound in Great Britain by
MPG Books Ltd, Bodmin, Cornwall

British Library Cataloguing in Publication Data
A catalogue record for this book is available from the
British Library

Library of Congress Cataloging-in-Publication Data
Hughes, Pat, 1945-
    Principles of primary education/Pat Hughes. — 3rd ed.
        p. cm.
      1. Education, Primary—Great Britain.   2. Primary school
    teaching—Great Britain.   I. Title.
    LB1507.H858 2008
    372'.941—dc22   2007042485

ISBN10: 0–415–45324–0 (pbk)

ISBN13: 978–0–415–45324–0 (pbk)

Contents

Illustrations

Figures

Tables

Acknowledgements

Ken Bevan, Adam Chamberlain, Helen Clegg, Kath Cox, Janet Evans, Cath Carson, Geoff Farrell, Steve George, Wendy Hall, Philip Hallman, Les Hankin, Pat Holden, Norman Jones, Arthur Kelly, Sam and Suzanne Kerr, Hilary Letts, Paul Lock, Keith McDougal, Ila Miller, Jean Robb, Jan Rowe, Lisa Seddon, Julie Sheriff, Keith Skinner, Eric Smith, Abigail Williams, Richard Wood.

Challenging and enthusiastic primary PGCE students – full-time and distance-learning – who helped to form and develop this ever-evolving course over many years. Knowsly PCT.

The following primary schools provided critical documents, advice and support:

Cheetham Hill CE, Eccleston Lane Ends, Deepdale Infants, Longview CP, Overdale CP, Prescot CP, St Patricks, Eaves CP, St Martins.

Abbreviations

ADD/ADHD	attention deficit (hyperactivity) disorder
AfL	assessment for learning
ALPS	accelerated learning in primary schools
ARG	Assessment Reform Group
BECTA	British Educational Communications and Technology Agency
BEM	beginning, ending and middle
BERA	British Educational Research Asssociation
BLP	building learning power
BSF	building schools for the future
CAF	Common Assessment Framework
CLC	city learning centre
CoRT	Cognitive Research Trust
CPD	continuing professional development
CPR	child protection register
CRB	Criminal Records Bureau
CVA	contextual value added
DCSF	Department for Children, Schools and Families (from 2007, replacing DfES)
DED	disability equality duty
DfEE	Department for Education and Employment
DfES	Department for Education and Skills (now DCSF)
DH	Department of Health
EAL	English as an additional language
ECDL	European computer driving licence
ECM	Every Child Matters
EiC	Excellence in Cities
ESCalate	Higher Education Academy Education Subject Centre
EWO	education welfare officer
EYFS	early years foundation stage
EYP	Early Years Professional
FACE	family and community education
FE	further education
FSMs	free school meals
GTC	General Teaching Council
HE	higher education
HLTA	higher level teaching assistant

ICE	information, communication and entertainment
ICS	integrated children's services
ICT	information and communications technology
IEP	individual education plan
ITT	initial teacher training
KAL	knowledge about language
KS	Key Stage
L2L	learning to learn
LA	local authority
LAC	lower achieving children
LSA	learning support assistant
LTR	learning and teaching responsibility
MFL	modern foreign language
MHF	Mental Health Foundation
MIS	management information systems
NAGC	National Association for Gifted Children
NCSL	National Council for School Leadership
NFER	National Foundation for Educational Research
NHSS	National Healthy Schools Standard
NLC	network learning community
NLS	National Literacy Strategy
NNF	National Numeracy Framework
NQF	National Qualifications Framework
NQT	newly qualified teacher
NUT	National Union of Teachers
Ofsted	Office for Standards in Education, Children's Services and Skills
PANDA	performance and assessment data
PCT	primary care trust
PDA	personal digital assistant
PE	physical education
PFI	public funding initiative
PGCE	Postgraduate Certificate in Education
PMFL	primary modern foreign language
PIPS	performance indicators in primary schools
PLP	personal learning plan
PSHE	personal, social and health education
QCA	Qualifications and Curriculum Authority
QTS	Qualified Teacher Status
Raiseonline	reporting and analysis for improvement through school self-evaluation
SATs	Standard Assessment Tasks/Tests
SEAL	social and emotional aspects of learning
SEF	self-evaluation form
SEN	special educational needs
SENCO	special educational needs co-ordinator
SMART	specific, measureable, achievable, realistic, time-related
SMT	senior management team
SNA	special needs assistant
SNR	special needs register

SOW	schemes of work
SWDB	School Workforce Development Board
TA	teaching assistant
TASC	thinking actively in a social context
TDA	Training and Development Agency for Schools (replacing TTA from 2005)
TES	*Times Educational Supplement*
TLR	teaching and learning responsibility
TTA	Teacher Training Agency (now TDA)
VAK	visual, auditory and kinaesthetic
WALT	we are learning to . . .
WIIFM	what's in it for me?
WILF	what I'm looking for . . .
Y	Year (as in Y2, Y5)

Introduction

Welcome to the world of lifelong learning

The purpose of this study guide is to act as the framework for a basic course in the Principles of Primary Education. It provides an overview of the changing face of primary schools and covers the professional standards of education which initial teacher training (ITT) students require to gain QTS. The course is based on the Primary Education course taught over two terms to Liverpool Hope University full-time PGCE students; to distance learning students on their two-year part-time course; and to undergraduates on an Education Studies course. The latter course is on disc and takes the form of voice-over presentations with notes. It is supplemented by material from the final year of the BA QTS and from practice in a number of schools. This means that the majority of the activities recommended have been tried, tested and modified by students and by primary teachers. Good teaching demands constant refinement. It is a lifelong process and teachers are lifelong learners. This is just the start.

The *initial target audience* for whom this guide is written covers:

- *full and part-time student teachers*;
- *trainees* on the variety of non-traditional routes into primary teaching;
- *students on undergraduate courses* such as Education Studies, Advanced Study of Early Years or Childhood Studies, who wish to see how formal schooling links with aspects of their course;
- those taking a *foundation degree* and those thinking of topping up to become a teacher;
- *school mentors*, who will find it useful to know the type of course their students are undertaking and ways in which the QTS standards can be exemplified;
- *experienced teachers* – as an opportunity to update reading in the area;
- *teachers considering taking a higher degree* – as a first step to getting back to academic reading;
- *new teachers* – supporting them in their induction year;
- *teacher returners*;
- *staff development officers* – to identify starting points for courses, particularly those for newly qualified teachers (NQTs);
- *colleagues in higher education (HE)* – and in school-based training schemes who need to devise distance learning materials for primary teacher training;
- *new primary school governors* interested in looking at how primary schools work today;
- *secondary teachers* who wish to follow a conversion course for primary teaching;

- *multi-agency workers* in health, social care, etc. who spend considerable time in primary schools and would like to understand more about how they work and the impact this has on children.

How to use the guide

Student teachers will find it most useful to work through the guide a section at a time. Although the text is presented in a linear progression, earlier units will need revisiting in order to support later ones. Other readers may prefer to pick out different sections in accordance with need. For example, a school governor with responsibility for special needs would look initially at the chapters on 'Special Children' and the last three chapters on current issues. Secondary teachers using the guide to familiarise themselves with primary education might turn first to Chapters 11 to 15 on planning and curriculum.

Activity and thinking tasks have been included to provide opportunities for critical reflection on both text and school experience.

Updates

Education is changing rapidly and readers are advised to consult Government websites. These include the Office for Standards in Education, Children's Services and Skills (Ofsted); Department for Children, Schools and Families (DCSF); and Qualifications and Curriculum Authority (QCA). The Every Child Matters (ECM) website provides a useful insight into integrated children's services (ICS). However, it is useful to remember that all these websites have a political dimension and can be usefully balanced with information from the teaching unions, the educational press and 'teachers TV'.

Writing style

The guide has been written informally, in order to convey the personal flavour of a taught course. It is not an academic piece of work, but guides readers to more academic texts to encourage self-supported learning. Children's names used in examples have been substituted with fictitious ones to avoid offending anyone.

This style of writing presents more of a challenge, because the view of the writer is more obvious and sometimes controversial. So if you do find yourself disagreeing, getting cross or angry with the text, good. This means it's succeeding! There are few easy answers, quick fixes or foolproof plans for teaching. We all need continually to try and learn.

The course

The course aims to give students a flavour of proven, research-based practices employed by thousands of other effective teachers. Educational research is not exclusively theoretical and the course seeks to improve primary practice by using what the research has identified as effective practice. This is becoming more important now as more PGCE courses look towards providing both a post-graduate teaching qualification and a gateway towards a Master's degree. This is reflected in other agencies that are becoming more closely linked to schools through the ECM agenda.

Educational research is a fluid process, and teachers need to contribute to it as well as update themselves. It has also acquired a powerful new partner: technology. Readers interested in looking at recent research findings in education should consult websites such as that for the British Educational Research Association (BERA) and the Higher Education Academy Education Subject Centre (ESCalate). These both provide useful weblinks for educational research in the UK.

Organisation of the guide

The guide is divided into four sections – People in Primary Schools, Learning, Planning and Curriculum and Current Issues/Changing Patterns. This reflects changes in the organisation of schools; the key role of understanding how children learn; how teachers and other adults plan, monitor, assess and feedback; and finally, the key role primary schools are playing in areas such as integrated children's services.

1 Understanding primary schools today

QTS Standards

5, 6, 20, 21b, 32, 33

Learning objectives

- to be able to identify different personnel working in a primary school;
- to examine the roles of the teaching assistant (TA), learning mentor and parent mentor;
- to gain some understanding in the multi-agency dimension of primary schools;
- to acquire skill in creating a situation analysis.

Changing personnel

Activity/Thinking Task 1

Write down as many people as you can think of who might be working in a primary school. Next time you go into school, look again at who is working there and add any personnel you missed when you did this task the first time. You will find the school prospectus useful in identifying the posts of some of those you may have met. Most schools have their prospectus on the school website.

Most people, outside the primary sector, when asked this would probably start off with teachers. Then, if there remained a pregnant silence, would move on to other school-based workers such as site managers, cleaners and a secretary. When children are asked this, they generally include themselves very early on. It is as if we retain a memory of the old Victorian and Edwardian photographs of classrooms with a teacher, pupils and perhaps the odd pupil monitor. Today's schools are staffed very differently and the primary purpose of this chapter is to help readers to identify some of the less obvious but extremely important personnel working in today's primary schools.

A tour round a primary school

I spend a lot of time in primary schools and this is an example of a brief tour I took round a school last week. I arrived at the school at 8.30 and standing on the playground, talking to a parent was Adam, the learning mentor. Later we will look at his role more closely. It is useful to remember at this stage that the titles, roles, responsibilities and pay of many of the support workers varies from school to school and from one LA to another.

I entered the school, pushing the doorbell to check me into the building. The small office is staffed by a secretary and two administrative assistants. Also sitting there at 8.45 was the site manager and the head teacher. Both of these had been in school since 6.45 and were having a well-deserved cup of tea. A TA was using the photocopier.

After signing in and saying my hellos, I then turned left into the school and walked down a small set of steps, which were altered some years ago to accommodate children, staff and visitors with mobility issues. Turning into the first room, I met with the parent mentor, three parents and one eight-month-old baby. We chatted briefly about the work they were going to be doing and I moved down the corridor to meet with a teacher with whom I work. Her senior management post changed recently from being a subject co-ordinator to holding a post as a LTR (learning and teaching responsibility). There were three other adults with her in the classroom. One was a TA and the other a special needs assistant (SNA). Neither would be in the same classroom all day. The third adult was a student teacher undertaking a placement. On another day in this same classroom, there is a trainee TA. All four adults have children's learning as their key responsibility and, at the time of my visit, the class teacher was organising her team for the day to ensure that maximum learning takes place.

I then came out of this classroom and entered another one. This was my reason for visiting the school. For on Tuesdays, I am a student taking a European computer driving licence (ECDL). The class is run by a further education (FE) lecturer from the local community college. The other students are either parents or people working in the school. We are all doing different courses and are at different stages. The provision is part of the LA programme called FACE – family and community education. Its aim is to 'skill up' members of the local community, to give them confidence as well as skills to improve their and their children's life chances.

When I left the school three hours later, I met with the local safety inspector who was running a cycling award course on the playground for the Y5 children.

All these people were school based because it was seen that their work enhanced children's learning. This has been made even clearer under the Every Child Matters agenda (DfES, 2003), although at least two of those I met on my tour would not be under the remit of the ICS department of the local authority (LA).

Roles and responsibilities

There were many other workers in school on my tour day. These include the welfare staff, who supervised the children at lunchtime and who have had several courses on outdoor play; the cook and catering staff who had been involved with courses on healthy eating and hygiene; voluntary workers; specialist support staff; professionals from other public services; professionals from charities; and once a week one of the local priests who takes an assembly in this non-denominational school. He is also a school governor. In this chapter we are concentrating on identifying those different groups whose work is directly linked to enhancing children's learning. They can be categorised into four different groups:

1   those employed directly by the school;
2   educational support workers, not employed by the school, but whose service may be paid from the school budget;
3   external providers who are employed by other public and private agencies;
4   volunteers.

These adults are often given the generic title of paraprofessionals. The Training and Development Agency for Schools (TDA) calls them support staff. I prefer the term allied educational professionals as it recognises the professional work they do with children within a formal educational context.

Allied professionals employed by the school

The teaching assistant, the special needs assistant and the learning mentor whom I met would all come into the category of allied professionals. They and other allied professionals may:

- work semi-autonomously with pupils throughout the day and report to a line manager within the school;
- give generic learning support in classes or learning units with work or assessment tasks prepared by the class;
- work with a child identified with special learning needs;
- work or manage a unit or centre within the school such as a nurture group for children who need particular support in the school situation;
- work in more than one role, e.g. a TA in the morning and a learning mentor in the afternoon;
- have variable training and qualifications.

The government is determined, quite rightly, to try and ensure that all those working in schools have the appropriate qualifications to do so. These are still very variable and can be school based; cluster based; LA, FE or HE based; nationally based – including on-line provision; self-determined professional development and life-experience based. Many allied professionals have qualifications prior to their employment by a particular school.

Not only does training vary but so does salary. Some allied professionals are on yearly full pay, like teachers; many are paid 'pro-rata' – for example, paid for only 45 weeks of the year, rather than 52; some pay may be based on qualifications and specialist skills held; some on recommended national rates. Some may be school based, often through more informal negotiation and some are negotiated at local level via trade unions.

Educational support workers – not employed by the school, but whose services may be paid from the school budget

There is a range of other workers, not employed by the school directly, but whose work can be closely linked to improving and enhancing children's learning. They are often employed in more than one school and may cover secondary as well as primary pupils. These include:

- counsellor
- pupil attendance and education welfare
- special needs integrated support
- behaviour support
- ethnic minority support
- integrated children's services manager
- educational social worker.

External providers – employed by public and private agencies, including charities

Table 1.1 Some of the educational professionals who provide services to schools

Generic LA (integrated services, leisure, libraries, etc.)	Emergency duty team (safeguarding)	Youth offending team
CAFCASS (Court and Family Court Advisory Support Service)	Primary Care Trust (NHS), e.g. school nurses, dentists	Child and adolescent mental health services
Substance misuse	Anti-smoking	NSPCC
ChildLine	Barnardos	Children's Society
Before and after school clubs	LA initiatives linked to specific strategies such as literacy, numeracy and citizenship	Play and holiday schemes
Theatre in Education	Author/artist in residence schemes	Creative partnerships
Police/road and/or rail safety	Faith workers	

Volunteers

There are also, particularly in primary schools, unpaid volunteers. Some may spend whole days in school, others just a couple of hours a week and others may work in several schools. These include:

- parents and carers and other relatives;
- community workers;
- partnership workers;
- governors;
- student teachers;

- work experience/trainees;
- former teachers;
- charity workers, where the school pays an agreed amount to the charity for administration but the worker is unpaid, e.g. Volunteer Reading Help (VRH).

Activity/Thinking Task 2

Revisit your original list of allied professionals and try to identify who you meet on a daily basis. You may like to organise them under headings and make a brief note of their major responsibilities, as you understand them.

Exemplars

In the following section we look very briefly at three of those whom I met on my visit around the school. They are the learning mentor, the TA and the parent mentor.

The learning mentor

Twelve years ago it would have been rare to find learning mentors in the English education system or indeed many of the other allied professionals found now. Learning mentors have a generic brief to 'break down barriers to learning'.

The history of their introduction and success in schools provides a useful rationale for many of the role definitions we now find assigned to allied professionals. For this reason, a brief look at their development provides a useful practical as well as theoretical base for this chapter. A much fuller version is available in Campbell and Fairbairn's (2005) book on support staff.

Table 1.2 Template for Activity/Thinking Task 2

Name or title of member of staff	Responsibilities	Employed by
Comments:		

Background

Learning mentors came from one strand of the DfES Excellence in Cities (EiC) programme. This was introduced in March 1999 to tackle 'specific problems facing children in our cities. Through a combination of initiatives, EiC aimed to raise the aspirations and achievements of pupils and to tackle disaffection, social exclusion, truancy and indiscipline and improve parents' confidence in cities' (Hughes, 2005).

The EiC initiative had come out of some good practice projects from within the UK, but also had imported ideas from the US (e.g. magnet schools). The programme was largely met with enthusiasm by the schools where it was originally introduced, who saw it as a recognition that more than words were needed to raise aspirations and hope for pupils in their schools. Since then the initiative has expanded across most schools in the country and has been subject to two excellent National Training Programmes. These training programmes provided mentors with a formal qualification in mentoring.

The current DCSF website on learning mentors defines learning mentors as:

- salaried staff who work with school and college students and pupils to help them address barriers to learning;
- a bridge across academic and pastoral support roles with the aim of ensuring that individual pupils and students engage more effectively in learning and achieve appropriately;
- a key ingredient in many school and college approaches to improving the achievement levels of pupils and students.

The overall purpose of their role is to promote effective participation, enhance individual learning, raise aspirations and help pupils achieve their potential (Hayward, 2001). This involves mentors having a good knowledge as well as skills base. Many learning mentors have degrees and some are former teachers. Particular aspects of the mentor's role are useful to see in relation to other allied professionals whose role it is also to raise achievement in schools. Table 1.3 shows just a few of the tasks learning mentors undertake to break down barriers to learning.

The teaching assistant

When I first started teaching in a primary school in the late 1970s, the only classroom support in the school was a nursery nurse, who worked across two reception classes. Since then there has been a massive increase in the number of support workers in classrooms. In this section we are looking at the growth and changing role of such TAs, while being aware that other workers in the classroom may have a different name but be doing much the same role. They are all working to break down barriers to learning.

The number of TAs in English schools rose from just 60,000 in 1997 to more than 153,000 today. They are nearly all expected to have or to acquire some basic related qualifications, if they do not already have some:

- one out of ten has completed training in order to become a higher level teaching assistant (HLTA);
- a survey by the Institute of Education in London shows that one in eight TAs is educated to degree level or above;

but

- one in five has no permanent contract; and
- only one in seven was paid during school holidays;

and

- 98 per cent of all TAs are women.

Initially, the sharp growth in the number of teaching assistants, since 1997, can be linked to three different factors: the inclusion of special educational needs (SEN) pupils into mainstream schools; the introduction of National Literacy and Numeracy strategies, which required additional adult support in primary schools and technological advances. During this time, both training and responsibility for teaching assistants developed. In the government publication, *Raising Standards and Tackling Workload* (TDA, 2003) the work of the teaching assistant was linked to teacher workload, but it impacted significantly on

Table 1.3 A few of the tasks learning mentors undertake to break down barriers to learning

Strategy	Rationale
1 Monitor and improve attendance – this involves developing whole-school and individual strategies to encourage reluctant attenders to come into school	Ensure students build up a habit of attending school and reinforce to both carers and pupils that this is important. Ofsted inspections see attendance as a crucial issue and government legislation distinguishes between authorised and unauthorised absence.
2 Establish one-to-one mentoring and other supportive relationships with children and young people	To support individual pupils who are failing to learn effectively for a variety of reasons. Mentors draw on their knowledge and skills to provide effective strategies to enable pupils to feel more 'relaxed and alert' about coming to school and being confident about learning. They may run specific activities to help pupils with issues such as anger management, emotional development, anti-stress. These areas form an important part of their training.
3 Support the PSHE curriculum within schools – often through individual work, but also via direct teaching with whole classes, e.g. circle time	Mentoring training involves drawing on new insights into PSHE. They are often the only ones in schools who receive regular training on these issues and their knowledge of individual pupils can help inform other integrated children's and young people's services such as health and social care.
4 Establishment of schools councils and parliaments	Empowering students to feel that they have a voice in their community; providing practical exemplars of citizenship; identifying key issues about the inner workings of the school that may be missed by adults, e.g. bullying.

changes in the roles and responsibilities of teaching assistants. Table 1.4. shows some of the tasks today's teaching assistants might undertake.

Activity/Thinking Task 3

Interviewing a teaching assistant

1   find a teaching assistant who is willing to be interviewed about their work;
2   find out how long they have been employed as a teaching assistant;
3   ask what sort of jobs are they doing;
4   ask what they enjoy most about their job;
5   have a look if possible at their job description and evaluate whether the job description fits with their current responsibilities.

The status – if not the pay – of teaching assistants was raised when the Teacher raining Agency (TTA) became the TDA and in its revised remit was charged with training responsibility for all those working in schools. Their roles are very directly related to breaking down barriers to learning for individual pupils, and often providing non-contact or supply cover for teachers. It can be argued that this provides continuity and is more effective than employing supply teachers. However, it can also be argued, mostly notably by the National Union of Teachers (NUT), who were not originally party to this agreement, that this extension of the role can be a cheap way of fulfilling the government's promise to decrease teacher workload.

Table 1.4 Some of the tasks today's teaching assistants might undertake

Provide specialist support for literacy, numeracy, ICT	Run booster classes	Be early years managers
Work as 'nurture' group leaders with small groups of children in separate units within schools	Become behaviour support specialists; either in classrooms monitoring behaviour and devising strategies, or in separate units	SEN specialists
Act as cover supervisors	Teaching assistant manager	Travellers pupil specialist
Provide EAL support	Be counsellors	Carry out the 20 administrative tasks under the 2003 Workload agreement that teachers no longer have to do
Act as invigilators and markers for SATs	Be resource administrators	Support parental liaison administrators
Anything else created uniquely to suit the school's needs and TA expertise		

Table 1.4 shows how comprehensive the role of the teaching assistant has become. Some of it is administrative, some teaching, some pastoral. It will vary from school to school, as do the names for those performing the role.

Parent/carer mentors

Educating or 're-educating' parents and carers has been seen by several governments over many decades to be one of the ways in which children's learning, behaviour, sense of citizenship, etc. can be improved. It has been school based and area based. A considerable slice of the adult education budget in many authorities has been linked with the second aspect of parent mentoring, namely equipping parents with the skills to produce the sort of citizens who know their responsibilities. At the time of writing, 'parenting' is receiving a good deal of attention by central government and parenting officers are being appointed by LAs, often at quite a senior level. This initiative is often seen as part of Community Education and involves new courses being created. These are nearly always school based. They may be called parenting courses, but they often hide under other names such as Family Learning, and a number of 'Helping your child . . .'.

I should confess here, that I have mixed views about 'parenting' courses. As a parent I would never have attended one and wonder about those who are so confident in what makes a good parent. Paid parent mentors tend to be found in economically disadvantaged areas, where central government targets parents and carers in order to support their own children's learning and development. It is worth remembering that poverty does not make a poor parent; nor wealth a good one. So why does the concentration on 'parenting' always seem to focus on those living in deprived areas? Our newspapers show only too clearly that the children of the wealthy and/or aristocracy undertake many of the anti-social activities their poorer and less privileged peers do.

One major advantage in these types of courses, is that they are often a safe and convenient way back into education for parents and carers. They usually provide opportunities to develop new skills and qualifications. Many primary schools have a good history of providing such courses for their local communities, so the current parenting initiative is not a particularly new one, but builds on good practice.

On my tour, the parent mentor was employed in a LA where there had been a recently created Family Learning service. This aimed to provide a range of courses and activities that:

- helped parents/carers engage with and support their children's learning and development;
- provided opportunities for parents/carers to develop new skills and gain qualifications;
- supported children's learning;
- provided a rage of other support, e.g. credit union, health awareness, volunteering.

The service acknowledged that because learning was a whole family, inter-generational process there was more than one way of working than a set of specific 'parenting programmes'. The parent mentor programme was therefore just a very small part of a much wider initiative, funded initially by central government through a programme known as the 'New Deal for Communities'.

Activity/Thinking Task 4

Tracking an allied educational professional working and employed by the school.

1   Identify the role and responsibilities of an allied educational professional working in a school. Ideally look at their role description.
2   Track and later record their work for the equivalent of two half days. Remember you are not a trainee Ofsted inspector and the purpose of doing the tracking is to learn about the role itself. Ideally, do the written recording *after* the tracking. If you do not understand elements of what you have observed, ask.
3   Evaluate what you have learnt about the work of this specific allied professional and the implications for the role of the class teacher.

NB. If you can manage it, track the role of more than one allied educational professional, e.g. an NNEB (National Nursery Examination Board) working as a teaching assistant, a special needs worker.

Situation analysis sheet

It is useful for you to build up information about any school that you are going to work in. This is the same whether it is work experience, attachment, a long term placement or permanent post.

Basic details

Collect a copy of the school prospectus, if possible prior to the work in school. Many primary schools have their own websites and usually put the prospectus on it. Some schools have really excellent sites and you will gain a great deal of information about the school, its curriculum, projects the children are involved with and lists of staff. A prospectus should have the following information:

*   practical details about the school;
*   information about admissions;
*   dates of school holidays;
*   the times at which each school session begins and ends;
*   charging and remissions policy;
*   ethos and values;
*   curriculum statement, teaching methods, special arrangements including SEN;
*   a SEN policy statement;
*   details of religious education provided and parents' rights to withdraw their child from religious and collective worship;
*   any affiliations with a particular faith or religious denomination;
*   complaints handling;
*   sporting aims and provision;
*   KS1 and 2 assessment results – school and national;
*   rates of authorised and unauthorised absence.

Additional useful information to collect:

- The number of free school meals (FSMs) – this gives some idea of the economy of the catchment area. The national average for FSMs is about 19 per cent. Central and local government use this as part of the 'contextual data' that is built up into a figure for contextual value added (CVA). Schools are placed in local clusters according to the number of FSMs. Standard Assessment Tasks/Tests (SAT) results are then related to this.
- numbers of children with English as an additional language (EAL);
- numbers of children on the special needs register (SNR);
- provision of extended services such as Kids Clubs, pre-school provision, adult and community courses, extended school provision.

The school's latest Ofsted report will provide this information and can be obtained from the Ofsted website.

The local community

Walk round the immediate catchment area of the school. A faith school is likely to have a very much wider catchment area than the local community school, but looking at the catchment area is important. Later we look at how planning the curriculum has to be related to both the needs of the pupils and the needs of the local community. When you walk round the catchment area note:

- amenities – the presence or absence of shops, parks, community centres, places of worship, libraries, swimming pools;
- different types of housing – flats, bungalows, houses, town houses, caravans, farms. Note whether the housing is privately owned or council/housing trust;
- quality of the environment – tidiness, noise, general pollution, graffiti;
- physical features – rivers, hills, factories, local industries, farmland;
- physical evidence of the history of the community – monuments, war memorials, buildings, street names, movements of people;
- cultural diversity.

Activity/Thinking Task 5

What implications do these features have, if any on:

1 planning
2 teaching and class management
3 attainment and progress.

For example, the presence of a local swimming pool and swimming clubs, makes it much more likely that pupils can swim. A local library gives opportunities for borrowing books and using IT outside school hours. If possible, discuss your findings with someone who works in the school.

---

2 Teachers in a changing role

Learning objectives
- to identify the changing role of the teacher in today's primary schools;
- to re-examine our own experiences of schooling and teachers;
- to begin to develop an understanding of standards relating both to teaching and other allied educational professionals working in primary classrooms.

The role of the teacher

A good teacher

Several years ago the TDA ran a series of television advertisements, showing a number of celebrities who made statements about the names of teachers who had made a difference to their lives. It is this idea that the individual can make a difference that guides many people into teaching. They want to be that person who makes a difference to children's lives. Interviewees for ITT often give this as one of their prime reasons for wanting to be a teacher.

Activity/Thinking Task 1

Maybe, like me, you didn't immediately think of a good teacher. I remember Mrs A very well. She was my class teacher when I was nine. She once threw chalk at me because I could not do fractions. I feared and hated her and later blamed her for my maths O-level failure, because I became frightened of the subject and believed I was no good at it. It took another teacher, at evening class, to convince me that my maths was recoverable and I eventually passed the exam in my early thirties. Looking back, I can see a tired, impatient and bored woman, who found the subject easy herself and could not understand why an A-stream child was having problems. She made a difference to me, not only because of my maths failure, but also when I did become a teacher, I remembered my fear of her.

My favourite teacher of all time was Mrs Crawford, who inspired a love of literature that has stayed with me all my life. Why? She loved it herself and could sell Chaucer and Donne to a group of cynical sixth-formers. She was also a very happy woman and clearly enjoyed her life both inside and outside school. I knew nothing about learning and teaching strategies then, but the contrast between these two teachers has stayed with me for life.

We all have a rich experience of teachers through our own schooling, and it is worth thinking through this carefully because we learnt about the role of teachers and schooling with them. Yet schools, teachers and children have changed with the demands of society and the role of the teacher has changed with it. In later chapters we look at how our knowledge about learning has changed with developments in neuroscience and technology and how this has also changed roles within schools.

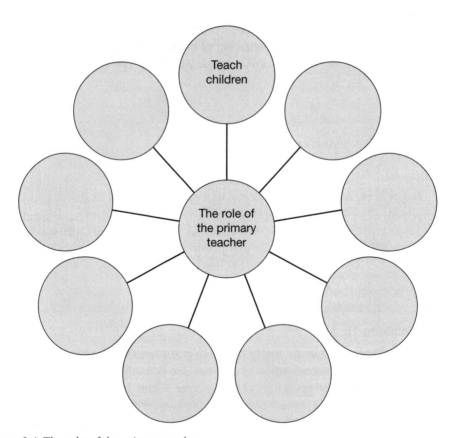

Figure 2.1 The role of the primary teacher

Activity/Thinking Task 2

Photocopy Figure 2.1 and fill in on it what you feel is the role of the teacher. Don't think about it too much, the idea is that it is what you are thinking at this stage of reading the book. Look at it again when you finish the course and see how your views have changed. Take a second photocopy and ask someone else to complete it. Compare the differences. Differences may be due to age, gender, experience and/or culture.

Compare your sheet with the one in Figure 2.2, which has been filled in by a primary Ofsted inspector. Schools are inspected to specific criteria and the inspector linked these criteria to her perception of the role of the teacher in today's society. It is not comprehensive and you should be able to think of at least five additional roles. And you may disagree with some of those suggested. Try looking at this week's *Times Educational Supplement* (*TES*) and that will probably carry several stories that document at least one additional role for teachers!

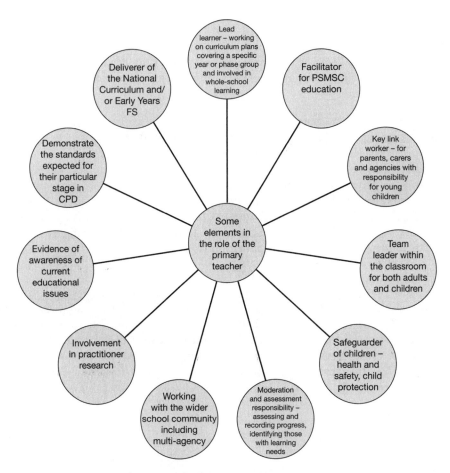

Figure 2.2 A personal view from an Ofsted inspector

Teachers in some other countries might be very surprised at some of the roles suggested for our teachers. A friend who trained in Ghana said that he was amazed when he came to England to find that schools expected him to be concerned about the social welfare of his children. He had come from a system where educational knowledge was perceived very differently and children had a different concept both of their role and that of the teacher.

Table 2.1 shows a generic job description for a classroom teacher. Does this provide anything else that should be recorded under the role of the primary teacher?

National Standards for Qualified Teacher Status

In 1992 the DfES (now the DCSF) published a series of 'competences' for student teachers. These changed over the years and in 1998 were published as Standards by the then TTA. The National Standards for QTS identified for the first time the professional knowledge and skills required by trainee teachers to gain full qualified status. These standards are now on their third revision and can be found on the TDA (2007) website.

Progression

The standards form a progression from student teacher to teacher, followed by the induction year, which must be passed in order to progress. The standards for NQTs cover three interrelated areas:

1   *Professional attributes*: relationships with children and young people (Q1 and 2); frameworks (Q3); communicating and working with others (Q7–9).
2   *Professional knowledge and understanding*: teaching and learning (Q10); assessment and monitoring (Q11–13); subjects and curriculum (Q14 and 15); literacy, numeracy and information and communications technology (ICT) (Q16 and 17); achievement and diversity (Q18–20); health and well-being (Q21).
3   *Teaching*: planning (Q22–24); teaching (Q25); assessing, monitoring and giving feedback (Q26–28); reviewing teaching and learning (Q29); learning environment (Q30–31); team working and collaboration (Q32–33).

And if you were wondering the 'Q' stands for 'Qualified'.

No teacher can begin their induction period before they have met all of the standards, which are also underpinned by the five key outcomes for children and young people identified under the ECM agenda and the six areas of the common core of skills and knowledge for the children's workforce. This formalises, for the first time, the need for QTS standards to fit in with the much wider agenda for those working with children. It is also worth noting that the 2007 standards defined the characteristics of teachers at each career stage:

- the award of QTS;
- teachers on the main scale;
- teachers on the upper pay scale;
- excellent teachers;
- advanced skills teachers.

Table 2.1 Job description for classroom teacher at Sundale Community Primary School

Job description for classroom teacher

General duties

a) To be responsible for the education and welfare of the class to which they are assigned in accordance with the requirements of the Conditions of Employment for Schoolteachers.

b) To have due regard to the requirements of the National Curriculum, the aims of the school, its objectives, ethos, schemes of work and policies.

c) To share in the corporate responsibility for the well-being and discipline of all pupils.

Specific duties

- To carry out the duties of a school teacher as set out in the School Teachers' Pay and Conditions document.
- To take responsibility for the progress of a specific group of children in all aspects of the National Curriculum and its cross curricular elements.
- To take pastoral responsibility for a specific group of children.
- To plan and record each pupil's attainment in all areas of the curriculum.
- To contribute to curriculum development in conjunction with colleagues. All areas are to be developed for the 3–11 age range.
- To ensure that there is continuity, progression, breadth and balance in the delivery of the curriculum.
- To create a safe, stimulating learning environment that encourages children to work and behave to the best of their potential.
- To ensure the classroom reflects the best standards of work displayed to full advantage.
- To organise the classroom so that all resources are easily accessible to pupils, used correctly and with respect.
- To ensure the safe welfare of the pupils.
- To plan and prepare lessons in advance, evaluate as necessary and present records to the head teacher on a regular basis.
- To mark and access regularly and constructively.
- To monitor each child's progress effectively by keeping regular records available for the head teacher and parents when requested.
- To bring to the attention of the head teacher and the SENCO [special educational needs co-ordinator] any child with SEN.
- To produce written reports for parents and to keep parents informed of their child's progress through regular meetings.
- All teachers will be expected to accept such responsibilities as the Headteacher shall determine from time to time.

Note 1 You will be required to ensure that all duties are carried out within the context of the school and LA policies on race, gender and special needs.

Note 2 The job description may be reviewed and amended at any time after discussion between the named teacher and the Headteacher.

Note 3 Grievance procedure: The LA's Grievance Procedure for Teachers as recommended to Governing Bodies applies in relation to any grievance arising in connection with this Job Description.

Activity/Thinking Task 4

Visit the TDA website and look at the standards identified under the heading 'professional attributes'. How might you evidence any one of these?

This looks like a daunting task, but you will soon become familiar with them and skilled in being able to unpick what you do and relate it to specific standards. The vast majority of student teachers quickly become confident and competent in what is required of them. This happens because there is some sort of progression through the standards. At the start student teachers spend most of their time looking at how teachers manage their classes and worry about whether they will have a riot on their hands once they take over. In learning how to 'manage' a class and/or a small group, they realise that they must look at content as well. This involves observing and investigating planning, monitoring, explaining, questioning, giving feedback and assessment, but the initial comments of most student teachers are often limited to the 'survival' standards of child behaviour. Later, they look more carefully at how they can exercise their role to help children make progress and raise their attainment. These strategies involve other standards, such as motivating children; establishing a purposeful and safe learning environment; and collaborating and team working with other allied professionals, within the classroom, and in the wider school community. Assessing, monitoring and giving feedback are closely linked to planning, since all planning has to be informed by learners' progress. There is little purpose in ploughing through a scheme of work if learners have not followed key elements of it.

Above all is the real acknowledgement that successful teachers need to have and continue to develop a strong body of knowledge and skills in order to be effective in their work. This body of knowledge is massive and growing all the time. It obviously covers the pedagogy of teaching, but it also covers knowledge about children's and young people's development and skills in being able to observe and respond to such development. Take just two examples: neuroscience and technology. None of this 'new' pedagogy is fixed and requires us all to have interpretative and evaluative skills as we are introduced to new ideas.

Qualifications and standards for learning support staff

The School Workforce Development Board (SWDB) was set up in 2004 to advise the TDA about professional training and development for all support staff working in schools. By 2007 there was a reasonably well-established support staff framework linking the NQF with the different roles of support staff in school. If we take a teaching assistant for example; at Level 1 they would be expected to hold a qualification such as a foundation award in caring for children. At Level 3 a teaching assistant might have an A-level or its equivalent, such as a certificate for teaching assistants or certificate of professional development in work with children and young people. A foundation degree would be at Level 5 and an undergraduate degree in education or any subject would be at Level 6. The PGCE comes in at Level 7. And many PGCE courses today, cover the early stages of a Master's course. Of course it does not mean that teaching assistants are all paid at the appropriate rate – but that is another story. This approach to professional qualifications and standards has been an important development in recent years and was part of the rationale for changing the name of the TTA to TDA. Formerly the

TTA had only been concerned with the training of teachers. Its remit now covers all support staff in schools.

This is certainly an area where the expression 'watch this space' is very relevant. The extended schools initiative, for example, is likely to provide additional roles for learning support staff. Further details about qualifications and standards for learning support staff can be found on the TDA website. The support staff framework provides a very useful guide to some of the qualifications required by support staff employed by the school.

The General Teaching Council

The General Teaching Council (GTC) is the professional body for teaching in England. It is similar, but not as powerful, as other professional organisations such as the General Medical Council for doctors and the General Nursing Council for nurses. Their stated purpose (from the GTC website) is 'to help improve standards of teaching and the quality of learning in the public interest. We work for children, through teachers.' All these bodies have their own professional standards and regulations and all teachers must register with the GTC. The GTC's Registration and Regulation committee oversees its disciplinary functions to ensure that professional standards are upheld fairly and transparently. A look in the *TES* most weeks will show one or two cases where teachers have been seen to fail to meet these professional standards and must then satisfy the regulatory body that they can meet requirements. Penalties that the GTC can impose are:

- Reprimand: kept on the register for a fixed period of two years;
- Conditional Registration Order: the teacher can remain on the register under certain conditions;
- Suspension Order: the teacher is suspended from the register and cannot work as a registered teacher for a stated period of time – up to two years. After this they are automatically eligible to register again;
- Prohibition Order: the teacher's name is removed from the register and they cannot work as a registered teacher. The committee may allow them to reapply after no less than two years, if they wish to do so.

The professional journey

The effective teacher

Activity/Thinking Task 4

Think of four characteristics of a well-managed classroom or nursery that help your class teacher and other adult workers to organise and manage teaching and learning time effectively. Would you expect big differences between the nursery and a Y3 class – between a Y2 class and a Y6 class?

You may see this as a fairly easy task, but if you discuss the task with others, you will find that people have very different views about what makes effective classrooms and schools.

And this includes the many research findings that have sought to discover the 'perfect' formula to maximise learning.

In my view the four characteristics that immediately spring to mind are:

1   a focus on learning rather than teaching – the teacher and other adult workers taking the role of guide, rather than 'sage on the stage';
2   children deeply involved in their work – and this includes the youngest as well as the oldest;
3   very little wasted time – allowed that we do all need 'time out' and keeping busy is no guarantee that learning is taking place;
4   a task orientated, purposeful working environment. Sometimes teachers photograph examples of children at work and put the pictures on the wall as an ongoing reminder of how learning is conducted in the classroom. This also gives parents and carers an opportunity to see how learning takes place in a variety of different ways.

Teachers must also maintain a good pace to the lesson and set appropriate targets for children to achieve during the lessons and small group activities. These need to be monitored and assessed systematically. Provision of meaningful continuation and extension work for those who complete the set tasks early, and presentation of pupils' outcomes can also be a factor in achieving an appropriate commitment to work. The physical environment and resourcing of the classroom will provide the background for a purposeful working atmosphere. Ask yourself how the adults communicate expectations about the way in which children should behave, and how children know what the objectives of the lesson are and the targets they should reach.

Effective teaching areas

Activity/Thinking Task 5

Think of other areas in the school where children are working, for example a school library or canteen. How are these areas enhanced to provide a positive and purposeful ethos?

Recently, I visited a refurbished dinner canteen in a two form entry primary school. The original building dated from 1952 and externally looked much the same. However, the refurbishment has completely changed the ethos of the dining space. Not only do the walls, ceilings, furniture and floor look brand new, they look fit for purpose in terms of 'eating out' in a restaurant. The long tables have been replaced by tables that will seat four, and both tables and chairs look like those you would be quite happy to have in your own home. A salad bar breaks the room up and the whole impression is one of relaxed dining; this is aided by small seating corners with sofas, cushions, etc. from a large departmental store. This also helps to give it a 'grown up' feel. Staff and pupils are delighted because they find it more peaceful and restful. And it is. Behaviour is respectful of others and the dining experience has been turned into a pleasant one. One of the aims is to build up again the number of children wanting to take a healthy school dinner, rather than packed lunch.

Focus on teaching activities

Table 2.2 shows an example of a very basic lesson/activity observation form for either a small group or the whole class activity. The focus for observation is on the teaching activity in the widest sense of 'teaching'.

Table 2.2 Early lesson/activity observation schedule

Early lesson/activity observation schedule: focus on teaching activity		
Date:	Teacher or lead adult:	Age range:
Other relevant information:	Other support adults:	Number in group/ class:
Activity prior to observed activity:		
Transition between prior activity and this one: Resources made available during course of lesson:		
Narrative of lesson/activity with approximate timings:		
What I learnt:		

Table 2.3 Internal lesson observation criteria

Internal lesson observation criteria		
Date: .... Name of teacher:	Lesson:	Observed by: ....
Leadership and management • Clear and effective routines • Identification of potential barriers to learning • Organization and management of the classroom and resources • Effective use of ICT to support teaching AND learning • Encouragement of independence in children: managers of their own learning • Curriculum design and planning • Effective deployment of TAs/other adults		
Culture and ethos • Inclusion – provision for all groups of children • Positive pupil response • Presentation of work: adults and children • Active listening skills: adults and children • Celebration of achievement		

Raising standards

- Evidence of high expectations
- Standards achieved by children
- Progress made within the lesson
- Use of assessment for learning
- Use of marking/target setting
- Verbal feedback/use of dialogue to elicit challenge

Teaching and learning

- Structure and pace of lesson
- Achievement of lesson objective
- Effective use of demonstration and modelling
- Creativity and inspiration

The way forward:

Table 2.3 provides an example of early lesson/activity observation carried out on qualified teachers in school. It is identified at this early stage in the book, because as you move through, you will be observing effective learning, rather than teaching. Some teaching can look very charismatic, but unless it results in effective learning, it stays as a 'performance', rather than an effective medium for supporting children and young people. Such performances can motivate learning, but they can also be rather like the good after-dinner speech, where you can remember it was entertaining, but not what it was about.

This observation format can then be adapted for more detailed analysis of the lesson/activity content. For example, observation of a traditional literacy or numeracy lesson may be broken down into parts:

1 general introduction
2 introduction to the lesson
3 development
4 plenary.

If the class is put into ability groups and different tasks given, then the lesson observation needs to record the nature of groups as well as the differentiated tasks.

Teachers are now very accustomed to being formally observed by students, colleagues, line managers, head teachers, local authority (LA) personnel (e.g. School Improvement Teams), Ofsted inspectors, etc. These all have a particular focus and it is usual to identify what the focus of the lesson or activity should be. When the student is looking at the teacher as 'the sage on the stage'; they might find it useful to focus in the next observation on how and what a small group of children are learning.

Table 2.4 What teachers (and other adults) bring to teaching

Knowledge of the learning process	*Views of what pupils should learn*	*Personality*
Expectations of children as learners	Management of resources	What is valued by (a) themselves and (b) by society
Beliefs about the pupil's role	Personal experience as learners	Understanding the curriculum
External constraints – size of room and number of children and adults; funding and resources; central and local government initiatives; school and network/ cluster initiatives	Organisation of the physical environment	Organisation of children
Views about the purpose of learning	Knowledge of individuals	Personal values and attitudes
Structured learning experiences (planning)	Teaching style	Nature of learning activities

What teachers bring to teaching

Table 2.4 acknowledges that teachers and other adult colleagues are not robots, they bring a great deal of themselves into the classroom or early years setting. This partly explains why children may react differently to different teachers. The table also acknowledges that there are many other influences on what happens in teaching – such as the size and shape of a room and number of other adults in it.

Further reading

When you first start out in a classroom, you are learning the basic techniques of the role of the teacher in supporting children's learning. Much of the knowledge and skills behind the apparent calm that an effective teacher creates are hidden. Some of this skill comes from school based research that has used the findings from many observations of children, pupils, teachers and teaching areas. Both educational psychology and sociology look at the role of the teacher in much greater detail. Psychology texts look at the different factors involved in the teacher's role and use role theory to analyse different types of role conflict and strategies that can be used to resolve these. It is often useful to look at this role theory at the start of a course because it can identify and name some of the processes that may be going on in your lives. Think of some of the roles you have – family roles such as parent, daughter, brother, aunt or cousin; work roles such as student, bar person, cleaner; community roles such as charity worker or football coach. For example, the work role may conflict with social or family role. Role theory enables us to stand back and look at how different elements of the teacher's role may conflict and cause stress. No wonder so many books on teaching finish up with suggestions about relieving stress.

Educational sociology texts have been much less fashionable over the past few years, but the move towards more multi-agency work, means that all those working in schools need to have a broader understanding of the world outside the school and how schools are fitted into that. Sociology looks at the role of the teacher much more broadly and often very controversially. Schools can be viewed as microcosms of society and the inequalities within society are not only reflected in schools but can be reinforced by the school. How society views the role of the teacher can be expressed locally or nationally and can influence the ways in which teachers view themselves and the work they do. This in turn influences the education children receive.

3 Learning from children

4, 5, 10, 18, 19, 21a,b, 22, 25, 28, 29, 30

Learning objectives

- to develop knowledge and skills in small group observation and teaching;
- to recognise some of the internal and external factors that influence children as learners;
- to identify ways in which these insights can be used to enhance learning.

> Better learning will not come from finding better ways for the teacher to instruct but from giving learners better opportunities to construct.
>
> (Seymour Papert, Professor Emeritus, MIT Media Lab)

From child to pupil

I am not sure that I entirely agree with Papert, unless he replaces 'instruct' with 'tell'; but I certainly think we need to work to enable children to have more opportunities to 'construct' their own learning. We look at this in more detail in the next few chapters. In this chapter we look at ways in which we can learn from the children themselves and so 'construct' our own learning about children learning from what we observe, rather than some idealistic concept of what a child should or should not do in an early years or school setting at any particular age.

Developing constructs of a pupil

When a child is born, s/he is not a pupil. One of the many things babies and young children learn in the UK is how to become a pupil at a very early age. Indeed, statutory schooling in the UK starts well before it does in many other European countries. Being in an early years setting and being a pupil are very different experiences from being at home, learning from siblings and adults around you. A pupil is a social construct, not a natural part of development like being a baby or a toddler. There may be no formal standards for a pupil – as yet – but most of us have a very clear idea of what makes a good pupil and conversely what makes a difficult pupil. Most of these are shared constructs, but there are often differences between the social construct of a 'good' pupil in one school and a 'good' pupil in another school. You will also see this within a school, where children can become very different 'pupils' and children (Jones, 2008) depending on their teachers. This is also about differing constructs of pupils. One of the reasons we involve children in creating rules and routines within individual classrooms and early learning centres is to provide shared constructs about 'standards of behaviour' for 'pupils' in this early years setting, this classroom, this school.

Inclusion and constructs

Most obvious are the differing constructs that teachers and other adults have about boys and girls. A quick look in any toy or clothes shop demonstrates the very differing constructs the commercial market has for boy babies and girl babies, boy toddlers and girl toddlers. We hold more hidden constructs for children who come from different heritage and cultural groups from our own and for children with SEN. Fortunately, constructs are not fixed and we can, if necessary, change the constructs we have of individual children, but in order to do this we need to be open about change and reflective about our evaluations of what we observe in early years settings and classrooms.

Evidence for forming a particular construct needs to also contain evidence about the circumstances in which the construct is being formed. Little girls who stand on the edge of the playground in small groups, may not be choosing to be more active for a variety of reasons – the playground is being occupied by a group they do not wish to challenge; they may have unsuitable clothing and footwear for active play; they may have been told to keep clean; or there is nothing for them to do. I did a piece of fun data collection after noticing how in some KS1 classes after physical education (PE), some girls were unable to do their hair without adult support because they had so many hair accessories. In my region I found that the less the number of hair accessories the higher the SATs results. I felt it might be linked with the encouragement of independent dressing at home! So I now hold a construct about pupils with bands, ribbons, etc.

A key standard for QTS, is that students need to have high expectations of children and young people and this must include a commitment to ensure that they achieve their full educational potential. If, when you reflect on constructs you hold for different children, you realise that some of these are basically labels for low performance, you need to challenge yourself to look more carefully and widely at why you hold these constructs.

Changing pupil constructs

Let's take a historical example of a child as a social construct, which has changed. The Victorians had a construct of the child as someone who should be seen and not heard. Actually reading literature on Victorian childhood, this construct was far from universal, but it is the construct that comes to us from the upper classes of the Victorian elite. This has certainly changed to the construct we have of children today.

Turning to education and the construct of a pupil, the 1967 Plowden Report on Primary Education (CACE) constructed a view of the pupil as 'active, engaged in exploration or discovery, interacting both with the teacher and with each other. Each child operates as an individual, though groups are formed and reformed related to those activities which are not normally subject-differentiated.' This is not the image you and I probably have about the pupils in today's schools; although it may be one we hold of children in early years settings. The Plowden pupil construct was also criticised at the time as being the image of a male pupil, rather than a female one.

I would like to think that all pupils are naturally curious, but see enough of classrooms to know that this isn't necessarily so. Later we will look at some of the reasons why, and strategies schools use to promote this innate curiosity and motivation to learn.

The focus in today's schools and early years settings is on the construct of 'pupils as learners'. In 2007, the terminology of the Standards for QTS was changed to reflect this. The term 'pupils' from the previous standards was changed to 'learners'. When primary Ofsted inspections started in 1995, inspectors were told to write of 'pupils' when writing their reports on children at KS1 and 2, and as children when writing about the under fives.

We also tend to assume that everyone had the same understanding about a construct of learning. This is just not so. Politicians, for example, make many public statements that show that they have very distinct views about what learning is and how learning takes place – or should take place – in school. And there are massive differences between their views. Different philosophies about learning are closely linked to the particular social construct of the pupil. The Victorians had a concept of the pupil as a blank slate. What the teacher taught, the pupil learnt. Sometimes it seems as if politicians and advocates of particular teaching strategies still have this blank slate approach. In this chapter, we begin to look at why learning is far more complex.

A philosophy of learning

When you apply for any post involving teaching in its widest sense, you are often asked to write something about your own personal educational philosophy. You are then often asked to exemplify this at interview. This recognises that what teachers and other adult support workers do is to bring with them their own personal school experience, parental experiences and academic study.

Table 3.1 gives you a chance to look at what you believe about learning.

Activity/Thinking Task 1

Use Table 3.1. as a checklist to decide what you believe about learning. No one is marking this, so don't tick what you think is the 'right' answer, tick what you actually believe. There is no need to discuss it with anyone else unless you want to. But you will probably find it helpful as well as interesting. An insight into our own beliefs should make us more reflective about assuming that everyone holds the same beliefs.

The table was adapted from Guy Claxton's (2005) work on building learning power (BLP), which we look at in greater detail in Chapter 17. As Claxton writes:

> all learners sometimes find learning difficult. It can be messy and confusing and often defies detailed planning. Good learners are able to work independently but they also

rely on learning with and from other people – including teachers. Good learners know when to give up: at least for the time being, until they find a suitable resource to help combat the difficulty. They make plenty of mistakes, but are always on the look-out for ways to learn from them.

Thanks to the television advertisement about not knowing the answer, but knowing someone who does, we all have a better idea that being a good learner is not about how much you know, more about how you go about getting to know more. It is particularly important for children to learn and see models of learners in their teachers and other supporting adults. Learning is not just a matter of skill; it involves personality and values. Self-esteem by itself does not improve learning, but it will increase whenever learners become more competent. One of the characteristics of a good learner is that they can recognise when learning is difficult, but are unafraid to try different strategies to improve their skills and knowledge.

Table 3.1 What do you believe about learning?

What do you believe?	Yes	No	Evidence from own experience as a learner
1 Good learners find learning easy			
2 Good learners are well organised			
3 Good learners never give up			
4 The best learners are totally independent			
5 Good learners don't make mistakes			
6 Being a good learner is about how much you know			
7 Good learners are very logical			
8 There is usually one best way to learn			
9 Self-esteem is the most important influence on learning			
10 Success at school means you are a good real-life learner			

Now look at the children in your group. How do these beliefs link with your own observations of children in

1 a classroom/early years setting;
2 out-of-school activity (children in a shop, learning a new skill, playing sports, etc.).

Part of learning from children is recognising that one's own school and personal experiences are partial and should be influenced and informed by further observing, reflecting, reading and discussion with peers and teachers. This involves developing a professional view of education, schools and learning; as well as an ability to change deeply held ideas. One of the most exciting things to observe is a teacher, or other school based professional, teaching something in a completely different way from one you would use – and then watching as you observe some extremely successful learning coming out of it.

School beliefs

Schools also have surprisingly different educational philosophies about how their children learn, and this is sometimes possible to identify in their initial mission statement or stated aims and objectives. One example is how the rapid growth in the number of faith schools is influencing what appears on their timetables. Proportions of time on different subject areas may vary. Some faith schools have religious education timetabled for every day. In some other faith schools, areas of the curriculum may completely disappear, e.g. ICT, because the faith school has particular views about IT and Internet access. The public sector of education must comply with government legislation and cover all the National Curriculum; but the private sector has more freedom, provided they can convince Ofsted of their effectiveness.

So by the time you have finished reading this book, undertaken the tasks related and spent a considerable time in school, we would expect your views to change. This would include:

- Your knowledge about the learning process. This covers both how children develop as well as how they learn. This should also cover your own learning process, unless you are supremely confident that your learning strategies are totally effective.
- Your beliefs in the child's role in learning. There are some very fundamental differences in values about this. At one extreme, children are seen as blank slates onto which governmental and commercial packages can be written; at the other end of the spectrum, children are seen as creating their own learning environment that is personal to themselves, and all teaching must be centred towards the learning needs of the child. The political pendulum swings backwards and forwards between the two extremes, and most teachers adopt a pragmatic approach that leans towards their own particular philosophy and that of the school in which they work. There is sometimes little choice; some of our most troubled children have to have a very distinctive personalised curriculum.
- Your views about the purpose of learning. School learning can be viewed as functional and utilitarian aimed at equipping the workforce with the skills it needs, or it can be seen as developing the whole child.
- Your views about what children should learn. A brief look at the history of education in England shows very different views over time. The Victorian Sunday Schools limited the education they provided to teaching children to read the Bible, which was later extended by the Board Schools to basic literacy and numeracy. Initially, it was thought that if the masses could write it might produce revolution! By the 1950s and 1960s there was a wider view of what was important. The National Curriculum in 1988 formalised this into subject areas. By the mid-1990s, it was narrowed again to increase the percentage of time spent on the direct teaching of literacy and numeracy.

The new millennium has seen many other aspects thrown into the primary school cauldron – modern foreign languages (MFLs); citizenship – both global and national; outdoor education and awareness; creativity and health education in its broadest sense.

• Your personal experience of education – both the good and the bad.

Activity/Thinking Task 2

Write down very quickly what you feel makes a 'good' pupil. Then discuss your concept of a 'good pupil' with someone else. What does it tell you about yourself? Were you a 'good' pupil? How might it influence you when you are teaching?

A definition of learning

One simple definition of learning is that it is a process that goes on inside a person. Teaching then becomes an attempt to effect change in someone from the outside. This is relatively easy if you are measuring learning in terms of behaviour, as the behaviourists did. It is much harder when you want to see whether a child has 'understood' a concept or changed its attitude about something.

Clearly the processes of learning and teaching are distinct but interrelated, although the relationship is rarely straightforward. The mistake the media and politicians make is that they think it is straightforward. Everyone is an expert on education. After all, we have all been through it.

During learning the following things can happen:

1 learning arises without direct teaching – for example sometimes when children are trying to make sense of their world and hypothesise about their ideas;
2 learning arises as a result of teaching – for example, when learners are encouraged to mix paints to produce different colours;
3 learning arises in spite of teaching, either positively or negatively – for example, when children learn that they can avoid going outside at playtime by offering to do jobs for the teacher;
4 learning is different from that intended by the teacher – this could be as a result of an inadequate, confused or incorrect explanation.

Activity/Thinking Task 3

Next time you are with a small group of children, inside school, try to find some examples of each type of learning.

You may be quite amazed by what children learn without direct teaching (1) and 'get a buzz' from the knowledge that the children are learning from activities you plan and teach (2). Different emotions arise from learning taking place in (3) and (4). This can cause frustration and annoyance, but it can also be amusing and puzzling. It helps to imagine what it is like to be a learner in any group with whom you may be working.

Now try the exercise with a child or children outside the school setting.

Small group teaching and learning

Challenges of small-group teaching

After student teachers have been into school on a couple of occasions, they sometimes feel that the small-group work to which they have been assigned is in some way inferior to the whole-class work that the teacher is undertaking. It is, in fact, probably the one time in most teachers' careers where they have the opportunity to sit down to observe and reflect on children's learning and learn how children learn. If we can develop some understandings about how children learn this gives guidance to planning for effective teaching to improve learning. Both knowledge and skills in this area are enhanced through a careful combination of theory and practice. Educational psychology informs practice, but it needs mediating, as there is no simple formula for enhancing children's learning. Small-group teaching develops skills that can later be translated to planning, teaching and assessing work for the whole class.

Setting small-group tasks

One of the main learning advantages of being assigned to a small group and working one-to-one with individual children is that the class-management aspects of teaching can be delegated to someone else, i.e. the class teacher. It then becomes possible to set individual and small-group tasks and watch as children tackle them. At first many of these tasks will be set by the class teacher, which frees the student teacher from the planning aspect of teaching so that he or she can observe, analyse and assess the learning taking place.

Several of the standards require an in-depth knowledge about children's learning, which can only be gained through working with individual children and in small groups. This requires both watching and listening carefully to children, analysing their responses and responding constructively in order to take their learning forward. Good assessment is heavily dependent on being able to gauge how successfully the learning objectives have been achieved and using this to improve specific aspects of teaching.

Small-group work is also a good opportunity to evaluate the effectiveness of different teaching strategies to improve children's learning. It soon becomes clear that children's learning styles vary and teaching strategies must be multi-sensory. Some children in your group may have ineffective learning styles and therefore you need to identify what strategies they are using in order to help them to try out more appropriate ones. One of the most common ineffective learning styles is that anything that looks challenging is greeted by the child as requiring adult help. Adult support therefore needs to help child develop other strategies as well as asking immediately for adult help. Depending on the activity, these strategies can include re-reading the task, looking back at what has been done before, asking someone on the same table, moving on to the next task and returning to this one later.

Activity/Thinking Task 4

Table 3.2. is designed as a simple method of recording learning within a group. It provides an opportunity to record simple background information, but the focus is on the learning. The quality of the observation should be informed by what you have read, including those definitions of learning that examined learning arising without direct teaching, as a result

Table 3.2 Early observation schedule on learners

Early lesson/activity observation schedule: focus on learning		
Date:	Teacher or lead adult:	Age of child(ren) observed:
Other relevant information:	Other support adults:	Number in group:
Planned learning outcome(s) – these can be taken from an activity or lesson plan:		
Prior understanding of the learning outcome: (you will need to ask the child(ren) probably)		
Resources made available to the child(ren) during course of lesson to support learning – include those that are added later by you or another adult:		
Narrative of activity with a focus on pupil learning:		
Record a piece of evidence to demonstrate that a particular child as a result of this activity has: Shown interest in the activity: _____ Understood what they were doing: _____ Applied intellectual, physical or creative effort: _____ Understood how well they have done: _____ An understanding of how they can improve: _____ Worked independently: _____ Worked collaboratively: _____		
What were the strongest aspects of learning and why? What needs improvement?		

of teaching, in spite of teaching and learning different from that intended. As with all observations of children, you need to focus on them and use the template after the event to note and reflect. It should take more than one side of A4, and you may want to start with one child, rather than a whole group.

Observing children learning

> There is nothing more unequal than the equal treatment of unequal people.
>
> (Thomas Jefferson)

What children bring to learning

Children are all unique, both as human beings and as learners. Our children come into school with different out-of-school experiences, interests, learning styles and levels of development and ability. Their maturation and age levels vary; they come in different sizes, shapes, colour and genders. The opportunity to work with individuals and small groups for a sustained period of time is a perfect opportunity to gather information about this uniqueness as well as more generic understandings about children as learners. This helps to broaden your construct of what being a child/pupil means.

Table 3.3 identifies some of the features that children bring to learning. You can probably think of some more.

Multiple intelligences

You will have already come across the term multiple intelligences and we will look at it in conjunction with some other learning theories later. Howard Gardner in *Multiple Intelligences* (1993) suggested that there were seven different intelligences: logical-mathematical; verbal-linguistic; musical-rhythmic; visual-spatial; bodily-kinaesthetic; interpersonal-social and interpersonal-introspective. This is often shortened in schools to visual, auditory and kinaesthetic (VAK). Later he added four other possible ones – naturalist, existential, spiritual

Table 3.3 What children bring to learning

Views of them-selves as learners	Influence of home on attitude to learning	Stage of development	Attitude to school
Relationship with the teacher	Existing knowledge skills, concepts	Understanding the activity	Perceptions of an activity's purpose/relevance
Perceptions of worth	Perceptions of 'achievability'	Response to learning experience	Involvement
Influences of culture, race, gender	Physical and emotional well-being	Ability to build positive relationships with other children and adults	Previous experience(s) of educational institutions

and moral. His more recent work looks at a theory of five minds – disciplinary, synthesizing, creating, respectful and ethical. His work has been heavily criticised, particularly by those looking to 'measure' these intelligences.

However, he does make some important points including the very obvious point that we have to move on from the idea that intelligence is a single, measurable entity. The 11-plus introduced after the Second World War, was the English equivalent of this. Primary children of 10 and 11 took the 11-plus examination as a means of assessing whether they should go to a particular type of secondary school. These were created out of the 1944 Education Act as 'modern' schools, 'technical' schools and 'grammar' schools. The grammar schools provided the strictly academic curriculum, while the modern schools provided a less academic more craft-orientated curriculum. The 11-plus examination was believed to be able to measure fixed intelligence for the appropriate school. The 11-plus is still in operation in some parts of the UK and grammar schools are still highly sought after in those areas. Gardner's multiple intelligences enable children and adults to have preferred intelligences, and schools need to broaden their curriculum content to ensure that all children experience these wider dimensions of life.

Later when you profile children in the class, it is important to make sure that you collect data on attainment in a variety of different areas of their lives. This will involve watching children at leisure as well as when they undertake tasks across the whole curriculum. It involves seeing how they create visual-spatial representations of the world and use their bodies. Gardner's theory should have major implications for curriculum planning, because it requires curriculum design to cover all these intelligences. The QTS standards reflect this view of multiple intelligences through their requirement for student teachers to set high expectations for all children – notwithstanding how progress and well-being can be affected by a range of developmental, social, religious, ethnic, cultural and linguistic influences.

The work of Alistair Smith and Nicola Call (2000) on 'accelerated learning in primary schools' (ALPS) has successfully adapted this learning theory for primary classrooms. The resource book accompanying the main text provides some very useful support sheets. It looks at the journey of learning and ways in which teachers can 'extend the horizons of possibility'. This will be examined in more detail in a later chapter.

Activity/Thinking Task 5

Which of Gardner's multiple intelligences are often seen as the most important in drawing up a profile of an individual child? What sort of constructs does this produce in terms of the 'good' primary pupil?

Contexts for learning

Learning takes place inside and outside school and individual learning styles may be influenced by diverse individual preferences. You may be reading this text surrounded by your family and drinking a cup of tea, whereas the author might have written it in a quiet, well-lit, warm room, with fairly regular breaks! Others may be reading in front of the television, in bed, or while moving around.

Individual preferences include those of temperature, sound levels, seating, lighting, group size and eating and/or drinking while concentrating. It is difficult to establish and maintain a purposeful working atmosphere in a classroom that caters for such different preferences.

No one preferred context is better than another, it is just different, although some children's preferred learning contexts may be more appropriate for effective learning in our conventional classrooms. For example, a child who likes to wander around the room can distract others and avoid completing learning tasks. They need strategies to settle down, since a mobile learning style in a room of 30 children is difficult to accommodate and becomes a management problem. Sometimes the strategies exist outside the child; for example, the teacher plans for less passive learning, so that the 'movers' get the opportunity they need to move around.

One of the major advantages of having enough room to provide different types of learning centres in a class is that these areas can provide different types of activity, lighting, seating and sound. They can include reading, interactive science and role-play areas. It is also useful to remember that children, like adults, vary their preferences for different areas of learning, at different times of the day, at different periods of their life and for different types of learning activity. Unfortunately, one of the side issues regarding the greater number of adults working in classrooms and early years settings is that space is often at a premium and the idea of many different learning areas becomes virtually impossible. Ironically, the old Victorian classrooms, in which sadly some of our children still work, usually provide this extra space needed.

Working with individuals and small groups can significantly alter the organisation and management of children's learning. You may find that some children prefer the small group situation and closer adult support. Their behaviour improves, they maintain concentration and become more effective learners. Some children may be disconcerted by the close adult to child ratio and transfer it to their experiences outside school. They may ask personal questions and wish to move from the more formal and professional relationship of child and teacher to child and older sibling. The advice to most student teachers is to avoid this. Keep your role as teacher and encourage the child to develop a small-group learning style that can use the adult to better effect. It is also worth noting that if a child reacts to you like this in a small-group situation, other adults working with small groups may need help to avoid the same scenario.

The growth in allied educational professionals working alongside teachers, often with small groups of children and young people, has significantly altered the dynamics of the classroom. It has also heightened the potential for children's learning. Part of your small-group work, should include identifying effective learning promoted by allied educational professionals, identifying what strategies are being used and how their support improves learning generally in the classroom.

Activity/Thinking Task 6

What learning styles are supported through the teaching and classroom organisation and management in a class you have observed? Are some children having difficulties with this? How might you develop additional teaching strategies to promote a greater variety of learning styles?

Culture, gender and special needs

Earlier we looked at social constructs of what being an effective pupil means. In this section we look at four forms of labelling and classification that can have an important influence in the constructs that both adults and children form of them.

Culture

Culture relates directly to the way in which others see us. Too often, we not only fail to understand people who are different from us, but also view them negatively. Genuinely valuing cultural diversity means that we can establish and maintain a purposeful learning environment that knows about cultural diversity, acknowledges cultural differences and plans for them. Examples of cultural differences that may influence learning are:

- the extent to which children are encouraged to 'speak up';
- attitudes to teachers – male, female, same culture, different culture;
- the use of gestures, eye contact and non-verbal cues when a child communicates with an adult;
- the importance of time;
- oral communication, rather than written;
- a community language spoken at home.

Gender

As we saw earlier, constructs of boys and girls as pupils are often gender related. Boys and girls may often exhibit different behaviour and learning styles, but are entitled to the same chance to participate and learn. Gender research (Hughes, 1991) shows that it is easy to discriminate unknowingly through the type of praise given, the tasks assigned, the questions asked and the time given for a response. Boys, for example, tend to be given more direct instruction, approval, disapproval and attention. Girls tend to get more teaching attention during reading instruction and boys during maths. Girls tend to be engaged with more social interaction with staff than boys. The heavy female bias among both teachers and allied professionals means that boys are frequently faced with a very overt feminine environment. This may influence the particular types of learning styles promoted.

Special needs

Constructs here have moved over the past twenty years. Today, the overriding ideology is that many children labelled with learning difficulties have average or above average intelligence and many are gifted. There is a distinction made between learning difficulties and learning disabilities. The latter are neurobiological disorders that interfere with the ability to store, process and retrieve information. This mostly affects reading and language skills, but can also influence computation and social skills. It may also make no difference at all in the children's ability to do well in school.

The term 'special needs' is less commonly used in the UK to describe very able or gifted children. Definitions, particularly of gifted children, vary considerably, although it is generally agreed that special needs result from both genetic inheritance and environmental opportunities.

Teaching programmes for children with special needs vary considerably. Giftedness covers the multiple intelligences mentioned above, so teaching strategies would need to include physical, musical, intellectual and social challenges.

There are a number of different learning disabilities and most LAs provide good support in terms of identification. Broadly speaking, identification tends to be based on difficulties in more than one of these areas – language, memory, attention, fine motor skills and other functions, such as poor learning strategies and grasp of abstract concepts. Financial restrictions often limit the amount of practical support that can be given, but Ofsted inspection reports indicate huge disparity between different schools within the same area. Some of the major learning difficulties are dyslexia, dyspraxia, visual perception, auditory discrimination, dysgraphia and attention-deficit disorder (ADD). These categories are in themselves controversial, as the discussions in the media about dyslexia demonstrate. Educational consultants such as Jean Robb and Hilary Letts (2002, 2003) are concerned that this type of analysis leads to labelling children, who then respond to low expectations of their learning abilities. They also point out that a whole industry has been created out of special needs provision, while the number of children identified as having difficulties grows, rather than decreases.

Whether or not we agree with Robb and Letts, it is worth observing practical learning strategies that are being used in the classroom or nursery. They tend to be good tips for working with all children:

- applying what has been learnt, discussing what they are doing and what has been learnt, recording through pictures, photographs, role play and construction;
- breaking down stages of learning into small steps, including the purpose of the exercise, clear, precise directions and instructions for task completion;
- ensuring that teaching and class management demonstrate clear structure and routines;
- providing practical experiences to support the learning of abstract concepts;
- paying careful attention to children's errors/misconceptions and helping to remedy them;
- recognising what is achieved successfully and rewarding it, so that children with learning disabilities gain in confidence.

Children in crisis

Children's learning can also be influenced by factors such as poverty, death, the absence of a loved carer, emotional and/or physical abuse, racial prejudice, homelessness, alcohol and drug abuse. This type of stress often leads to behavioural and learning difficulties, but many children in crisis do manage to overcome these. Teachers and other allied professionals in school can be focal support for such children. This adult may be the one reliable adult in that child's life and, through their care and trust, can give the support the child needs in order to learn successfully.

There is an increasing recognition of the need to get extra, specialist help for children when the crisis is too difficult for them to handle. Warning signs include unusual aggressiveness, withdrawal, depression, fearlessness, fearfulness, poor concentration and repetitive and disturbing behaviour such as headbanging.

The Common Assessment Framework

The Common Assessment Framework (CAF) is a standardised assessment that was a direct outcome of the ECM agenda. It was designed to get a complete picture of a child's additional needs at an early stage, rather than multiple assessments from different agencies. In relation to learning it requires evidence about the following:

1 *Understanding, reasoning and problem solving*
Organising, making connection; being creative, exploring, experimenting; imaginative play and interaction.

2 *Participation in learning, education and employment*
Access and engagement; attendance, participation; adult support; access to appropriate resources.

3 *Progress and achievement in learning*
Progress in basic key skills; available opportunities; support with disruption to education; level of adult interest.

4 *Aspirations*
Ambition; pupils' confidence and view of progress, motivation, perseverance.

It might be useful to profile an individual child's learning under each of these categories and use the evidence of your observations to identify evidence of its completion. If you do not have any, it would be useful to find out why; for example you may be only looking at a very narrow element of a child's learning. This reflects a narrow construct of a child as an academic learner. The section on 'aspirations' makes for good small-group discussion material in both Key Stages.

The whole of the CAF can be found on the ECM website (www.everychildmatters. gov.uk), together with a toolkit for its use. It is also possible, through a generalised search to look at the advice given by LAs for its completion and examples of completed CAFs.

Increasing children's learning

It is easy to feel overwhelmed by all this information about what characteristics directly affect children's learning. This is why the initial opportunities for individual and small-group work should be seized upon and used to the maximum. We return to this area of learning needs in Chapters 5 to 10, where the most important thing is to have high expectations for all children and resist labelling.

The effective teacher

School-based research shows over and over again that the three major characteristics of effective teachers are:

1   they have high expectations for children's behaviour and learning;
2   they are extremely good class managers;
3   they know how to design lessons and activities that motivate and help children to learn.

Table 3.4. shows what children from reception to Y6 feel makes a good teacher. We can learn a lot from them.

Table 3.4 Children's views on what makes effective learning (with thanks to all the children at
          Prescot CP who let me know)

Reception
- Happy teacher
- Being with friends
- Not being silly
- Sitting nicely so we can listen.

Year 1
- We like it when we can do it by ourselves. We know the rule and where everything is
- It helps us remember if we know WHY
- Lots of praise
- When it gets a bit harder
- When we are given reasons, not orders.

Year 2
- When Miss brought in a skeleton
- Doing new things
- Working all the time – lots of work
- When everyone is working together, sharing and getting on
- Learning to do new things.

Year 3
- Teacher talking to us and not shouting
- Getting stars
- Celebration of each other's achievements
- Listening to each other, helping each other. When we make mistakes, not laughing.

Year 4
- Energetic teacher
- Good resources.

Year 5
- Everyone giving 100%
- Good teamwork
- Being able to use equipment, more visual, hands on
- The teacher having a sense of humour
- Challenge
- Being able to trust the teacher
- No one having a cold.

Year 6
- Different perspectives and new ideas
- When we are inspired
- The use of demonstration and concrete examples
- We need to feel we can ask for help
- We need to feel secure
- Remember our names
- Sweets.

One very honest Y5 child wrote 'I enjoy sitting down talking about things other than work'.
This was well balanced by another child in the same class writing 'I think it would be better if
there would be more lessons in the day'.

This guide to effective teaching also raises issues. The school now has healthy school status and
there are no sweets given as rewards or allowed in school from home. The whole business
about rewards links with questions about intrinsic and extrinsic motivation examined in
Chapter 5.

Observing children inside and outside school teaches us a lot. It helps to see the child as both a pupil and as a child. In the classroom, it helps in particular to show the variability of pupils as pupils and how they learn. It also can show how children learn at different times, with different adults and children, and on different tasks.

Two particular texts that you may find useful to support your work on observing children are, first, an American book: *How People Learn*, 2000, which provides examples of exciting new research from the American National Research Council (2000) that has come out of observing children. It examines these and discusses their implications for what we teach, how we teach it and how we access what our children. It is also free as an e-book. The second is Blakemore's and Frith's *The Learning Brain*; this won the Society for Education Studies best book award in 2006, when it was published.

4 Establishing a safe and purposeful learning environment

QTS Standards

30, 31, 32, 33

Learning objectives

- to identify ways in which a purposeful learning environment can be created through the physical layout of the classroom, pupil grouping, routines and learning areas;
- to examine organisational and management strategies to ensure effective teaching of whole classes, of groups and individuals within the whole class setting, so that teaching objectives are met and the best use is made of available teaching time.

Overview

One of the aspects we examined in the previous chapter, and will return to later, was that learners have different learning preferences. In this chapter, we look at some very practical strategies to organise and establish a safe and purposeful learning environment that supports the needs of different learners. You go into classrooms and other learning areas where you feel very comfortable and others where you do not. This is the same for all learners, whatever their age. In either case, you need to observe and record carefully so that you can analyse and develop your own teaching and learning. Specific aspects are involved in classroom organisation and management. As a student teacher, or allied professional, it may be possible to alter some of these, but not in others. Increasingly, many schools are taking a whole school approach and you need to make yourself aware of some of the key areas as soon as you set foot in the school. Visiting different classrooms and activity areas can alert you to differences and similarities and so give you an idea of what it is possible to change and what has to remain the same.

The word 'classroom' is used generically to mean any sort of learning and teaching area i.e. it covers the whole school, the extended school and pre- and post-school provision. In essence, this involves looking at particular aspects of learning and examining how they reflect different learning styles.

The physical environment

Activity/Thinking Task 1

Draw a diagram of the physical layout of a classroom or learning area known to you. Now ask yourself what learning and teaching style this reflects. Particular features to look for are ways in which the teacher arranges the space; organises the placing of desks and chairs; caters for individual children's environmental preferences such as temperature, lighting and noise; the type of display, whether they have been created by children or adults and their purpose; specific learning areas and storage arrangements. Teachers often change seating arrangements and may move furniture to enable different activities to take place – art, drama, and science for example.

Several books recommend different methods of organisation. As a visitor to the classroom or learning area, even as a working visitor, you are not expected to reorganise an established teacher's layout. Some teachers are very willing for students to experiment – and learn from their mistakes! However, always ask first if you wish to move furniture and be quite clear about what you are hoping to achieve.

Risk management: some safety tips

Effective teaching has to take place within a safe environment. Establishing this seems commonplace and UK schools carry out regular risk assessments to ensure that they follow the latest safety guidance. In most cases guidance is provided by the LA and adopted by the school via the governing body. It is teachers' common-law duty to ensure that children are healthy and safe on school premises and when they are involved in school-related activities elsewhere, such as educational visits, school outings or field trips. In an increasingly litigious society, all institutions have become paranoid about being sued. The *TES* provides an almost weekly article on a particular aspect of school practice that has driven a parent or carer to take legal action. Ironically, it was the Royal Society for the Prevention of Accidents at the 2007 International Play Safety Conference, which voiced concern about today's children having the right to access wild places so that they can take risks. Policies and guidelines may cover, among other things:

- named persons as health and safety contacts;
- procedures for the safe supervision of children, including restraint procedures;
- child protection;
- accident reporting procedures;
- fire precautions;
- first-aid procedures;
- bomb alert procedures;

- telephone threat report procedures;
- hazard reporting procedure;
- electrical safety;
- hygiene and health;
- contracts;
- medicines;
- school ponds;
- training on health and safety;
- good working practices;
- safe practice in PE;
- coping with the sudden death of a pupil;
- emergency planning, including human flu pandemic;
- environment and traffic;
- school access and security;
- visits: short educational, residential outdoor education, swimming.

Obviously you need to prioritise about what you really need to know as a student, since many of these guidelines and procedures are aimed at guiding the governing body and head teacher in the event of a particular emergency. As a starting point, I would suggest health and safety guidance; safe supervision of children; restraint procedures; child protection. Teachernet and union websites provide more detailed guidance.

Classroom safety checklist

- Ensure carpets, rugs and tiles are fastened down.
- Make sure windows and door are unobstructed – lay inspectors on Ofsted teams frequently record fire exits obscured by chairs, tables and general clutter once the class starts working.
- Make sure children are always visible.
- Make sure anything breakable, sharp or toxic is carefully displayed or stored and labelled in a safe place.
- Avoid congestion in high traffic areas, such as those giving access to reference materials, pencil sharpeners, rubbers, etc.
- Create individual space, where possible, so that children can store their belongings safely.
- Make sure that any electrical plugs are checked, wires not left trailing and electrical appliances (including those owned by staff) are checked regularly.
- Make sure instructional support, such as cards, clipboards, whiteboards and shared reading support can be seen by everyone. This includes not only those with special needs in relation to visual materials, but also pupils squashed together on a small carpet trying to follow instructions from a small board or chart. If you wear glasses or contact lenses yourself you will understand why reading from a 45-degree position is not easy.
- Your name, the class and room number should be displayed on the classroom door, so that carers and children can find you and your class easily.
- Children also need to feel personally safe and secure. Most schools have policy statements that outline strategies on child protection, equal opportunities and bullying policies. The growth of information technology has also led to other safety issues such as the growth of cyber bullying; Internet access to children by strangers and easy access by children to inappropriate materials.

Make yourself familiar with all of these and be aware of new guidelines related to children's safety as they come out. You may be the first person a child approaches when their personal safety is being threatened.

Environmental preferences

- Provide opportunities for children to move around.
- Establish informal as well as formal seating arrangements – many children do not learn best when sitting up straight in a hard chair. Learning areas can provide different forms of seating arrangements, e.g. soft cushions and beanbags in a book corner.
- Provide different types of lighting, so that some areas are very well lit and others more relaxing – too much light can make some children hyperactive; too little can make other children passive.
- Encourage children to modify their clothing, depending on the temperature. A surprising number of children keep jumpers and sweatshirts on when it is very hot.
- Keep the room well ventilated. Classrooms can become quite smelly and stuffy if the air is not moved around and changed.

Teaching area displays

Primary schools and nurseries in England have long been known for their bright and colourful displays (CACE, 1967). And certainly most primary schools do give a general impression of colour and light. However, since 1967 more work has been done on the 'display journey' and display is far more than just a colourful way of brightening up a room or area. Many schools now follow a more traditional – almost Victorian – approach to classroom display. There is considerable evidence that pupils learn from the displays that surround them (Smith and Call, 2001) and it therefore makes sense to have displays that support this learning in the classroom, where pupils can refer to them and look at them regularly. In particular, the purpose of display is seen as being a visual means of focusing on specific learning outcomes, which form part of the current curriculum.

Displays have a direct teaching purpose and are often teacher or commercially led; for example, alphabet and numerical charts, historical time lines, globes and maps. Some of these displays may be directly linked to the testing regime and remind children of technical terms, key words and concepts. This is particularly true for literacy and numeracy displays, both two- and three-dimensional ones. Some schools, which have a particular focus on raising pupil expectation, have posters with messages directly linked to raising self esteem – 'You have never lost until you quit trying' for example. There is also concern about pupils, particularly young children, becoming too over-stimulated by colour and in fact unable to make sense of the displays.

Displays in more public areas are often used to celebrate children's work; to inform other pupils, professionals, parents and carers and other visitors to the school what is going on within the school.

The Reggio Emilia approach to the role of the physical environment for learning in the early years settings has had an important influence in many schools, as well as in nurseries. This environmental philosophy is often referred to as the child's 'third teacher'. It is closely linked to the findings of the Plowden Report and draws on and develops aspects of the work of other early years gurus such as Maria Montessori, Rudolf Steiner, etc. These included the use of natural materials such as wood, rather than plastic; found objects, rather than commercially made products; use of indoor plants; and plenty of natural light. Teaching areas should open into other areas and children encouraged to move between them. The provision for outdoor play, for example in the foundation stage, is a direct product of this tradition.

Grouping

School grouping

Schools generally group their children into classes, usually classes where children are all the same age. There are exceptions to this, where children are grouped across age ranges. This is sometimes by choice, but it may also be for a number of other reasons, such as:

- Vertically grouped classes, sometimes known as family grouping. This occurs when schools believe that children work best in a mixed-age environment. Older children support younger ones and reinforce their own learning. Family grouping is often found where the school places particular emphasis on its children's social development. It is less popular in the UK now than it was 30 years ago.
- Mixed-age classes exist in some schools, where it is impossible to fill one class with children of one age group. Schools with falling rolls are often forced into doing it and having to justify it to parents. The trend towards themed planning may help to make curriculum organisation easier to manage in these circumstances.
- Towards the end of Key Stage (KS) 2 some schools prefer to mix Y5 and Y6 children, finding that they work and behave better.
- In recent years there has been a move towards cross-year ability grouping for English and mathematics. This is often between Y3 and Y4 and then between Y5 and Y6.
- The foundation curriculum is being opened up in some schools to Y1 and sometimes to Y2 classes to support learning. This is made easier if the design of the building allows for more flexible learning centres. Ironically, this is planned for all secondary schools under the building schools for the future (BSF) programme. And a look at this website can provide some very inspirational design ideas for primary schools, which could influence grouping considerably.

Activity/Thinking Task 2

Find out how a school you know or work in organises its classes and whether all teaching takes place in one class grouping for all the children in the class.

First you need to record the number of children in the school and the number of classes. This information can be found in the prospectus. School prospectuses are increasingly found on the school website. These numbers may also be found at the front of the school's most recent Ofsted report. You will have to ask about the school groupings. A single-form entry is the simplest method of organisation, but not all schools can or choose to organise like this. If the school has more than one form of entry, find out how the children are sorted into classes. Many schools put older reception children into one class and younger ones into the other. This can have important implications for overall attainment at the end of the KS if children remain within this grouping. Other schools mix the children up; sometimes alphabetically, often at random. Sometimes, children carry on in the same class grouping through the whole of their primary school career; sometimes they are moved around. Mixed-age classes occur for a variety of reasons and individuals within those classes may have had different class grouping from other children. If new children come into the school in the course of the year, find out how they are accommodated.

Class grouping

Once inside the classroom, children are often grouped even further. Some teaching and learning takes place in whole-class settings. Sometimes it is divided into smaller, working groups. Such a grouping is often an instructional strategy, as in the case of grouping for collaborative learning or ability grouping in maths and English (e.g. guided reading). It may also be an organisational strategy designed to establish and maintain a purposeful working atmosphere. In some classrooms these groups are fixed, particularly if they are organised according to reading ability. Flexible grouping occurs when children work in differently mixed groups, depending on the task in hand. Flexible-grouping strategies may be random, co-operative, by ability, by interest, by task, by knowledge of a specific subject, by skill and by friendship.

Look also at how children with SEN are grouped in any one class. Do they always sit together? Do they always remain in the same year grouping, or do they work with children in other year groups? How are children who speak English as an additional language grouped? Are children withdrawn from class? What do they miss when this happens?

Activity/Thinking Task 3

How are the children grouped in a class known to you? Is there an academic, racial, behaviour and gender balance?

In some schools boys form the bulk of those children identified as having SEN. They may spend all day sitting in the same group, assimilating patterns of learning behaviour from each other, or sitting alone. The key features of these groups tend to be poor reading ability and/or an inability to sustain concentration. In some areas a disproportionate number of black boys are excluded from school. If these imbalances occur in your school, what attempts are being made to analyse them and provide strategies to ensure that these children become effective learners? There is no research correlation between success and family background, race, national origin, financial status or even educational accomplishments. The two correlations are postcode and attitude. Knowing what you can and cannot achieve is called expectation; the classic research on expectations producing success in classrooms was carried out in the 1960s by Rosenthal and Jacobsen (1968). Some grouping arrangements produce children who use up a lot of energy – their own, their peers and adult support workers – achieving negative results. The same amount of energy can be directed towards achieving positive results.

Characteristics of a safe and purposeful learning environment

Routines – the three Rs

Routines can be seen as the three Rs – rules, routines and regulations – all of which have to be in operation before effective teaching and learning can take place. Routines are the backbone of daily classroom life. Regular procedures known to the class make it easier for children to learn, enable them to make progress and achieve more. Of course, routines make it easier to teach, although naturally they differ from teacher to teacher and class to class. Recording these differences enables students to improve their own practice. They eliminate many potential disruptions and help to establish a safe environment that supports learning.

It is often difficult to see these well-established routines, particularly when they work well. The routines for getting attention and signalling for help are likely to vary from class to class. Effective teachers model the behaviour they want and practise it with the whole class, giving the children time to demonstrate that they know and understand it. These routines can be reinforced through photographs, lists of class rules (often made with the children themselves) and written support.

Below are two suggestions for establishing routines for seeking help. The first one is designed as a poster to which children can refer. The second is a procedure. Like all strategies they need to be practised by the whole class and understood before it will work for individual children.

Example 1

How do I spell a new word?

Use a 'Have-a-go' card:

- Think about meaning. Does it give any clues to spelling patterns?
- Say the word slowly. Listen carefully.
- Write the word syllable by syllable.
- Make sure you have represented each sound with a letter or letters.
- Look carefully to see if the pattern looks right. If not:
    - try a different pattern
    - see if you know another word which is similar.

(example given in *Education Department Western Australia*, 1997)

Example 2

Signalling for help

One example of a successful routine for signalling for help is given in an American book issued to all NQTs in Arizona. The authors suggest that each child is given an index card folded and taped into a three-sided pyramid. One side is blank, one side reads 'Please help me' and the third side reads 'Please keep working'. The blank side normally faces the child. But when the child needs help, he or she signs by turning the 'Please help me' side towards the teacher. This in turn, puts the 'Please keep working' side towards the child as a reminder to continue quietly until the teacher comes. This is a silent procedure that secures the necessary help without disrupting the whole class. It also avoids the very public admission of difficulty involved in raising a hand for help.

Most practical books on teaching strategies provide plenty of similar strategies for managing to maintain a purposeful learning environment. It is also useful to remember that the strategies will need practising – even very obvious ones such as raising a hand to answer a question. Look at the tentative hand-raising in many KS2 classrooms. Next time you ask a large group of children a question, try raising your own hand, enthusiastically and high, to model what you are wanting. Point out that learning is about trying, having a go. None of us is right all the time and we can only learn by asking the questions and practising the answers.

Activity/Thinking Task 4

Observe a primary classroom with a focus on the three Rs. Try to place them into different categories and add to them as you observe more teachers and allied professionals in action. Try using the checklist from Table 4.1 as a starting point.

Table 4.1 Three Rs checklist

Category	Examples	School practice
Start of the day	Registration – including self registration, money collection, children arriving late, walk-in work routines, parents/carers seeking access to the teacher	
Work routines	Naming and/or heading paper and books, use of pencil/pen/ rubber, presentation, incomplete work, number of pages completed, registration for tasks	
Instructional activities	Signals by teacher/child for attention, talking during seated tasks, getting work marked, activities when work completed, movement around class, expected behaviour, number of children in learning/activity area	
Ending the session	Putting materials away, tidying up, leaving the room, moving from one activity to another (transitions)	
Interruptions	Rules, talking to other children, handing in work, monitoring	

Table 4.1 Three Rs checklist *continued*

Category	Examples	School practice
Other procedures	School dinners, packed lunches, changing for PE, assembly, moving from one place in school to another, milk/snack time, adult support workers	
Room/school area	Teacher's desk, books, computer, toilets, pencil sharpener, rubber, learning areas, playground, movement around the classroom (adults and children)	
Checking work	Working collaboratively/ independently, giving in homework	
Academic and personal feedback	Rewards and incentives, communication with parents, written comments on work, self-recording equipment	
Use of ICT	Rules relating to its use, number of machines within the classroom, activity of machines	

Class management

Class management refers to all of the things that a teacher does to organise pupils, space, time and materials so that teaching and learning can take place. Effective class management and leadership can be seen when both pupils and adult support workers are on task, deeply involved with their academic work and rarely misbehave. Remember, the teacher is ultimately responsible for organising a well-managed classroom or nursery so that pupils can learn in a good working environment. Observation of existing good practice provides the first step to learning the craft of establishing a safe and purposeful learning environment:

- A high level of pupil involvement with their work.
- Pupils who have clear and accurate expectations of what is required of them. They know (and understand) the purposes/objectives/outcomes/focus of the tasks set for them as individuals. They need to know the purposes of both written and non-written tasks such as when they are involved in speaking and listening activities. Many teachers record their activity/lesson objectives on the board, so that they and the pupils are reminded of them.
- Relatively little wasted time, confusion or disruption.
- A pleasant, relaxed and work-orientated atmosphere.

Maximising children's learning and minimising disruption

This involves:

- High levels of preparation – activity content, the furniture, the floor space, work areas, wall spaces, bookcases, teacher area, teaching materials, use of other professionals working in the classroom. Observe carefully how the physical environment of the classroom contributes to good management.
- Identifying strategic locations for less motivated pupils. Behavioural challenges will occur from time to time.

The extract below is taken from a handbook issued to NQTs. The author compares disruptive behaviour in class with infractions in hockey. When the infraction occurs in hockey, there is an area, or strategic location set aside for the offender. The author argues that the same needs to occur in teaching. As always it is important to remember that the focus is on the unwanted behaviour, not the children themselves.

Infraction behaviours

- *Aggressive behaviour* – hyperactivity, agitation, unruliness.
- *Resistance* – not wanting to work or take part in activities.
- *Distractibility* – difficulty concentrating.
- *Dependence* – wanting help all the time, unwilling to take risks on the tasks set.

Strategic locations

- *Separate* – separate the pupil from the class or at least from other problem students. This is most appropriate when behaviour is aggressive and/or resistant.
- *Close by* – keep the pupil close to an adult. This is most appropriate for distractible, dependent and occasionally resistant pupils.

Being a well-organised teacher

Remember the first day is the most critical. Pupils, teachers, other allied professionals and parents will be observing you; even when you are in a classroom as an observer. Their opinion of you may be based on the first 5 minutes they meet and observe you. They will expect you to perform effectively.

1. *Positive expectations*: for the children you are teaching and for yourself as their teacher. Expectations are different from standards. Standards are levels of achievement. Positive expectations help produce high standards. Say to yourself: 'This is an exciting class. This is going to be the most memorable professional experience I have ever had. As a result we will all do well.' The most successful schools have expectations that everyone will succeed.

2. *Time management*: teaching takes time; learning how to teach takes even longer. Time management is likely to be one of the biggest challenges in classroom management. You need to be able to manage your own time well so that you can manage both yours, other adult workers' and the children's. Time management is a thread that runs through good class management – organising the day, organising the classroom,

organising the day-to-day and weekly timetables, recording pupils' progress and keeping disruptions to the minimum. Below are some suggestions:

- Set goals – professional and personal – and review them regularly. Don't attempt to do too much. Target the possible.
- Make a daily list of the things that need doing.
- If possible do the hardest task as early in the day as possible, so you get it out of the way and don't have to spend time and energy worrying about doing it.
- Identify your personal working habits. Do you work best first thing in the morning? If you arrived at school half an hour earlier would you accomplish more than staying two hours after school?
- Learn to say no to activities for which you do not have the time. Students need to have a social life, but kickboxing followed by a few drinks may not be the most effective way of spending the evening preparing for the next day's lessons – despite how some television dramas present teaching.
- Delegate – family responsibilities will need to be delegated and shared. Do not even try to be superhuman.
- Learn to concentrate and stick to tasks.
- Avoid perfectionism – an additional two hours on a worksheet may just not be worth it.
- Set time limits for tasks and set deadlines for yourself and your class – work expands to fill time.
- Operate a one-touch policy for mail, including e-mail. Put it into the waste bin, virtual or actual, or attend to it immediately.
- Have an answerphone so you can monitor phone calls.
- Monitor your texting and chat room habits and assess how much of your time they are making.

Hopefully, time becomes your ally, rather than your enemy. And you can help pupils to manage their own lives more purposefully.

3   *Create a good initial impression* – you do not get a second chance to make a first impression.

(a) Arrive early. The time of arrival depends on the school in which you are working. In some schools, teachers arrive as early as 7.00 a.m., in others the majority may arrive about 8.15 a.m. In many schools there is a short staff briefing before the day begins. You should ask if you can attend this, if you have not already been told to do so. These meetings are often the key to learning how the school day is to be organised, what visitors are expected, where attention may need to be focused. Many schools encourage students to attend staff meetings and professional development sessions that occur after school and at weekends. Again, you should make the most of these opportunities and, if not asked directly, politely enquire if you can attend.

(b) Remember you are treated as you are dressed. In an ideal world, we would be accepted for ourselves, not our appearance. In the real world, appearance is under constant scrutiny. Dress for respect, credibility, acceptance and authority. Then you can go wild at the weekends!

(c) Welcome pupils with a smile. In some schools, I have seen head teachers greeting parents and children when they come into the playground. Most teachers prepare their children for visitors. But you too should make sure that the children know your name and that you are given an opportunity to get to know them. Whenever you work with a small group, make sure that they know who you are and if possible conduct some form of 'getting acquainted' game. Avoid creating a 'family group' and children calling you by your first name, unless that is the practice within the school for all staff. This may be difficult for you, if you are used to working with children in more informal settings, e.g. youth groups, summer schools and play schemes.

(d) Show you are interested in the children. You may find it useful to spend time with children out of the classroom, for example during playtime, having a school dinner and in the pre- and after-school clubs. Consult with the class or nursery teacher. Remember if you agree to take on additional responsibilities, such as a residential weekend, you must do it. Nothing is worse than a volunteer who backtracks at the last minute.

(e) Don't spend time on clerical tasks in the classroom. Observation schedules, evaluations, etc. can be done when the children are not around.

(f) Encourage invitational learning – whatever task you are doing, make sure that you create a welcoming and invitational atmosphere.

Learning areas

Activity/Thinking Task 5

Look back at your original plan for the classroom or early years setting. Can you identify any part of the classroom where the teacher has planned for independent learning activities? Record this on your original plan if you have not done so already. What are the children learning in this small area and how is the learning being evaluated?

Planning and designing effective learning areas is one of the hardest tasks for the teacher because it is so dependent on ensuring children's self-sustained concentration. Direct teaching, provided class management is satisfactory, is much easier. The teacher remains in control. Once children are working by themselves in a learning area, control is subcontracted. When planning for these areas is well done, it helps children not only to learn efficiently, but also to develop self-control and independence. Judging by Ofsted inspection reports, this is often planned better in nurseries and infant classes than at KS2. Clear learning objectives are required for any learning area, such as a role-play section, science discovery corner, maths display, listening centre, computers or class library. These learning objectives will change over time as pupils achieve their learning outcomes. Learning areas are the real test of whether teaching methods are sustaining the momentum of pupils' work and keeping them engaged through stimulating curiosity and communicating enthusiasm. They create an ethos of consolidation and extension of directly taught activities.

Allied educational professionals

The learning areas used by allied professionals when working with individual learners or small groups should be attractive and conducive to learning. Most primary schools are good at doing this now and gone are the converted, windowless, dark broom cupboards for special needs pupils, and the cold, windy corridor for volunteers hearing readers. Allied educational professionals, whether employed by the school, the LA or acting as volunteers need to be well briefed. They should have a clear idea about the purpose of the activity and their role within it. Sometimes their task may simply be observation, which can be recorded and later assessed and analysed with the teacher. This informs them both about future planning for the area and the best use of continued adult support. Well-trained adult support workers can provide excellent support for children's learning, but Ofsted reports still record some poor use of this valuable personnel resource.

The increased use of technology such as personal digital assistants (PDAs), hand-held computers and tablets have enormously enhanced the skill of observing children. This is sometimes known as 'Owling' – Observation, Wait, Listen.

Planning

Planning is the most important aspect in establishing a safe and purposeful learning environment. It is linked closely to assessment for learning (AfL) and target setting. Unless you assess what has been learnt you cannot move on to the next learning stage and this needs to be embedded in the planning process. Planning includes arranging the physical environment of the class, deciding rules and regulations, collecting materials and organising the other adults working in the classroom. The other side of planning is that for teaching the academic content of the curriculum. Increasingly, this has meant those areas tested – English, mathematics and science. This is dealt with in greater detail in Chapters 5 to 10, which are on various aspects of planning. Student teachers rarely become effectively involved in more than short-term planning, although they need to understand how it draws on both medium- and long-term planning. Indeed, student teachers are often part of planning meetings that draw these up.

Good planning takes a lot of time and practice, but much can be learnt from looking at the ways in which different schools plan. There are still considerable differences in how schools plan, despite the mass of formal documentation on planning from central government, local government, independent websites and commercial companies. And this is what would be expected if schools plan for their own community. Perhaps the most important thing to remember is that planning cannot be limited to content. It is far more professional than that. A good teacher can look to an inexperienced observer as if he or she is teaching 'off the top of their head'. In today's primary schools, no one can do this. Substantial documentation exists in all schools to inform planning, teaching, class management, assessment, target setting, reporting and recording. The skill for the student teacher and other allied professionals is learning how to make sense of these plans and use them most effectively to support their own teaching and learning.

Efficient and effective teachers know what they are doing and do the right things consistently. The effective student gains skills and knowledge about the ways in which the class is taught and managed by their regular teacher and support workers. They can then develop this knowledge and use it in their planning for their own teaching, adapting and changing as well as replicating existing practice. Once routines are changed, children need to be informed and encouraged to practise new procedures.

5   Approaches to learning

QTS Standards

10, 18, 22, 29

Learning objectives

- Insight into:

    - child development theories;
    - theories of learning; and
    - learning style theories.

- to gain skills in identifying aspects of these theories when observing children who are learning in classrooms and nurseries;
- to develop skills in utilizing their knowledge to inform their planning for teaching.

Introduction

In this chapter and the following six chapters we look directly at what is known about learning and the implications of this knowledge for motivation, planning and behaviour management. It would be wonderful if this were a very precise science; where, if we did this and then that, we could be assured that effective learning had taken place. Sadly this just is not so and there are still wide differences and disagreements between theory and practice and also ways in which learners differ themselves. Sometimes, people have believed they have 'the answer' and of course there are many resources that claim to be the 'answer'. You need to reflect on your readings and practice and although you will never have 'the answer', you will have some partial answers and this will help you to become a more effective teacher. Informed observation is fundamental to learning about learning. This chapter aims to support such informed observation. There are many excellent books on the market and I have included a couple in the bibliography. In addition, any good educational psychology text will provide you with a broad overview of learning. These can be found in local libraries as well as those in university and college. If you have not done any psychology before, you might find it useful to start with an A-level text, before moving on to an undergraduate one.

In many of the later chapters in this book we look at the revolution in the study of the mind over the past 40 years and examine the important implications this has on planning, targeting, teaching, assessing, monitoring and giving feedback. In this chapter we will provide an introduction to this topic, and there are many good educational psychological texts that can provide a much broader insight. It is a fascinating subject, which provides real insight into informing good practice.

The three areas that all those working in classrooms with children need to know, are:

1   child development theories
2   theories of learning
3   learning style theories.

Child development theories

Child development theories used to form an important part of every student teacher's course about 15 years ago. Indeed, undergraduates would often have a whole year covering the topic. Table 5.1 on language development is just one example of a topic that would be studied for a couple of weeks in such an undergraduate course. This looks at the development of language from birth onwards and was linked into language in the home, early years setting and then primary school. Child development was gradually squeezed out for student teachers with the introduction of the QTS competences in 1992, which did not require this sort of phase knowledge. This has now changed. The 2007 QTS standards require both primary and secondary teachers to cover child development and

Table 5.1 Typical progress of language development from birth to adolescence

Approximate age	Behaviour
Birth	Phoneme perception Discrimination of language from non-language sounds Crying
3 months	Cooing
6 months	Babbling
9 months	First words Holophrases (single words used as a sentence)
12 months	Use of words to attract adults' attention
18 months	Vocabulary spurt First two-word sentences (telegraphic speech)
24 months	Correct responses to indirect requests 'Is Daddy cooking?'
30 months	Creation of indirect requests 'Sabba is on my slide' Modification of speech to take listener into account Early awareness of grammatical categories
Early childhood	Rapid increase in grammatical complexity Over-generalisation of grammatical rules
Middle childhood	Understanding of passive forms 'The ball was taken by Muff' Acquisition of written language
Adolescence	Acquisition of specialised language functions

the ECM agenda requires all those working with children who have a common core of skilled knowledge. This includes child development.

It is generally recognised that there are three theory groups within child development theory – maturationists, environmentalists and constructivists.

Maturationist

One of the main maturationist theorists was Arnold Gessell. He and other maturationists believed that child development was a natural biological process that occurred automatically in stages over time; as, for example, shown in Table 5.1. In an education context this can result in the assumption that children will acquire knowledge naturally and automatically as they grow physically and become older – provided of course that they are healthy.

Environmentalists

The main theorist here was B.K. Skinner. Environmentalists challenged the maturationist approach. They argued that the child's environment shapes learning and behaviour. This means that human behaviour, development and learning are reactions to the child's environment. In a school context this assumes that young children can develop and acquire new knowledge by reacting to their environment.

Constructivists

This is perhaps the most well-known group in child development. They include Piaget, Montessori, Bruner and Vygotsky. They all believed that environment by itself was not enough, the key to learning and development lay in the way in which young children interact with the environment and the people around them. Constructivists saw young children as active participants in the learning process. They also had the very optimistic belief that young children initiate most of the activities required for learning and development.

Central government perspectives on child development

Of course child development is much more complex than this, but it is useful to look at these theories in relation to the guidance produced for the early years foundation stage (EYFS) by the DfES. Figure 5.1 provides the areas of learning development seen as essential for the under fives according to the DfES (2007) publication *Statutory Framework for the Early Years Foundation Stage: Setting the Standards*.

The Statutory Framework provides an easy to follow overview of early child development. It provides overlapping developmental stages:

- birth to 11 months
- 8–20 months
- 16–26 months
- 22–36 months
- 30–50 months, and
- 40–60 months.

It is important to refer also to psychology texts for greater depth and broader understandings about this.

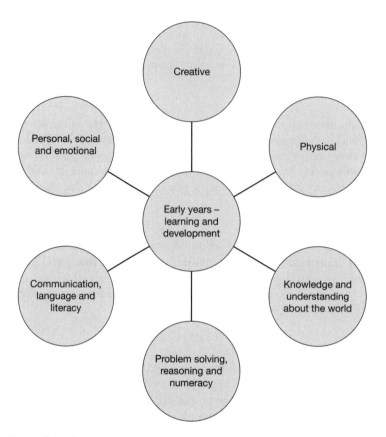

Figure 5.1 Areas of development – EYFS

Activity/Thinking Task 1

Access the *Principles into Practice* cards in the *Setting the Standards* pack. Look at one of the areas of learning; for example knowledge and understanding of the world. Read through some of the suggestions made for developing this area in terms of positive relationships, enabling environments and learning and development.

How are these theories about child development – maturationist, environmentalist or constructivist informing some of the statements?

There is a slight word of caution here for those of you who decide to watch the short clip on the CD in the pack. As with any video clip, the practitioners who agree to be videoed are of course under considerable pressure to demonstrate a particular bit of teaching. This sometimes comes over as a bit didactic and very much in the 'performance mode'. Also, a short clip of any video allows very little time for children and adults to be seen exploring, observing and discovering things. As we have all observed, a very young child can spend half an hour exploring an activity. A video often brings it down to two minutes of concentrated learning outcome, with the adult playing the key role.

Reflection

Setting the Standards is perhaps an unfortunate sub-heading for the foundation stage document, it sounds rather like a pre-SATs document. Although the *Principles into Practice* cards do provide useful definitions and examples of how settings can effectively implement each particular area of development.

Below are two controversial issues that have engaged child developmental theorists from early days in the field – identifying stages and sequences and nature versus nurture.

1   *Identifying Stages and Sequences.* The government documentation for the early years presents child development in stages. Each is seen as a discrete entity with some overlap. The child in each stage approaches tasks differently and sees the world in a different way. More recently researchers have argued for 'sequences of development'. This allows for individual sequences of development in every area. A child may be particularly advanced in one sequence, but not in another – for example linguistic development, rather than physical development. As a child, I did not walk until I was about two, but was able to chat away quite happily to ask for what I wanted well before the allocated 'stage'. My brother on the other hand, had two elder sisters who did everything for him and did not need to speak much at all until he went to school at five. Since then he does not seem to have stopped. The great danger of holding too closely to tight age-related stages is that some children may be identified as 'slow learners' before they have reached statutory school age. The ability grouping of reception children is just one example of how this is evidenced.

2   *Nature versus nurture or heredity versus environment.* This used to be one of the most controversial areas of research among psychologists. In the Victorian era in England it was accepted that each person had their own particular station in life and this was an essential part of their nature. That old Victorian hymn 'All Things Bright and Beautiful' contained the verse:

> The rich man at his castle
> The poor man at the gate
> God made them high and lowly
> And ordered their estate.

Victorian and Edwardian biologists and, later, psychologists provided extensive evidence for why white, wealthy, European men should be at the top of the hierarchy (Tracy with Rose, 1995). There is still a strong element of this hidden in deficit theories about particular groups in our communities.

Developmental psychologists asked whether a child's development is governed by a pattern that is built in from birth or whether it is shaped by experiences after birth. The answer is a complex one and difficult to unpick. A mother's lifestyle during pregnancy, for example, can affect a child, particularly if there is a history of drug or alcohol abuse. Puberty can be influenced by environmental factors such as diet. I am a strong believer that children's life chances are not just down to their heredity. Schools, and the adults working in them, can make a difference to children's lives through the provision of learning experiences, learning opportunities and raising aspirations. How they do this most effectively, is really at the heart of this book.

Activity/Thinking Task 2

Find out about the 'Mozart' effect for unborn babies. How does the nature/nurture inform this commercial venture?

Look at some of the health education initiatives for parents of unborn and newly born babies. Can you identify some of the influences that are informing their promotion? You might like to look at the healthy eating advice given to pregnant women and the advice about feeding babies, toddlers and older children. It is also worth noting the direct commercial response, in supermarkets, to this advice, which is aimed specifically at parents.

Theories of learning

These can be divided into four theory groups (Fetsco and McClure, 2004):

1 behavioural learning
2 cognitive learning
3 social cognitive learning, and finally
4 cognitive development learning.

Behavioural view of learning

The behavioural view of learning is a very basic theory and is used by many schools as a means of managing behaviour as well as learning; for example schools using 'Assertive Discipline' have adopted a behavioural approach to behaviour management (Chapter 9).

Behaviourism implies that (1) the teacher is the most important force in the classroom and (2) modification of a child's behaviour is possible. The classic example of behaviourism comes from the work of Ivan Pavlov. He found that ringing a bell could induce salivation in dogs, even when no food was present, if the dog was trained to associate the bell with food. The link with behaviourism and dog training is what has made many educationalists unhappy about it as a means of reinforcing learning.

Activity/Thinking Task 3

Provide some examples of behavioural reinforcers used in classrooms and early learning centres that help children to learn.

- social reinforcer – demonstrated by teacher approval (such as a smile/frown from the teacher);
- activity reinforcer – behaviour or privilege earned ('golden time');
- tangible reinforcer – physical object earned through behaviour (good work sticker);
- natural reinforcer – behaviours that contain their own reinforcement (intrinsic motivation).

Cognitive learning theory

There are four main principles behind this learning theory – prior knowledge; organisation of knowledge; appropriate matching of new knowledge and skills with working memory; acknowledgement of learning as an active process.

- *Prior knowledge*: To link new knowledge and skills to the learners' existing knowledge and skills. Learning occurs when the learner can add to and modify existing knowledge. This is often the reason why students are advised to include prior knowledge in their planning sheets.
- *Organisation of knowledge*: in order to encourage learners to organise their learning. This is often done through a process of 'scaffolding' and is done in a number of ways. Some of these are specific, we do this and then we do that. Many pupils are asked to write the learning outcomes in their books prior to starting on a written activity. The cognitive learning theory supports this because the children are being asked to identify and record what they hope to gain from doing the activity. It organises their learning into required outcomes.
- *Working memory*: knowledge about this is necessary in order to ensure learners are not required to learn more than their working memory can cope with at any particular time. This forms part of a theory about how information is processed and involves different forms of models that describe thinking and memory. Working memory is seen as a memory story where information is temporarily maintained before it is stored in long-term memory.
- *Learning as an active process*: This principle recognises that learning is an active process and needs to be goal directed. These goals need to be personal. Today this is often known as the WIIFM (what's in it for me?) factor.

Cognitive learning theory is a much more personal, individualist approach to learning than behaviourism. It signifies the difference between extrinsic and intrinsic motivation, which we look at later in this chapter. Behaviourism encourages the desired learning through external factors such as rewards (extrinsic). Cognitive theory encourages the learner to make the learning meaningful for themselves by linking it with what they already know and identifying what they need to get out of it.

Activity/Thinking Task 4

Can you think of a recent occasion when you have felt that your 'working memory' has been over-stretched? What effect did this have on you? What sort of factors influenced your ability to remember?

Social cognitive theory

Current social cognitive theory is heavily based on the work of Albert Bandura. He suggested three main features that learners need to have:

1 Models of learning from which they can acquire knowledge and behaviours about how to learn. One example you may observe in classrooms or nurseries is the teacher,

or other relevant adult, 'thinking aloud'. There might be a mathematical problem on the board and the teacher models the process by which the problem can be solved. The 'thinking aloud' can test out a hypothesis and reject it as well as a hypothesis that works. Puppets and soft toys are often used to model learning with younger children.

2   Belief in themselves as effective learners and their potential to control their own learning process. Many of us can identify strengths and weaknesses in our own learning. These are not always accurate or realistic of course, and a great deal of work has to be done with some children to raise their self-esteem about their ability to learn. A less obvious challenge is children whose self-esteem is quite high, but who are actually failing to acknowledge the amount of effort that they will need in order to succeed at a task. Most of us recognise this in adults, who seem to know a great deal about something and then you find out that they know a lot less than they think they do.

3   The opportunities and abilities to regulate their own learning processes. This is fairly obvious; we learn better when we want to learn something and can create the best conditions in which to do this. In the real world, many learning activities are determined by others and there is little choice about what and how to learn. In essence, self-regulation of learning is challenging.

Activity/Thinking Task 5

Who has provided you with a good role model for learning?
Where would you identify your greatest strengths in learning; what do you have most difficulty learning? Can you identify any reasons for this?

Cognitive development theory

This theory suggests that learning is more effective if:

*   learners actively construct their own understandings;
*   those who work with learners take into account their cognitive development levels. This is often interpreted as age related;
*   learning is assisted by the nature of the interaction with people and objects in their environment.

Key constructivists for cognitive development theory are Piaget, Vygotsky and Bruner. Piaget used to be one of the key psychologists for teachers to read, together with some of those who critiqued his work. He placed learning into stages. These were sensorimotor (birth to 2); preoperational (2 to 7); concrete operational (7 to 11); and finally, formal operational.

Key strategies for the classroom from this learning theory involved:

1   opportunities for discovery learning, so that pupils can use problem solving techniques to create new knowledge;
2   comprehensive learning experiences that enable knowledge to be integrated and viewed from different perspectives;

3 opportunities for thinking and working collaboratively with their peers, teachers and other educational professionals;

4 means whereby pupils can self-regulate their learning and design their own learning experiences;

5 authentic learning experiences.

There is very little about these ideas to disagree with in theory, but in practice in schools and early years settings they are extremely challenging.

Activity/Thinking Task 6

Use an educational psychology text to find out more about the ideas of Piaget, Vygotsky and Bruner. Most educational psychology texts will also provide you with practical examples of how their findings can be exemplified in schools and early years settings. You will find plenty of critiques about their work, but also much that you do recognise that takes place in schools.

Andragogy

There is a tendency to see adult and children learning in much the same way, and indeed this chapter follows that precedent. There is, however, a strong theory (Nottingham Andragogy Group, 1983) that adult learning has its own methods and philosophy with a different type of teacher. The term 'andragogy' is used to describe this and can be contrasted with pedagogy. The current growth in use of the term pedagogic to describe the knowledgeable person in the education setting is interesting therefore for two reasons. First, it distinguishes the child and adult learning setting, and second it raises awareness of a specific specialism related to teaching – pedagogy.

Learning style theorists

I expect everyone reading this has done at least one questionnaire to identify their preferred learning style. These exist on-line as well as in psychology and general educational texts. They are available for children as well as adults;but do need to be treated with care. This section outlines three different learning style theories. There are far more than that

---

Activity/Thinking Task 6

If you have not done so, find a learning style preference questionnaire online. Do it and print it out. You should evaluate how accurate it is, and then try it again at the end of this book. Some commercial companies offer a 'free' sample questionnaire to entice you into buying their products, but you obviously do not need to follow this up.

You might like to try the children's questionnaire in Table 5.2 that comes, with permission, from a teacher in a primary school, who used it as a starting point for some action-based research on mind-friendly learning (see Chapter 7).

Table 5.2 Learning styles children's questionnaire

Name	Date
What do you think?	
Question	Smiley scale ☺ ☺ ☹
1 I usually enjoy learning	
2 I am always organised for lessons	
3 I always understand what my lessons are about	
4 I always try to take part in lessons	
5 I can record my work in different ways	
6 I enjoy listening to the teacher talk	
7 I enjoy learning in groups	
8 I enjoy learning on my own	
9 I can always explain what I have been doing at the end of a lesson	
10 I enjoy talking about my work to other pupils	
11 I learn better when I am doing practical things	

on the market and they do not all necessarily adapt easily to work in primary schools. What is certainly true is that the educational professional needs to know more than a tabloid newspaper version of what is meant by a learning style.

Howard Gardner

In Chapter 3 we looked at the work of Howard Gardner on multiple intelligences and how he himself has acknowledged that he has moved on from his original thinking. In relation to the multiple intelligences theory, this has been to extend them from seven intelligences to nine intelligences and then to speculate on another two – spiritual and

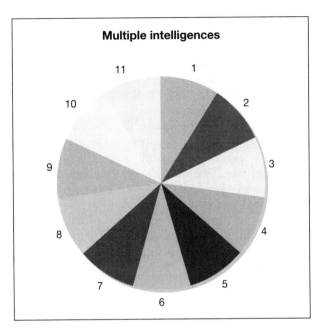

Multiple intelligences

1 Linguistic
2 Mathematical
3 Visual
4 Musical
5 Bodily
6 Interpersonal
7 Intrapersonal
8 Naturalistic
9 Existential
10 Spiritual
11 Moral

Figure 5.2 Multiple intelligences

moral. Whatever Gardner may now feel, the idea of multiple intelligences has certainly taken on a life of its own; Figure 5.2 provides a visual view of this.

The sense of what is covered by most of these intelligences is fairly self-evident, although the latest four – existential, naturalistic, spiritual and moral are more difficult to identify. The inability to measure any of them is less important than the acknowledgement that we are made up of more than one single intelligence. Yet, some classrooms do not reflect this much broader approach to intelligence and in the interests of differentiation set children into groups based on their reading ability. This seems to make sense when activities are linked to reading worksheets in any subject area, but may hide the fact that some weaker readers have much to offer in other areas. There are also issues, which will be examined later, of equality of access to the whole curriculum.

David Kolb

Kolb's learning style model identified four different learning styles. This theory sorted learners into four types, who at the extreme ends of the model were:

- *Divergers.* These are learners who prefer to learn by concrete experiences and reflective observation. The initial school attachment experiences that generally start all teacher training courses play very much to this learning style. The student teacher can be part of a school and have plenty of time to learn through concrete experience of and working with groups of children. They observe and then reflect on their observations.
- *Assimilators.* These also learn by reflective observation, but this reflection is informed by abstract rather than concrete experiences. If we continue with the education example above, this assimilation learning style suits those students who enjoy studying

the broader elements in education as a subject discipline in itself, rather than the focus on the teacher training element. This is reflected in the massive growth of education studies as an undergraduate degree in its own right. Assimilators are theoretical thinkers, building up ideas and hypothesis about the subject they are studying from its ideas, rather than the practical outcomes. You might argue that this is what politicians and other policy makers do. They look at education from their perspective and make policy decisions based on the abstract ideas.

- *Convergers*. These learners prefer to learn by active, physical experimentation and abstract conceptualisation. I suspect the changing role of the lead teachers in primary schools requires this as more of a preferred learning style. Certainly some of the government initiatives encourage this. Two examples are the TDA 'fast tracking' for beginner teachers and the National Council for School Leadership (NCSL) courses such as 'Leading from the Middle'.
- *Accommodators*. This learning style prefers active experimentation and concrete learning experiences. The recent growth in seeing the teacher as an action-based researcher fits into this learning model. It involves being willing to try/experiment with new ideas, resources, curriculum designs, etc. In order to be successful, it does have to involve reflection.

Kolb acknowledged that although almost everyone makes use of all these learning models – diverger, accommodator, converger and assimilator – each of us has a preferred learning style.

Dunn and Dunn

These researchers looked at how learning was influenced by 'instructional preference'. This might seem very obvious to us, but if you have an image of the child as a blank slate, the idea of instructional preference challenges this. Dunn and Dunn identified five basic stimuli

---

Activity/Thinking Task 7

Very quickly write down your own preferences for learning in terms of:

- the physical environment in which you prefer to work – temperature, noise level, seating arrangement;
- emotional factors, such as the amount of independence you are given and the structuring and scaffolding of the tasks set;
- sociological – whether you prefer to work alone or in groups;
- physiological – kinaesthetic, visual, auditory learning preferences;
- psychological factors – cerebral preferences, whether you feel yourself to be very analytical or are more creative.

You should then compare your list with someone else. There should be some differences between the lists and you have probably noted differences for your own list in terms of what you are learning, what time of day it is and even what time of the year. What will be a lively, colourful and cheerful classroom for some children, may be seen as a cluttered, confused and disorientating mess to others.

---

that affected an individual's ability to perceive, interact with and respond to the learning environment. This was out of a learning model that identified more than twenty. The basic five were environmental, emotional, sociological, physiological and psychological.

There are many other learning style theorists, but these three sum up for me those that are most influencing our views about learning in primary schools today. The actual models and theories may not be known to many of those who use elements of them. Later, in Chapter 17, when we look at schools as learning communities, we will look at some of Guy Claxton's strategies on L2L.

6 Personalised learning, motivation and implications for planning

QTS Standards

4, 10, 19, 26

Learning objectives

- to evaluate initiatives on personalised and customised learning;
- to examine Prochaska's and DiClemente's motivational cycle and evaluate differences between intrinsic and extrinsic motivation;
- to demonstrate these understandings in relation to drawing up individual child profiles and personalised learning plans;
- to apply these understandings to observations on individual children.

In this chapter we look at how current initiatives on personalised learning have been informed by research findings on learning and motivation and some direct implications this has for planning. The chapter will cover:

1 personalised and customised learning;
2 practical outcomes on preferred learning styles;
3 motivation and learning;
4 child profiling;
5 personal learning plans (PLPs);
6 differentiation.

Reminder

In Chapter 5 we looked at some theories on child development, learning and learning styles. These were based on research evidence, mainly from several fields within psychology, but increasingly from other disciplines.

- Cognitive psychology, which covers areas such as memory, language processing, perception, problem solving and thinking.
- Developmental psychology, which shows how young children learn through their experience.
- Social psychology, cognitive psychology and anthropology help us understand how learning is influenced by cultural and sociology norms.
- Neuroscience is just starting to show how learning actually changes the physical structure of the brain and with it the functional organisation of the brain. This is looked at in more detail in Chapter 13.
- School-based action research has helped to show how design and evaluation of learning environments can yield new knowledge about the nature of learning and teaching.
- Finally, emerging technologies are enhancing learning for us all in ways unimagined in the past.

One key feature which does come out of the previous chapter is that many of the implications for learning are personal. Even the psychologists who saw child development theories and learning theories in stages, acknowledged that each of these stages were over a considerable period of time and could vary. It is a truism to say that this results in huge variations in learning and achievement in any single-aged class.

Personalised learning

Government definition

David Miliband, a senior government minister, in his 2004 speech to the North of England Education Conference defined personalised learning as something that all schools must invest in and which involved:

> High expectations of every child, given practical form by high quality teaching based on a sound knowledge and understanding of each child's needs. It is not individualised learning where pupils sit alone. Nor is it when pupils are left to their own devices – which too often reinforces low aspirations. It means shaping teaching around the way different youngsters learn; it means taking the care to nurture the unique talents of every pupil.

Activity/Thinking Task 1

Identify three different statements here that can be linked to the research findings identified in the previous chapter.

This particular minister was probably well aware of those research findings, but what is also true is that many of the statements that seem so obvious to us now, were far from obvious prior to about 1960. The Plowden Report coined the expression 'child-centred' education to describe their philosophy. This term had fallen into disrepute by the late 1970s and early 1980s, but is essentially the message behind the ECM agenda and personalised learning.

In 2004, the *Five Year Strategy for Children and Learners* published by the DfES (2004b) identified five components of personalised learning, which seem, at first glance, very different from the statement by Miliband. This policy document identified individualised learning as having five key components:

1   AfL;
2   effective teaching and learning;
3   curriculum entitlement and choice;
4   school organisation e.g. workforce remodelling;
5   beyond the classroom, e.g. extended schools (see for example Chapter 18).

Personalised learning has its critiques. Philip Beadle, writing in the *Education Guardian* (2007) quotes Professor David Halpin of the Institute of Education, who described it as a 'rubber bag' kind of expression into which almost anything can be fitted. And this is fairly obvious from the very different statements that have come from central government. By making it so wide a concept, Beadle suggested 'it ultimately signifies very little of consequence or substance'. Beadle, who was secondary school teacher of the year in 2004, suggested that personalised learning, when it finally reaches the classroom, will be a 'whip with which to force teachers to differentiate by task for every single lesson taught'. The idea of a PLP for each child is ideologically attractive, but as the Scottish trial mentioned later shows, it is virtually impossible to manage with current resourcing.

Customised learning

Bill Gates of Microsoft has been using some of his great wealth over the past few years to transform chosen schools all over the world. Indeed one of these schools is about 5 miles from where I live. He described this transformational learning as 'customised' learning and it involved among other technical innovations a laptop for every pupil. Love it or loathe it, ICT has had an enormous influence on the manageability of a more customised and personalised learning environment for schools.

Role of BECTA and ICT

In the UK, British Educational Communications and Technology Agency (BECTA) has been made responsible for delivering the e-strategy that is seen as essential to enable personalised learning. Initially, BECTA produced a short booklet *Learning Platforms and Personalised Learning* (2007). This is not without controversy. BECTA has shown that schools can fingerprint pupils without asking for parental permission and by mid-2007 the campaigning group 'Leave Them Kids Alone' estimated that 3,500 primary and secondary schools were using biometric technology systems, involving 750,000 fingerprinted children and young people. Among other things, biometric technologies were used to run cashless lunch queues, school libraries and attendance systems. Commercial systems aimed at parents are available that offer continuous location monitoring for a monthly fee. This enables the parent to view their child's position on a personalised mapping system, and to know whether the device is on or off or if it has been damaged while being worn.

ICT can also provide a greater range of classroom and school resources than ever before. It has the capacity to enable electronic testing, marking, targeting and report writing. It can analyse work undertaken by pupils and enable systematic feedback on learning and thereby inform on the effectiveness of the teaching. It can individualise work and enable instantaneous feedback.

The IT revolution is for all ages. I went into a nursery the other day and saw teaching assistants using PDAs to note down their child observations. These small handheld machines had the distinct advantage of getting rid of the numerous post-it observations. They also supply ready data to feed into ongoing records for each child. The latter statements come from the teaching assistants themselves, who would certainly not be engaged in something they felt was time-consuming with the children.

Personalised learning as part of the ECM agenda

Central government's interest and promotion of personalised learning is also linked to the outcomes of its ECM agenda. The location monitoring mentioned earlier, for example, is marketed to include 'being safe' and covers bullying. ECM is not a blanket statement that children matter – it is 'every' child from 0 to 19 years of age. This forces us also to rethink what exactly we mean by 'a child'. Just as earlier we looked at the social construction of a pupil, the ECM agenda involves a re-construction of what is meant by childhood and whether this really does cover sixteen-year-olds and over.

The personalised learning ideology does support a return to a far more holistic approach to learning and teaching and this links in directly with theories that attempt to look at and analyse different approaches to learning, in particular institutionalised learning that takes place in early learning centres and schools.

Practical outcomes on preferred learning styles theory

Learning styles

This section draws on the ideas about learning styles carried out by Gardner, Kolb, and Dunn and Dunn. It is also informed by many other researchers and practical advisers such as Smith and Call (2000) about physiological learning styles. We gain information about the world in which we live from each of our five senses – sight, touch, feel, smell and hearing. Many of us do not have all the five senses in perfect working order and some do not have use of one or more of them. Sometimes, this is compensated for by other means, sometimes it means that we identify the child as having SEN. When working with very young children and babies we see the most active use made of sensory receivers. As children become older the importance of different senses in industrial countries such as the UK tends to change. The current models on preferred learning styles reflect this and by the time children come into school, these tend to be divided into three key senses:

- visual
- auditory
- kinaesthetic (moving) or tactile (touch).

It is really important to remember that a preferred physiological learning style does not mean that the child – or adult – can only learn in one style. It means that they prefer to learn in one style and may for that reason learn more effectively in that style. As the crude learning preferences questionnaires demonstrated, it is often possible to have two learning styles, but usually one will dominate. It is important that children get the opportunity to develop learning styles in all three areas, and fortunately the fashion for setting children into VAK group learners seems to have finished. What this physiological insight into learning has done is to alert educationalists to the need to ensure that all learners get a variety of different opportunities to use their senses for learning. This is a powerful message for all teachers.

Table 6.1 VAK learning preferences

Visual learners

- Prefer to see information and instructions
- May forget information that has only been heard
- Enjoy writing, drawing, imagining
- Prefer to make their own notes and read for themselves, mind maps, flow diagrams
- Appear to daydream when read to
- See pictures and images in their minds when they remember things
- Are likely to be able to recall through the use of labelled diagrams or by re-writing pieces of text or other information, multi-media graphics, learning mats, key words display, picture sequence puzzles
- May be easily distracted by noise or movement
- Are organised and observant

Auditory learners

- Follow verbal instructions easily
- Prefer to hear information. They ask for information to be spoken to them, rather than to read or collect it for themselves
- Enjoy talking books, multi-media sounds, positive self-talk
- Express themselves well orally but may have difficulty when writing
- Can recall with some accuracy what has been said to them and may find little benefit in repeated additional reading or writing out facts
- Enjoy explaining to others and using positive self-talk
- Are talkative, enjoy music, use character voices
- May move their lips when reading silently to themselves
- May be confused by directions and have little spatial awareness

Kinaesthetic learners

- Are more likely to be the ones who can adapt less readily to the other two learning styles
- Demonstrate a need to be active; are anxious to 'do' and get 'hands-on'
- Enjoy making things and other practical activities
- Need few verbal or written instructions
- Can do and demonstrate to others readily – role play, dancing, sports, touch-sensitive whiteboards
- Fidget a lot and pay little attention to verbal or written instructions and activities
- Are not distracted by their own 'fiddling' and may even be unaware of it
- May learn little by the auditory or visual means that become more prevalent as they proceed through primary school, and are therefore the pupils who are most likely to become disaffected and disruptive
- Benefit from ICT features such as mouse/track/move

Source: With thanks to Julie Sheriff, deputy head and lead learner, Longview CP School.

Table 6.2 NLP language extension

General	Visual	Auditory	Kinaesthetic
I don't understand	I'm in the dark	That's all Greek to me	I can't make head nor tail of it
I don't know	It's not clear	I can't tell if that's right	I don't have a handle on that idea
I understand	I see what you mean I get the picture	That rings a bell	That feels right I get your drift
I think	My view is . . .	Something tells me	I hold these views
I'm confused	This is a mess	There's no rhyme or reason to this	I can't get a grip
	It's obscure	It sounds crazy	None of this fits

Remember that this is not a precise science, it is only offered to provide some guidelines. An interesting extension to this comes from the findings of the Neuro-linguistic Programme (NLP) researchers. They suggest that speech may translate differently for different types of learners. Table 6.2 provides some examples. I cannot say this really convinces me, but it is quite interesting to observe.

Teaching styles

Of course, as well as different learning styles there are different teaching styles, as we saw from the previous chapter. Student teachers and other educational professionals working in school become only too aware of this as they watch different teachers teaching the same children or different children.

Folklore has it that the majority of teachers are visual learners themselves and therefore tend to favour and understand the visual learners more easily in their class. Certainly, I have sat at the back of many classes and watched children being told off for fiddling with hair, doodling on small white boards and messing about with rulers and pens while they should be listening. I am often only too aware that during lectures and meetings I have done exactly the same and watched others doing the same as well. The 'fiddling' seems to help concentration and in some classrooms this is recognised by letting the 'fiddlers' play with a small piece of Blu-tack, which is less annoying and distracting for others. Auditory learners often get told off for not looking at the teacher or other educational professional when they are being instructed – looking down, gazing out of a window for example. It may be that for some of these learners, the visual is distracting and the looking away is a means of concentrating. It is also interesting to remember that in some cultures it is disrespectful for a child to look directly at someone who is talking. This may not only be an ethnic difference, but can be linked with children who come from homes where children are careful to keep out of the way of specific adults and develop an aura of invisibility in order to survive.

Activity/Thinking Task 2

Observe a group of children or adults at a meeting, lecture, lesson, etc. that involves quite a degree of concentration. It is also possible to do this activity watching a discussion panel on television. What 'fiddling' activities are being undertaken? How may this help/hinder concentration?

The beginning, ending and middle factor

Some years ago, I attended an inservice training course on accelerated learning. We were asked to listen to a list of unconnected words without writing anything down. We were told that there would be about twenty-five of these words and we should listen carefully. Then the twenty-five words were read aloud. Afterwards we were asked to write down as many as we could remember. Some of the audience were really excellent, demonstrating to the rest of us how useful it is to have a good auditory learning style and memory.

The purpose of the exercise, however, was not to test good auditory learning, but to evidence the beginning, ending and middle (BEM) factor in learning. This is the premise that people learn more successfully at the beginning and end of a learning activity than they do in the middle. It is assumed that this is linked with the fact that concentration, interest and motivation are usually highest then. Certainly the result of the reading out of those twenty-five words resulted in the majority of us being able to recall some words at the start, one or two in the middle and those at the end. The audience also demonstrated that an unusual word was also more likely to be remembered. Indeed, I can still recall it now – 'elephant'.

The lesson for learning in schools was a simple one – create more beginnings and endings. Both the literacy and numeracy hour/lesson in their traditional format did this; although I suspect this was accidental, rather than intentional. The oral/mental starter at the start of the numeracy lesson exemplifies this. Many of the plenaries at end of lesson involve a change in seating or a change in activity. This results, hopefully, in providing points where children remember more easily what they are doing. Some plenaries concentrate on reviewing the learning that has taken place, others provide homework tasks to consolidate the learning.

Activity/Thinking Task 3

Observe an activity or lesson and focus on the small beginnings and endings within that activity. Or plan an activity that contains a number of small beginnings and endings.

It is important that 'beginnings' are not wasted on mundane or routine activities. In my own primary school – a good few years ago – the head teacher would spend the first ten minutes of most assemblies telling us what we were doing wrong or might do wrong. It was obviously the most important point of the assembly for him; but for us, his child audience, it meant that what followed could never be an awe-inspiring, motivating experience. We were in daze mode.

The BEM factor also acknowledges that most learners – ourselves as well – need some sort of 'switching-off' time when we are learning. How many of you as readers of this book, will put it down and go and take a break while reading even small extracts. Certainly as the writer of it, I do. Good teachers implicitly acknowledge this. In Chapter 13 on 'Brain Breaks' we look at this in more detail.

Motivation and learning

This section turns to another important factor in learning – motivation. We are going to look at one particular theory about how we can motivate learners. This is a model of a motivational cycle, which has been found particularly useful with more challenging learners, but also quite useful for more personal action plans.

Motivational cycle

Figure 6.1 shows Prochaska and DiClemente's Motivational cycle for six stages of change. This is also closely linked to the work of those trying to help people beat addictions such as smoking and drug abuse. But it is also used very successfully with learners who need to become motivated to behave in order to learn.

This figure sets out six different stages of change. It starts with the arrow on the right at the pre-contemplation stage and then moves round clockwise to contemplation, determination (often called preparation), action, maintenance and relapse. Of course 'the

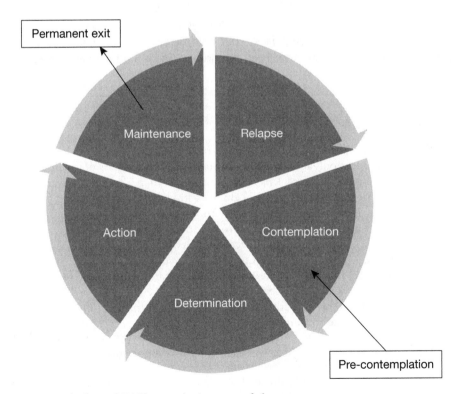

Figure 6.1 Prochaska and DiClemente's six stages of change

relapse' isn't an automatic stage, but one of the great honesties of this cycle is that it recognises and deals with relapses in behaviour. This is one of the reasons why it becomes a powerful tool in coping with children and young people with challenging behaviour, chronic addiction problems and risk-taking behaviour.

Table 6.3 shows what each different stage implies in terms of indicators and strategies to use. At the start of the cycle, we are completely oblivious to the problem we have and show great resistance to anyone trying to make us change our behaviour. We may say that we don't have the problem, deny that it is a problem, 'smoking never did my granny any harm', etc. In a primary classroom, this is the unmotivated learner being uninterested and unable to see that that in itself is an issue. The lack of motivation may show itself in misbehaviour, other children laugh and the child learns to misbehave to gain attention and, often, street 'cred' from his peers.

Activity/Thinking Task 4

Tom is nine. He is really unhappy in school. He finds it difficult to read and is always tired. He daydreams and gets told off for not paying attention. He doesn't seem to care what happens and does not seem to talk much.

- Where does Tom fit in on the cycle?
- What are the indicators for this stage?
- What strategies would you use to enhance motivation?
- What needs to happen for Tom to move on to the next stage?

If you have found this quite a challenging task, you might find it useful to start with something you have tried to change in your own behaviour – for example giving up smoking, not eating chocolate, etc. Then go through Table 6.3 again and see how the cycle works then.

Extrinsic and intrinsic motivation

Motivation is another important element in managing change. We are all familiar with the rewards systems in schools and have probably been the beneficiaries of it when at school ourselves. Over the past ten years, I have seen a massive increase in the rewards systems used in primary schools, which I actually think is linked with much more formal and traditional teaching. Rewards provide extrinsic motivation. We do this in order to get a specific reward. Intrinsic motivation comes from within. We do this because we want to do it. I read because I want to read, not because someone will give me five house points for finishing a book. Many of the techniques we are covering in this book – accelerated/ mind-friendly learning, brain gym, and thinking skills are designed to encourage children to want to learn for its own sake, rather than for a reward. Research (Kohn, 2001) suggests that extrinsic reward systems prevent the establishment of intrinsic motivation and there are ways into learning that concentrate on intrinsic learning.

Intrinsic motivators

Much of the learning we look at in the next two chapters concentrates on making learning meaningful, relevant and fun, so that there is less need for extrinsic rewards to encourage

Table 6.3 Stages and motivational tasks

Stage	Indicators	Motivational task
Pre-contemplation	The entry point to the process of change Child or adult oblivious to the problem Great resistance Not currently considering change; denying, ignoring or avoiding	Raise doubt – increase child's awareness of risks and problems with current behaviour
Contemplation	Ambivalent about change: 'sitting on the fence' Not considering change within the next month Apprehensive about changing See need to improve/change and begin to think about how to do it	Validate child/adult's lack of readiness Clarify that the decision is theirs Encourage evaluation of pros and cons of behaviour change Identify and promote new and positive outcome expectations
Determination	Aware of the problem Some experience with change and are trying to change 'Testing the waters' Beginning to consider the change and able to predict a future Planning to act within the next month	Need help identifying and assisting in problem-solving regarding obstacles Help in identifying support Ensuring the child has the skills and resources to change behaviour Gain encouragement (perhaps from others) for small initial stages
Action	Commitment to change Practising new behaviour for three to six months Visible change taking place Forward movement takes place towards the goal to produce a change in the problem area Learning has taken place	Focus on restructuring cues and social support Bolstering up self-efficacy for dealing with obstacles Combating any feelings of loss Reiterate long-term benefits
Maintenance	Continued commitment to sustaining new behaviour Change feels comfortable after six months	Plan for follow up support Reinforce internal rewards Discuss coping with relapse Acknowledge that maintaining a change may require different skills and strategies than were needed to achieve the change in the first place
Relapse	Resumption of old behaviours 'Fall from grace'	Evaluate what caused the relapse (trigger) Reassess motivation and barriers Plan stronger coping strategies

children/young people to 'do good work' or maintain good behaviour. Other suggestions are:

- giving learners control and choice;
- curiosity;
- offering challenges, problems and novelty;
- discouraging feelings of inferiority;
- stimulating emotional intensity in learning though discussion, music, drama and art;
- frequency of feedback;
- using learners learning style;
- making the environment physically and emotionally safe.

(Adapted from Module 4, *Learning Mentor Training Handbook*)

Kohn (2001) writes both academic and family-friendly papers and articles. The list below is slightly adapted from one of these family-friendly articles:

1   all rewards are bad;
2   rewards manipulate children;
3   rewards interfere with the real reason for learning;
4   rewards create praise junkies;
5   rewards devalue the task and the learner feels bribed;
6   rewards steal a child's pleasure;
7   rewards encourage children to lose interest once praise is gone;
8   rewards reduce achievement.

Most of Kohn's work has looked at how children/students can be taught how to be 'responsible' and 'respectful'. The goal of education is to 'help students realise that they can think, learn, act and change things.' And here I would agree with him. I am not so sure that I would say that all rewards are bad, since I quite enjoy getting rewards myself, even when I am intrinsically motivated to do something. But I do think we are encouraging children to become 'praise junkies' and later in schooling they 'see through this' and become virtually impossible to praise. If you visit his website, there is a lovely critique of the ideology of that 'super nanny' TV show.

Child profiling

There is no right way to construct a child profile, but you will need to collect relevant evidence from an early stage. When beginning a child profile, it is useful to have a record sheet on which you can gather information in note form. Evidence of a child's work can be written, taped, photographed and filmed – with the appropriate permissions of course. Most schools today have a generic ruling about photographs, linked with educational purpose; but some schools are still retaining a child-by-child policy. Any evidence should be dated and annotated.

The learning profile can be divided into three broad areas:

1   relevant background information;
2   strengths and areas for development in learning as identified by the class teacher and other adult educational professionals working with the child. This will also give you

an opportunity to meet with some of these professionals, such as the SNA, learning mentor, HLTA, etc.;

3 own observations.

Background information

Relevant background information includes facts such as date of birth, heritage language, gender. For both this and the next section you will need to consult the class teacher and/or other relevant adults to obtain general and background information to inform the two sections. Only include the first name of the child in order to ensure confidentiality of information.

Strengths and areas for development

Document strengths and weaknesses in learning as identified by the class teacher and other educational professionals. Make sure you have evidence for your records. Do not make assumptions or stereotype children. Children of single parent families, for example, are often given a deficit model label, but there are usually many other factors involved in family life. Large numbers of single parents do a wonderful job, with little money and support. See if you can use Gardner's multiple intelligences to broaden the remit of strengths and weakness.

Own observations

Your own observations should inform judgements about the child's development. These may be general observations that pose such questions as:

- Does this child relate well to others?
- Does s/he communicate well?
- Is s/he active or assertive in the groups in which they work? Are there differences?
- Does s/he understand instructions?
- Does s/he need a high level of support, reassurance?

You may find it helpful to relate these questions to specific areas of the curriculum. Do not forget to provide evidence for any statements you make and ask yourself if there are differences linked with the nature of the learning, time of day, peer/adult presence, area in which activity is taking place, etc.

Much of the evidence you need for this section can be obtained through careful observation. Make sure you observe inside and outside the classroom and in all areas of the curriculum. The timed observation schedule sheet in Table 6.4. provides one way of observing a child during the course of the day. It is worth doing well, asking 'What is the child actually doing?'. The answer to this question tells you what is taking place in the 'observed' learning. The analysis section should be used for making some evaluation of this 'observed' learning. You might also speculate on the experience as well as the formal and hidden curriculum involved. The twenty-minute schedule was designed several years ago in Leeds by a research team led by Joan Tough. It was used by full-time class teachers to record, as accurately as possible, two children during the course of a day.

Table 6.4 Timed observation schedule

Date		
Year		
Child (first name or letter only)		
Focus of observation: child's approach to learning		
Time	*Child activity*	*Comment*
8.50		
9.10		
9.30		
9.50		
10.10		
10.30		
10.50		
11.10		
11.30		
11.50		
12.10		
12.30		
12.50		
1.10		
1.30		
1.50		
2.10		
2.30		
2.50		
3.10		
3.30		
Analysis		

As the profile develops, information may be structured as follows:

- *Intellectual development.* This involves more than listing SATs results and other test scores. Again, Gardner's work on multiple intelligences is useful. Try to observe the child engaged in different activities in different contexts. Comment both on the quality of the end product and the learning processes. Remember to look at all four modes of language – listening, speaking, reading and writing. How does the child cope with problem solving or investigation activities? What are the child's talents and interests?
- *Physical development.* Comment on the child's build. How does s/he compare with others of the same age? You will need to read about the norms in physical development. There are often huge differences in any one class. You will also need to consider fine motor skills (writing, colouring in, using scissors, drawing, etc.) and gross motor skills (general movement, physical education, dance, in the playground).
- *Emotional development.* Is the child confident, self-assured, able to organise her or himself, able to organise others, happy, secure, etc. Does the emotional development vary in different subject areas or at different times of the day? Is the confident reader bullied in the playground? Are the quiet children for whom English is an additional language, chatty and confident in their own language.
- *Social development.* How does the child get on with other children? Does s/he have lots of friends/mix freely/have a few steady friends/exist on the fringe of the class/seem to be a loner, etc.? How does the child relate to you, the teacher, other adults, other pupils?

Analysis and findings

Both the profile and the timed observation schedule in this chapter are based on observing and gathering evidence on children's learning. The final analysis therefore needs to demonstrate how your thinking has been informed by your readings on developmental psychology theories.

Personal learning plans

These have been mentioned quite often in recent years and were trialled a few years ago in a small number of Scottish schools. The trials showed that the plans produced an 'enriched dialogue' between teachers and pupils, but were extremely time consuming. Schools also found it difficult to link PLPs to the formal curriculum.

The management of personalised learning in terms of individual PLPs is a real challenge for schools. It is not new, although the politicisation of the term is relatively new. Many schools you visit and work in do tailor their curriculum and teaching methods to meet the needs of their community. These are the schools that walk the talk of the stated principles behind the government rhetoric and adapt it for their own school community. These are the schools who may never have read the stated principles behind personalised learning but enshrine them in their practice. They:

- Make clear learning pathways through the education system and provide the motivation for children to become independent, e-literate, fulfilled, lifelong learners.
- Create a professional ethos that accepts and assumes every child comes to the classroom with a different knowledge base and skill set, as well as varying aptitudes and

Table 6.5 Personal learning plan

Personal learning plan based on the foundation	
Name of child	
Date of creation	
Review period	
Involvement of others in plan creation	
Area of learning and development	*PLP focus*
Personal, social and emotional development	
Communication, language and literacy	
Problem solving, reasoning and numeracy	
Knowledge and understanding of the world	
Physical development	
Creative development	

aspirations; and that as a result, there is a determination for every young person's needs to be assessed and their talents developed through diverse teaching strategies.

• Promote high standards of educational achievement and well-being for all pupils, ensuring that all aspects of organising and running the school work together to get the best for all pupils.

(Adapted from DfES, 2004a)

Activity/Thinking Task 5

Think of a child you know, perhaps the children on whom you did the child profile. How would you devise a PLP for that child? You might find it useful to use the headings provided in that profile – intellectual, physical, emotional and social development. You may want to add some yourself, perhaps in a faith school you might want to look for spiritual development. It would also be possible to devise PLP for any aged child based on the areas of learning and development for the foundation stage. I have used this approach because it represents a broader approach to thinking about the child themselves, rather than strict subject specialisms.

You may also need to think for how long this plan should last – one week, half a term, a full term. If it is a weekly plan, does it need to target every area? Who else needs to be involved with developing it. This sort of plan does not replace the AfL, which will be examined later, it is simply an exercise to help you think through how you would develop a plan for a specific child.

And finally, how manageable would this sort of activity be for every child in a class?

Differentiation

Differentiation as a formalised PLP

PLPs are a formalised record of differentiation, and this section looks more closely at exactly what this often-used term means as well as challenging it, using experience from France. As is often the case in education, this term means something very different from what it means in either mathematics or science.

Government publications provide three categories of differentiation:

1 by task: setting different tasks for pupils of different abilities;
2 by outcome: setting more open-ended tasks, allowing pupil response at different levels;
3 by support: giving more help (resources, adult support, etc.) to certain pupils.

Certainly if we use Bloom's taxonomy for learning objectives, there is a very distinct levelling both for setting and evaluating learning outcomes. So differentiation by outcome can be linked with whether the outcome involves knowledge, comprehension, application, analysis, synthesis or evaluation. This is not easy because it involves quite a detailed analysis of each child's outcome – both written and oral – to identify exactly what process has taken place and been evidenced. If tasks are fairly pedestrian it is easier, for example outcomes from an exercise of addition sums. It is much harder if the task is more open-ended. This difficulty of levelling for open-ended and creative tasks was a point well illustrated by Michael Morpurgo while he was the children's poet laureate. He undertook KS2 English Standard Assessment Tasks/Tests (SATs) and emerged with Level 5. A Level 5 puts him just into the secondary level!

Principles of differentiation

John Clare (2004) gives many different definitions of differentiation and points out how unhelpful many of them are. He does recommend the work of Carol Tomlinson and her five principles of differentiation:

1   intelligence is varied rather than singular;
2   the brain hungers for meaning;
3   humans learn best with moderate challenge;
4   there is an increasing variety in the students we teach;
5   differentiation is about a struggle for equity and excellence.

Tomlinson also provides some guidance to how differentiation would look in a classroom and this could just as easily be applied to an early years setting.
Table 6.6 sets out the eleven characteristics of a differentiated classroom. It is worth pointing out that several of the characteristics listed in Table 6.6 have been incorporated into the ideology behind many of the plans for new secondary schools under the BSF programme,

Table 6.6 Eleven characteristics of a differentiated classroom

1   Learning experiences are based on diagnosis of student readiness, interest and/or learning profile
2   Content, activities and products or other assessments are developed in response to differing needs
3   Teaching and learning are focused on key concepts, understandings and skills
4   All students participate in 'respectful' work
5   Teacher and students work together to ensure continual engagement and challenge for each learner
6   The teacher co-ordinates use of time, space and activities
7   Flexible groupings ensure consistently fluid working arrangements, including whole class learning, peer-selected groups, teacher-selected groups and random groups
8   Time use is flexible in response to student needs
9   A variety of management strategies (such as learning centres, interest centres, compacting, contract, independent study, collegial partnerships, tiered assignment, learning buddies, etc.) are used to help target instruction to student needs
10 Clearly established individual and group criteria provide guidance towards success
11 Students are assessed in a variety of ways appropriate to demonstrate their own thought and growth

Source: Adapted from Tomlinson in Clare (2004).

and also that most are really what we would expect from good primary practice. The Plowden Report stated its views about differentiation quite clearly, although it was not termed differentiation until much more recently: 'Teachers will have to adapt their methods to individuals within a class or school. Only in this way can the needs of the gifted and slow learning children and all those between the extremes be met.' However, just twenty years later the focus on the individual primary child was changed to a focus towards achievement in core subjects. The introduction of the National Curriculum in 1988 and later the National Literacy Strategy (NLS) and National Numeracy Framework (NNF) were linked with particular teaching practices, in particular whole-class teaching and various forms of ability grouping. Ten years later, this is the legacy found in most primary schools and one which theoretically means the move towards a more differentiated, personalised curriculum is challenging. However, the major challenge is still that while the focus is on achievement in mathematics, English and science; those will be the subject areas that form the bulk of the curriculum.

Differentiation in other countries

As part of the primary PGCE programme at Liverpool Hope, those studying modern foreign languages spend a teaching practice in a European school. One of their major findings in countries such as Spain and France is that not only is there virtually no differentiation, but also in both countries it is actually seen as illegal because it denies some children the right to a full curriculum. There are good historical reasons for this that are part of the differences between the core educational values of both countries. French education, for example, was informed by Republican ideas of emancipation and social justice, whereas English education was linked with a more utilitarian approach of needing

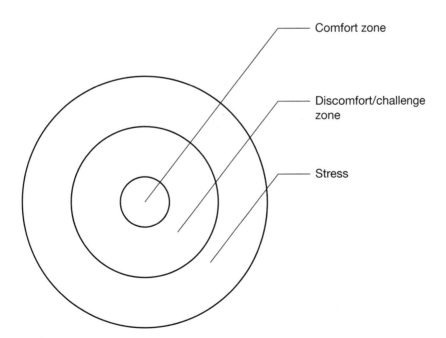

Figure 6.2 Change related to learning to cope with learning challenges

to ensure basic education so that workers were educated to fit 'their station in life'. More recently self-esteem has been rated as a key characteristic of successful learning in English schools and children encouraged to feel confident in themselves. This may result in children, who have few strategies for coping with challenge, remaining in their comfort zone. Differentiation can facilitate this and can also very effectively narrow the curriculum for some children.

Figure 6.2 shows how this can be seen in terms of change theory. If children are encouraged to remain comfortable, they miss learning strategies to manage challenge in their learning. They may maintain their self-esteem, but fail to progress. As this is a more generic model of change, we should be helping all children to be flexible, face challenges and be unafraid of new learning. Obviously we would want to avoid raising the level to stress point, where much less learning is likely to take place.

The English MFL student teachers found that whereas English teachers systematically provided differentiated tasks for written work, not one of their overseas schools did. Children were given identical tasks to complete and most work was undertaken either as whole-class instruction or individual work from a set book or worksheets. When discussed with the teachers, the French teachers were quite horrified that English children might miss out on parts of the curriculum.

There has been considerable criticism in the past about ability grouping and streaming in primary schools and classes in England and the tendency it has to replicate the inequalities outside school, with socially and emotionally deprived children being placed in lower groups.

Table 6.7 Differentiation in a cultural context

	France	*England*
1 Core educational values	Republican ideals of emancipation and social justice	Developing the full potential of each child, happiness and balance
2 Coping with mixed ability in the classroom	Differentiation of means (time, teacher and peer support)	Differentiation by task
3 Differentiation by task	Last resort for individuals with exceptional needs	Standard practice based on same-ability groups
4 Self-esteem	Inclusion	Succeeding to do a task
5 The pupil	A social being, entitled to equal expectations with peers	A happy and well-balanced child whose full potential should be developed
6 Cross-cultural criticism	English differentiation teaching practice perpetuates social inequalities	French universalism leads to lack of respect of individual needs and self-esteem; no stretching for the most able

Source: Raveaud (2005).

The French and Spanish results are not significantly different from those in the UK, so this very different approach to 'personalised learning' is interesting in terms of outcomes as well. Raveaud (2005) provides a useful table that certainly raises questions about our assumptions that we must differentiate, although there may be several variables which are unaccounted for – e.g. numbers of children with SEN within main-stream classes in English schools (see Table 6.7).

Personalised learning, learning style preferences and differentiation all have important components in common. They represent a current trend in English education to try to match curriculum content to the learning needs of pupils. This is a complex process in which there are no 'right' answers.

7 Planning for mind-friendly learning

QTS Standards

1, 2, 4, 8, 10, 14, 21, 22, 25a–d

Learning objectives

- to recognise links between learning theories in Chapters 5 and 6 and ideas on accelerated and mind-friendly learning;
- to identify four different types of curriculum;
- to recognise the need to set clear objectives for children's learning, building on their own prior knowledge and ensure they are aware of the substance and purpose of what they are asked to do;
- to be able to use a planning framework for mind-friendly learning that supports learning theories covered in Chapters 5 and 6.

This chapter will look at ways in which the aspects of our knowledge about how children learn can be developed into a viable way of planning for a small-group activity or whole-class lesson. In order to do this the chapter will explore the work of writers such as Alistair Smith, Nicola Call and Peter Greenfield.

Accelerated learning

A definition

Accelerated learning has been defined by Oliver Cavigolioli and Ian Harris in the book on mind mapping as a 'considered, generic approach to learning based on research drawn from disparate disciplines and tested with different age groups and different ability levels in very different circumstances'. This definition is probably as good as any for the term accelerated learning can be misleading. It is not for a specific group of learners, nor for a particular age group, nor for a particular category of perceived ability. It does not mean doing the same things faster.

It seems to have come originally from Colin Rose's book on *Accelerated Learning* (Tracy with Rose, 1995). At this time the idea of accelerated learning seems to have largely stayed within the American system and extended particularly into corporation and business management. A quick web search on accelerated learning exemplifies this move into business, where consultants in accelerated learning clearly found business corporations more open and profitable than education.

ALPS

The growth of expansion in the UK at the end of the 1990s and into the new millennium has been largely due to the work of Alistair Smith, the organisation Alite, and the publishing house Network Education Press, now known as Network Continuum Press. There are a number of independent consultants working in the UK on accelerated learning within local education authorities and the term 'accelerated learning' has sometimes been altered to 'mind-friendly learning'. Many of the teaching and learning strategies used now are such an inherent part of good practice that more recent practitioners are probably not aware of the history or the initial terms behind them.

Smith and Call in *The Alps Approach* (2001) explain that there is the accelerated learning cycle at the heart of the ALPS approach to classroom strategies and this should act as a framework for planning. It involves:

1   connecting the new learning with what has previously taken place;
2   providing learners with an overview of ' the big picture', i.e. what is going to take place in the lesson or activity;
3   describing the learning outcomes, so that all learners are clear what they are going to be learning;
4   providing the relevant input using a VAK approach (visual, auditory and kinaesthetic); this is sometimes called VARK (visual, auditory, reading, kinaesthetic);
5   activating understanding of the input through VAK support;
6   ensuring the learners can demonstrate – at their own level – their understanding of the task(s);
7   reviewing the lesson – this can be as a plenary review or as a homework activity linked to the outcomes, or as a review of how the learning took place.

Peter Greenhalgh, formerly a senior adviser for Cheshire and now an independent consultant, outlines a slightly different planning circle for mind-friendly learning in his *Reaching Out to all Learners* (2002) booklet. This starts at the all-important point of providing a supportive ethos for learning.

Accelerated and mind-friendly learning techniques have drawn heavily on knowledge about how learning takes place – both the internal and external processes. These include:

1   developments in neuroscience and how the brain works;
2   work on physiology and learning – closely linked to Maslow's work on 'hierarchy of needs', which we will examine in the following chapter;
3   teaching specific skills such as listening, paying attention, concentrating, good sitting, and modelling generic good learning behaviours;
4   strategies for providing a good, secure and purposeful working environment.

5   the creation and development of a positive learning environment based on three factors – resourcefulness, resilience and responsibility.

Network Continuum Press produces several excellent books that go into these strategies in much greater detail. They differ considerably from the 'Tips for Teachers' texts because they explain 'why' as well as 'how'.

Four types of curriculum

The curriculum

Pollard and Tann (2004) and Pollard (2002) distinguished between the official or formal curriculum, the hidden or latent curriculum, the observed curriculum and the curriculum as experienced. These are all part of children's learning experience and can deeply influence the effectiveness of the learning outcomes. Chapter 4 examined several aspects, but as we move through this book, we can provide a more technical and professional language to describe the process.

The hidden, observed and experienced learning experiences in the curriculum are particularly relevant to the overall aims of the school, especially children's personal, spiritual, moral, social and cultural development. The formal curriculum has to plan for these, but they are demonstrated through the other curricula. We can teach children that they should play well together, but it is only through observing them informally over a period of time, both inside and outside the classroom, that we know whether the teaching has been effective. Even then we cannot be sure that it was as a direct result of the teaching.

The official curriculum

When the National Curriculum was first introduced in 1988, it was a statutory instruction for all children and young people to be taught specific and recognised subjects. This has altered considerably since, but our Victorian ancestors would have recognised most of what was set down in the 1988 requirements. They would have questioned the right of all children to 'receive' it, pondering about the wisdom of teaching subjects such as geography and mathematics (rather than arithmetic) to working boys and girls.

The National Curriculum set out the law, and later published schemes of work (SOW) through government agencies such as the QCA. The SOW set out not only what children should learn, but when and how they should learn it. As the name suggests, they were non-statutory and schools were not required to follow them. The DfEE (the Department for Education and Employment), later the DfES and now the DCSF produced more extended guidelines for both literacy and numeracy for primary schools. This 'planned course' of study is also known as the official or formal curriculum. It makes planning much easier because the content is already defined. In recent years central government has made statements, for example in all the personalised learning documentation, about loosening its hold on what goes on in schools. But the need to demonstrate both nationally and internationally that attainment is rising in English schools means that results will still be published, league tables followed and inspection reports tightly monitored. This means that central government control will remain tight.

There is nothing new about this. Schools that have logbooks dating back to the nineteenth century have some wonderful descriptions of standards and the role of the central government inspector who visited and tested children to see if they had reached the required level. Then, as now, the emphasis was on literacy and numeracy.

The hidden curriculum

This curriculum is 'picked up' rather than learnt. The previous chapters of this guide have identified several aspects of the hidden curriculum, and the findings about children's learning have emphasised the importance of school and classroom ethos in terms of supporting effective learning. There are hidden messages about the role of the teacher; the role of other adult workers in the classroom and school; the role of the learner, in particular the role of the individual child as a successful learner; attitudes towards learning; ways adults expect different groups to behave and contrasts between this and peer expectations. Most primary schools have good personal, social and health education (PSHE) programmes that acknowledge the pervasiveness of the hidden curriculum and its influence on children's progress and attainment. There has also been a growth in the programmes that look at emotional intelligence/literacy within schools as well as moral and spiritual development. All this is an acknowledgement that programmes are needed to inform the hidden curriculum and ensure that the stated ethos of the school is supported by its policies and practice.

Figure 7.1 shows how different aspects of school life need to be audited to ensure that equality issues are addressed. Sometimes the areas under scrutiny are not relevant for one particular group, but are for others; for example staffing role models in most primary schools give hidden messages about both gender and ethnicity to all pupils.

Activity/Thinking Task 1

1   The SATs results identify several groups that do less well than other groups; why might this be a product of the SATs testing itself, rather than a 'failing' of the group to achieve?

2   How are visitors welcomed into a primary school you know? What is the hidden curriculum of this? You could include your initial telephone call to the school and how this was dealt with and the sort of reception you received when you arrived at the school. Many schools have welcome packs for student teachers; these provide guidance on the roles and responsibilities of both parties as well as other important support and organisational procedures. A member of the senior management team (SMT) often has overall responsibility for students and may take a particular interest, even when the more operational side of the work is delegated elsewhere. There are many hidden messages here.

The most important aspect of the hidden curriculum, is that it does need to be identified. A positive ethos for every child does not just happen, it needs to be planned for and created. There may be a specific time for it on the timetable as in a PSHE lesson, or daily circle time; but it has to permeate the whole life of a school to be effective. Planning any lesson or activity involves planning for children's personal, spiritual, moral, social and cultural development, although such learning objectives may never appear on the lesson or activity plan.

The government has issued a considerable amount of guidance and commentaries in the past few years on PSHE and most recently has linked many aspects of the hidden

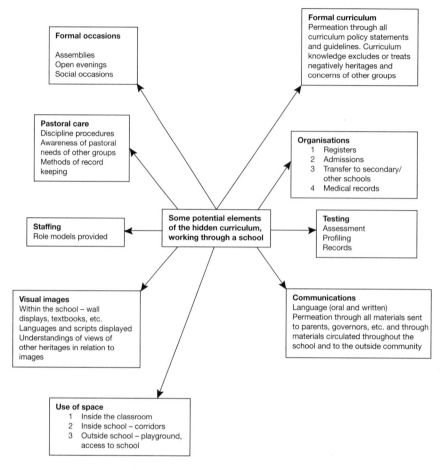

Figure 7.1 The hidden curriculum

curriculum to the concept of citizenship. More information can be found on this via the DCSF website.

The observed curriculum

The observed curriculum is what is actually taking place in the classroom: the lessons and activities you see. This may be different from the intended official curriculum, for a variety of reasons, and one of the skills in lesson observation is to note and evaluate the differences. The beginning teacher is much more likely to display differences between the planned and observed curriculum; but many excellent primary teachers make changes between planning and teaching. Indeed, you will observe lessons where teaching changes during the course of the session as the teacher responds to children's learning needs. The effective teacher has a sound educational reason for this, and the process indicates the subtle skills involved in good teaching.

The experienced curriculum

This is the curriculum as experienced by the children. This is what they take away from the lesson and it is particularly hard to monitor.

Planning for effective learning

In Chapters 11 and 12 we look in more detail about whole school planning in terms of the formal curriculum. At this stage we are just looking at very short term and detailed planning for small-group and whole-class activities.

Schools vary considerably in how they plan and in this chapter we are looking just at the sort of planning student teachers and other educational professionals are asked to do when they first start. This is planning in depth and is generally what is expected of inexperienced teachers, student teachers and teaching assistants – and of course when Ofsted decides to call.

Planning objectives

There are two schools of thought about this. First, those who believe that the planning objectives should be the same as the learning outcomes, and, second, those who say that learning objectives and learning outcomes are different. There is also a move towards having learning objectives, learning outcomes and success criteria. The apparent separation of learning objectives and outcomes is often conveyed to children with the use of two characters called 'WALT' and 'WILF'. WALT stands for 'we are learning to . . .' and WILF stands for 'what I'm looking for . . .'. The 'I' here, refers to the teacher. WILF indicates what are the success criteria that the teacher is defining as achieving the objectives and outcomes.

Here, we are looking at just learning objectives and outcomes being the same, because it is obviously easier and more efficient. This is the learning objective and therefore the outcome will be the achievement of that objective. You may, however, work in a school where this is not necessarily so, and you should therefore follow the advice provided. You will, however, still find it useful to follow the guidance here.

Planning objectives cover two different groups – the children and yourself.

For the children

The first involvement trainee teachers have in planning is generally writing lesson or activity plans, which are developed from the school's medium- and short-term planning. Writing learning objectives for these is one of the hardest aspects of curriculum planning for effective learning. You will learn by looking at objectives written by teachers, teaching assistants and HLTAs and fellow students, and through looking at particular words (usually verbs) as starting points. Teachers' manuals for commercial schemes of work often include lesson objectives and should be consulted before using any commercial programme. This includes government materials from the Internet. Be careful that you do not use either government or commercial schemes objectives, which are aimed at medium- and long-term planning objectives. You will also learn about identifying focused learning objectives by evaluating and reflecting on what progress children have made in the lesson and what you have learnt yourself.

Ineffective learning and teaching is about coverage: 'doing volume/alliteration/sound' for example. This is just too much for an individual lesson or activity. It is a medium-term objective, covering a term or half-term's work. Effective learning takes place when children are kept aware of instructional objectives and receive feedback on their progress towards these objectives. Although this sounds obvious, if children know what they are to learn, you increase the chance that they will learn it. This is easy to test in a small-group teaching situation, when you discuss with children the purpose of the activity. If children think the purpose of the session is to 'have fun', they may enjoy it, but they may not be learning. Mind-friendly learning requires clear focused objectives, which can be easily understood by the children. This does not mean reciting 'parrot fashion' a statement from a government document. Learning objectives need to be in child-speak and clearly understood by learners. Obviously, learning objectives for some children may be different from those for other children. But this is only one element of personalised learning and there are many others as we shall look at in Chapter 12.

For yourself

We are all learning all the time. Children are not the only learners in schools, so too are the teachers, student teachers and other adult support workers. So every lesson/activity has learning objectives for them as well. These are not generally written down in the formal lesson/activity plan, although it is useful to think through and record your specific learning objectives before you go into school each day and then evaluate them at the end of the day and week. The TDA teaching standards provide some of these, but the majority of the TDA standards are long-term objectives and need to be broken down. Some training institutions identify a 'focus' for the student teacher on their lesson/activity templates.

Working with student teachers over several years, it appears that learning objectives for them fall into a distinct pattern:

- Behaviour management – ensuring that the classroom has a reasonable working atmosphere. This is usually – and quite rightly – the first priority for student teachers.
- The focus then moves on and identifies that the most important means of ensuring this is a good working atmosphere that provides children with meaningful and productive lesson/activity content. This should motivate learning.
- The next stage seems to be identifying that this can only be done effectively if such learning tasks are targeted at children's learning needs. This in turn needs to be linked to their prior knowledge, prior assessment of learning and clear indicators for the next step or steps in the learning process. The learning needs vary from school to school, class to class and child to child. They need to be 'customised' for 'your' pupils.
- Finally, planning has to be linked to good observation, monitoring, targeting, assessing and evaluating and recording.

We look at all these stages later, but at this point acknowledge that planning a lesson or activity for children involves a complex and progressive learning continuum for all those doing it. The best teachers are those who will happily acknowledge that they make mistakes and learn from them. In most lessons and activities, you should expect to learn more than the children. Even highly experienced teachers often find this. 'Why is Sabba having difficulties with halves and quarters?' 'How can I increase John's confidence with his spelling?' Experienced teachers too, can be surprised at how children react to specific activities and lessons.

Identifying prior knowledge

Children often know more than we expect and have hidden skills. A simple brainstorming/
blue-sky-walking session at the start of an activity can reveal what knowledge and understandings children already have. There are already several commercial software programmes
on the market. Firms such as Rising Stars provide extensive testing and revision programmes which offer opportunities for regular testing at the start and end of topics.
Personally, I prefer the less text/exam-orientated method described above. When you first
start working with a small group, informal discussions at playtime and lunchtime can reveal
a great deal about what children have already covered. It will often identify what access
to resources they have out of school – a computer with Internet access, a digital watch,
regular visits to the local library, a good store of non-fiction texts, a knowledgeable adult,
family living overseas, family outings and trips at home and abroad, good knowledge about
relevant television programmes and interesting leisure activities, etc. Your own learning
objective for one day might be to find out more about the children's knowledge of authors,
for example. A walk around the playground and having a school dinner are two very good
ways of getting to know this as well as getting to know the children and more about the
culture of primary school children. Which children notice the big display on Janet and
Allan Ahlberg, which children have any of their books, who uses the public library? If at
lunchtime you sit with children from a class above or below your own, you can discuss
their knowledge of authors and from this begin to make some informal assessments about
progression in children's learning and enjoyment about literature. When identifying your
own learning objectives, children's needs must take priority, and this is shown in planning
documentation in the vast majority of schools.

The language of lesson objectives for children

Some of the documentation provided by the school, LA and central government gives
guidance on lesson objectives in particular subjects and phases of learning, but it can offer
no more than guidance. In the previous paragraph, we looked at the individual nature of
children's learning. However good a government or commercial scheme of work, it has
to be personalised for particular children in a particular school at the particular time. And
we look at how one primary school does this for its whole school planning in Chapter
11. Government and commercial schemes provide the current discourse, or language, for
learning, but date rapidly. The same is true for the many schemes and lesson plans to be
found on the Internet. This is why most schools have a rolling programme for updating
their schemes of work.

   Much has been written about writing learning objectives and most general texts on
learning to teach will contain some examples and rationales for their chosen method
(Pollard, 2002). In this chapter we are using some ideas based on the work of Benjamin
Bloom. Much of the advice given to students – and teachers, HLTAs and teaching assistants
– is based on this, although it may not be clear where it comes from originally. LAs, schools,
training manuals and institutions vary in the advice they give. Lesson and activity planning
sheets contain different headings. Some require extensive documentation; others are much
more open-ended. Sometimes lesson objectives can be written as bullet points; sometimes
they have to be full sentences. Practices can vary even within the same school or training
institution. These differences should be viewed positively as it enables the beginning teacher
to look at what is most effective to ensure effective learning and monitoring. There are
three aspects of learning objectives that are universal:

1   Objectives must be written down before the lesson or activity begins because they tell the teacher what is to be taught, why it is to be taught and, often, how it is to be taught.
2   Objectives should be shared with the children, so that they know what they are responsible for. This is usually done orally, although it may be written down. It helps to write objectives in 'child-speak'. It will also clarify your thinking and avoids lifting medium-term objectives from government documentation.
3   Objectives should be shared with all the adults working within the classroom prior to the lesson. Usually this happens in a joint planning meeting, with a quick briefing at the start of the day – as we saw taking place in Chapter 1 on our tour around the school. Adults need to know the purpose of the activity, their role in it and how to use any resources that can enhance the learning.

It is worth noting that many very effective teachers sometimes do not share the learning objectives with the pupils. They wait until the plenary to ask if the pupils themselves can work out what the initial learning objectives were. Many science activities lend themselves particularly well to this.

Content and targets

When objectives are written as bullet points, as the learning outcomes are in this study guide, they begin with verbs. These tell the learner what is to be achieved and tell the teacher and other adults what to look for in order to see if the child has accomplished it. This sounds very mechanistic, but it is just a starting point for planning. Ideally, particularly when working with small groups, adults and children plan targets together. For example, at the end of a session sorting plastic shapes by colour, the teacher may encourage the children to see if there are any other ways of sorting, and identify this as the next learning target. This is rarely solely child-driven – the teacher has a framework of objectives – but content and targets can be set with the children. For example, in a lesson on the Vikings, children could identify what they already know and then what they would like to know. The teacher could then ask them how they would find the information they need, how they would record it and how they would present it.

Figure 7.2 is taken from some work done with Y3s. The first diagram shows the children's initial response to the question 'What do we know about the Vikings?'. The second is the response to the question 'What else do we want to learn about the Vikings?'. Both questions were promoted by having a display of books and access to a CD-ROM, website, etc. on the Vikings available before the lesson. This gave the children an opportunity to gain some prior knowledge, even if this were limited to the covers of the books and software on display. Of course, the teacher has to be clear whether the key objectives are English- or history-based and these may influence both the content and teaching strategies used.

'Child-centred' education was always rather a misnomer – as indeed 'personalised learning' is, when it is used to suggest that children determine what they are going to learn. In the example given above, it is the teacher who is guiding the children's statements about learning objectives. Some of the very detailed coverage in published and online schemes of work seem to allow few opportunities for teachers to do this with their children, but the skilful teacher can still continue to 'sell' the idea of choice, so that children do feel as if they 'own' their own learning. This ownership of learning links closely to many of the findings in the previous three chapters about how to create effective conditions for learning. As adults, we know that choices help to motivate learning.

What we know

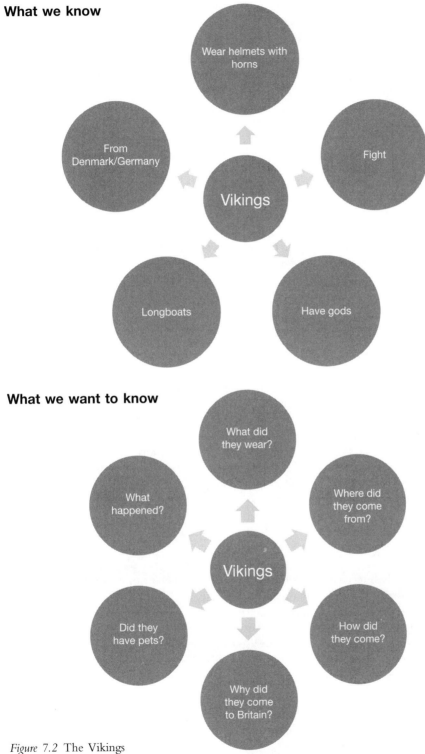

What we want to know

Figure 7.2 The Vikings

Writing objectives

When you first start to discuss and write objectives, it might be useful to think of them as requiring the learner to engage in different levels of thinking. This can also introduce a subtle, rather less obvious means of differentiation into what looks like the same task. Bloom divided verbs into six related categories, starting with knowledge and moving towards evaluation:

1   knowledge
2   comprehension
3   application
4   analysis
5   synthesis
6   evaluation.

This is not just a linear progression. Five-year-olds should be involved in evaluation, synthesis and application just as much as eleven-year-olds. Reviewing objectives alerts you to making sure they do not fit into one category, e.g. knowledge.

Remember, thinking skills are involved in:

*   *Knowledge* – defining, filling in, identifying, labelling and recalling information. Children are asked to remember material by recalling facts, terms, basic concepts and answers. Questions to monitor this learning are literal ones, using words such as 'who', 'what', 'why', 'when', 'show', 'spell' and 'list'.
*   *Comprehension* – describing, retelling, summarising and paraphrasing in order to show comprehension and understanding. Questions to monitor this learning would include 'What facts or ideas show . . .?', 'How would you summarise . . .?'.
*   *Applying* – demonstrating, investigating, showing, solving and using. These ask children to use their learning in a new situation. Questions would be linked to this, asking children to make use of facts in order to . . .
*   *Analysing* – categorising, classifying, examining and deducing. These require the learner to show that they can see parts and relationships. Questions would require children to make inferences and conclusions.
*   *Synthesis* – verbs such as changing, combining, planning, pretending and reconstructing. They ask children to take parts of the information to create an original whole. Tasks would involve adapting, changing and modifying.
*   *Evaluating* – words such as choosing, deciding, evaluating, justifying, ranking and valuing. These ask children to make a judgement based on criteria. Tasks would involve asking children how they would prioritise facts and justify their choices.

For the beginning teacher the most effective objectives, in terms of assessing his or her learning outcomes, are knowledge- and skills-based, i.e. what the children will know and what intellectual/social/physical and communication skills will be developed. Start off with these and limit the number per lesson or activity to one or two. Make them subject-specific or specific to particular areas of learning.

Attitudes

You may wish to include 'developing specific attitudes' as one of your learning objectives, but positive learning attributes such as curiosity, confidence, perseverance, responsibility and interest are generic. They form part of the overall philosophy of learning teaching. Many schools have policies on learning and teaching and these subsume all lesson objectives. There may be a very specific reason for including an attitude objective, for example one that is linked to the needs of the class; or it may be much more personalised for a small group or individual child. This is a clear example of 'personalised learning' and the next chapter looks at this in relation to emotional health and learning. The lesson/activity content needs to show how the attitude will be developed, and the evaluation needs to provide evidence of how it has been developed. The first condition for learning an attitude is to ensure that learners have opportunities to practise the behaviours and choices associated with that attitude. You can then connect attitudes with success by reinforcing the behaviours associated with that attitude.

Activity/Thinking Task 2

You may want to 'encourage a love of reading and experience reading as an enjoyable activity'. What sort of strategies have you seen being used to encourage the attitude towards reading as an enjoyable activity? You might like to think of school and class-based strategies and then out-of-school strategies in local libraries for example. How can parents and carers encourage reading? How can schools help with out-of-school strategies to enjoy reading? How might you measure the success of learning this attitude? Why might this only be a focused activity for some children?

Concepts

Intended learning involves understanding and developing concepts. Conceptual development has a huge research base. At this stage in your career, think of concepts as subject-specific vocabulary and target which concepts you wish to develop in any one session. Generally, technical vocabulary can be found in the scheme of work used by the school. The learning objectives for the scheme then move into key ideas and techniques. A specific lesson or activity objective is based on an understanding of the concept word, and content would look at the word and ensure that children have an understanding of it – at their own level of understanding.

If we take the example of the concept of a triangle. You would have no trouble with a quick definition of a triangle as a two-dimensional shape with three sides. A three-year-old might be able to tell you it had three sides, particularly if the triangle was put in front of them. They might of course tell you that it was blue, but then they would be investigating other properties of a specific triangle. As children learn more about the properties of triangles, they might spend time finding out about different types of triangles – irregular, equilateral, isosceles and right-angled. Later, they would learn about angles within a triangle and gradually their concept of a triangle would develop. They would learn to use and name different instruments to measure triangles and probably quite early on look at triangles in our environment and some of the design properties of a triangle. This might involve returning to constructional toys they played/experimented with when much younger. They would, of course, need to be presented with non-examples of the concept – and be able to differentiate for example between a triangle and a rectangle.

Planning a mind-friendly lesson in eight steps

Figure 7.3 provides one means of planning a mind-friendly lesson. This is adapted and extended from the Alite learning circle and covers eight different planning and execution stages or steps. First, before any effective learning can take place, the learner needs to feel that they are in a safe and purposeful learning environment.

Connections made with prior learning is the second step. This often links very closely with the concept development that was discussed earlier in the chapter. When learning anything we need to link it with something we have already learnt, so that it makes sense. For example, a young child will start to learn that a specific animal is called a 'dog'. Then will gradually, and often with the help of others, learn that there are different sorts of dogs, different colours, different characteristics. If you work in a farming area, children will often have a much better idea about farm animals, crops and seasons than those in an urban area. This is because they have built up their learning outside school and may often have a much better idea about farms than their urban-living teacher. Gervase Phinn has some wonderfully funny examples of this in his many books on working in primary schools in the Dales. The WIIFM is about selling it to the class.

Figure 7.3 Model for a mind-friendly lesson plan

Activity/Thinking Task 3

1   Identify and record ten ways in which teachers and other professionals working in schools try to ensure that children and young people have a classroom environment that establishes and sustains a positive learning mind state.

2   Identify and record five things that prevent children – or adults – feeling relaxed and alert about learning.

You might find it useful to look forward to Figure 8.1 (p. 113) 'Maslow's hierarchy of learning needs'.

The third step is to think about this in relation to your own learning. How do you feel when faced with learning something completely new. If you feel positive about yourself as a learner – and hopefully everyone reading this book does – then you are more able to face a challenge. If your experience hasn't been so positive you may feel stressed. Individual learners have different needs and obviously those teaching them need to be aware of how specific children with learning anxieties can be supported. They need to know why they are doing this activity. An overview – or 'big picture' is the section of the lesson where the teacher lets the children know exactly what they are going to do in the lesson. It is doesn't have to be long and often takes the form of a child 'speak' lesson objective. Selling the benefits again is important.

In step four, the teacher explains what the learner is going to achieve and how. Step five is the direct teaching input. Some activities and lessons don't contain this. They may be continuations of the activity, or the children may have had the input in another session. If you are observing or teaching the 'initial teaching input', these are important factors to remember. Learners need to use more than one sense and this may need to be provided by others. Accelerated learning has connected this to VAK, and inputs need to contain all elements. The same applies for step six. In the main activity, learners need to explore the learning, engaging as many senses as possible. They need resources and activities to enable them to make use of their many different intelligences. Filling in a worksheet does not do this, and although it may be appropriate sometimes, heavy use of worksheets is unlikely to motivate or teach pupils very much. The hidden curriculum of the worksheet is that learning is worksheets.

Visual activities will include plenty of pictures, check lists, information posters, photographic reminders, use and creation of mind maps, videos, DVDs. Many schools adopt colour coding for marking and for board work, so it is useful to know which children are colour blind. Auditory activities will including telling stories, modelling being a good listener yourself, direct teaching of listening and talking through the tasks.

Auditory listeners often like to recite and may ask more questions as they are more dependent on the spoken word. Kinaesthetic activities let children model their understanding through drama, role play, construction, design, drawing, painting, etc. Learning is encouraged through 'having a go', experimenting, exploring, touching, feeling and smelling. In order to apply the learning, kinaesthetic learners may prefer to demonstrate, show, solve and use, rather than read or tell. Kinaesthetic learners in particular need to have a real active content – field trips, museum visits, bus trips, local walks and more movement generally within lessons. This involves much more activity and in small, crowded and cramped learning areas, this is often difficult to do. Nevertheless, it is important and learners should not be expected to sit still for large periods of time. For many people – not just children – five minutes can seem a long time sitting still.

The seventh step is the demonstration stage. This is about consolidating learning. It is important that the showing and demonstrating is not just for someone else. Learners have to be able to show they know to themselves. Sometimes this is much easier than others. Learning a skill – for example how to drive a car – is much easier to demonstrate and feel achievement about than learning in more academic set-ups. The results there are often in terms of completion and examinations. Reviewing what you have done so far in this unit is a way of reviewing the unit to consolidate your learning. Finally, reflecting on how we learn is important. Again, taking this chapter, you need first to review what you have learnt and then think about how you have learnt it. This involves finding time for reflection, teaching yourself and those you are teaching how to reflect on their learning, acknowledging difficulties and seeking clarification, identifying ways in which learning can be improved, raising new questions to investigate (self-target setting) and exploring how this learning can be applied in other learning or in everyday life.

Activity/Thinking Task 4

Table 7.1 provides one way of evaluating a lesson in terms of this mind-friendly framework. The template provides an easy record for either a lesson/activity you observe or one that you plan. Not all lessons/activity plans move through all eight stages and you might like to think which ones are essential, step 1 for example, and which ones may change.

Always plan

Any activity carried out with children must be planned for. A lesson and/or activity plan is embedded within the school's short-, medium- and long-term planning. It has to provide a clear structure for the lesson and usually a sequence of lessons. These have to maintain pace, motivation and challenge for children. They will use assessment information on children's attainment and progress, so that future curriculum planning takes account of what children have already achieved; i.e. the next lesson plan will build on what has already been achieved, identify misconceptions and errors and look at how content, teaching strategies and resourcing can be adapted to support progression in children's learning.

As you become more proficient in lesson planning, you will find it easier to identify and plan for children with SEN as well as those who are very able and those who are not yet fluent in English. The purpose of the activities for these children must be clear, to you, the children and other supporting adults. This is true whether you are working with thirty children, or just one.

When you first start working in a primary school, you may be asked to carry out an activity with a small group that forms part of the teacher's planning. Make sure that you understand the purpose of the activity, otherwise it tends to become merely childminding, and the educational purposes of the session are lost. Children are quick to sense this and it prevents the establishment of a purposeful working environment. This is also true for

Table 7.1 Evaluating a mind-friendly lesson

1 How safe and purposeful was the learning environment?	
2 How was learning connected with prior knowledge?	
3 How was the overview of the lesson/ activity provided?	
4 How was the proposed learning explained?	
5 What sort of input was provided, how much of it used VAK resourcing?	
6 What was the main activity?	
7 How did children demonstrate their understanding?	
8 Was there any time for reflection? If so, how was this demonstrated?	

reading a story at the end of the day. This is not a time-filler; it has purpose, and this purpose needs to be recorded in terms of learning objectives. If you ask another adult to work with you, they should have a copy of your lesson plan or a special plan for their activity. This needs to cover the purpose of the activity, i.e. the learning objectives, which the adult is required to do to enable the children to gain these objectives. It needs to cover what children are required to do and the technical vocabulary to be used. Small-group activities are ideal for assessing children's learning and other educational professionals can be extremely insightful. Use them.

Assessing learning objectives: first steps

For children's learning

You will find out if the children have learned what you intended them to learn through:

- observing them;
- listening and talking to them;
- questioning them;
- marking their work – Theme 3 looks at this in more detail and you may find it useful to refer to this as well as to look at the school's marking policy;
- matching lesson objectives with learnt outcomes – quite often the learnt outcomes may not match directly because during the course of the lesson, the skilled teacher realises something else is needed before learning can be achieved; or that the children already have achieved those learning outcomes and therefore need to move on.

Children's learning must be recorded. The most manageable way of doing this includes:

- an evaluation of each lesson/activity plan;
- keeping daily records of children's progress – this can be done as a daily diary;
- daily discussion on child progress and attainment during the course of the lesson/ activity with the class teacher and anyone else who has been present during the lesson;
- using school-based checklists and records.

For teaching skills

You will find out if you have learned what you intended through:

- identifying whether your teaching-skill focus was achieved and what evidence you have for this (If it was not achieved, why not? How will you structure your next session to achieve it?);
- assessing what you did during the activity;
- assessing what you learnt.

Reflection and evaluation

A critical analysis of the activity/lesson is vital in order to identify the implications for future planning in terms of progression in learning for the children. It is also important in terms of progression in learning teaching skills. There are a wide variety of different aides-memoire for this, two of which are illustrated in Tables 7.2 and 7.3.

When reflecting and evaluating, you should consider the following aspects. This should always be done on the day of the lesson.

1 Has the intended learning been achieved?
2 What evidence can you use to support your conclusions?
3 Was the provision relevant to all the children's needs?
4 Did anything in the children's response surprise you?
5 Appraisal of your own teaching performance: communication, organisation and control.
6 The management of yourself and, where appropriate, other adults.
7 How can you use your assessment to inform future planning?

Tables 7.2 and 7.3 provide two templates for student lesson evaluation provided by a very experienced school mentor.

Table 7.2 Lesson plan evaluation sheet (1)

Evaluation
1   Comment on how you know whether the learning objectives were achieved and how well they were achieved. Comment on anything that surprises you.
2   Comment on whether your resources were adequate and pitched at the right level.
3   Comment on your timing and pace. Was it well matched to all children's needs?
4   How effectively did you manage other adults in the planning, delivery and assessment of this activity?
5   Evaluate your progress in terms of your focused target from your weekly review.
6   How will you use this evaluation to plan for your next lesson.

Table 7.3 Lesson plan evaluation sheet (2)

Lesson evaluation	Lesson ....
	Date ....
Achieved learning objectives?	
How did the children respond?	
Evaluation of own teaching	
Evaluation of resources used	
Management of other adults in the classroom	
Future planning	

8 Emotional health and learning

QTS Standards

1, 10, 18, 20, 21, 30, 31

Learning objectives

- to recognise how the emotional health and well-being of pupils is essential for effective learning to take place;
- to know that there are several different terms for emotional health;
- to explore some of the implications for those working with children and young people inside school, in particular those learners whose emotional difficulties may present themselves with behavioural difficulties;
- to review the way in which we ourselves show anger and how we manage it.

Emotional health

Chapter overview

As you have already discovered – or rediscovered – effective learning is heavily influenced by having a positive mind state. One of the most important roles of the teacher and colleagues is to create a positive, safe and purposeful learning environment. In this chapter, we are looking at emotional health of learners and some strategies used to promote this in schools. There are lots of different terms for emotional health, but I have called this chapter 'emotional health' because it links most closely to the idea that all those working with children and young people must be interested in the children in a holistic sense – this is very much the part of the ECM agenda.

It is of course not enough to know what the terms mean, but also to have strategies for supporting pupils to enhance their general well-being. It is about caring. Hopefully, this chapter will help you to recognise children who may be suffering from different levels of stress in the classroom. This can be either as a result of what takes place in schools, or of what is happening outside school. Schools are being held responsible for both of these areas now, and we will look at the role of the healthy schools programme later. Emotional health is also covered under the Education Act of 2004 and the ECM agenda. It appears at this stage in the book because of its overriding importance in terms of working with learners.

There are several excellent books (see Bibliography) in this field. These are all very practical books and of course there is plenty on the Internet; although do take care with Internet material as some of it moves into the more freaky side of personal development. The Catherine Corrie (2003) book covers a very broad spectrum of work with primary school and nursery children. It looks at understanding and managing behaviour, the emotional effects of grief, intrinsic and extrinsic motivation, self-esteem, spirituality and creating identity. Daniel Goleman's (1996) book is probably the most well-known text on emotional intelligence, although a search through the Internet reveals an ongoing dispute about his pre-eminence in the field. Call's *The Thinking Child* (2003) is aimed at the early years, but has strategies for children throughout the primary school. The DfES also sent to schools a quick guide to social and emotional aspects of learning (SEAL).

The four Fs of classroom survival

Alistair Smith (2000) in his book about the brain suggests that there are four easy ways to spot how learners respond to the anxiety that can accompany learning. He calls these the four Fs – flocking, freezing, fight and flight. These reactions occur because meaningful learning carries risk with it.

1   Flocking involves adopting 'the norms, values and behaviours of the herd' – in this case the peer group. The peer group will police and in some cases collectively suppress learning performance in a classroom . . . The flock or peer group shapes the perform-ance and it is difficult to be different' (Smith, 2002).

2   Freezing is a temporary paralysis. It happens when you get stuck or someone suddenly asks you a question out of the blue and you can't think of an answer. Note children who look as if they 'freeze' when you are in a nursery or classroom. It is often when the teacher or other educational professional is pouncing questions. I can still remem-ber oral tables tests when I was about ten. The teacher would shout out a question at the same time as pointing to a member of the class. I just froze and even writing about it now, my stomach is churning at the memory – and it is a long time ago.

3   Flight – this is an avoidance tactic we have all used. I had an appalling statistics lecturer at university. I was in a large group of about 180 of whom about thirty of us were women. And boy, did he pick on us. I spent three terms at the back of the lecture theatre with my head hung down every two hours on a Monday morning. This avoided him seeing me or at least making eye contact. I 'fled', and how I passed the course I just don't know. Certainly 'no thanks' to Professor Smith. Other common classroom tactics include doing the minimum. This hides the inability to understand and it seems that many children would rather be labelled lazy, than have attention drawn to their inability to do something everyone else seems to be able to do. Other tactics include – waiting in long queues, sharpening pencils, going to the toilet, daydreaming, copying. In some extreme cases, children do run from the classroom. I remember visiting one school to see a student, and one of the pupils from her class was literally on the roof. There

were obviously other factors going on in his life and the student not only passed the practice, but got a job in the school afterwards!

4   Fight – any form of tantrum, rebelliousness, bad behaviour. The behaviour then becomes the focus of the lesson, rather than the learner's anxiety or fear that they cannot do the task set. In some very challenging schools, fight mode can be exactly that.

The learned behaviour for children in classrooms when they panic is important. The four Fs prevent learning, and as educational professionals we need to identify and encourage more positive strategies.

Activity/Thinking Task 1

Identify a classroom situation in which you see a stressed child use one of these strategies. Then see if you can find other children using other strategies. Table 8.1. provides a means of recording this.

Table 8.1 The four Fs of classroom survival

Survival mode shown	Perceived reason	Management strategy used
1 Flock		
2 Freeze		
3 Flight		
4 Fight		
5 Other		

Definitions

Emotional health

I recently attended a conference on emotional health by an advisory teacher in Lancashire. During the introduction we were given the following characteristics of good mental health:

*   optimism
*   sense of achievement
*   being happy
*   feeling affection for family and friends
*   having a sense of fun
*   sleeping well
*   being energetic
*   enjoying life
*   looking forward to things
*   maintaining the ability to laugh at oneself
*   feeling valued

- being able to learn, work and achieve
- feeling creative
- having a sense of purpose for the future.

I think I am fairly emotionally healthy; but I cannot in all honesty tick each one of these at any particular moment in time. Yet probably, overall, I can tick most of them. It is the energetic one that seems hardest! Of course it is possible to disagree with aspects of this definition and you do not have to have a full tick list to be mentally healthy. Some people may not have a family, and friends may be very distant. Insomnia can be very difficult to live with, but many people manage with very little sleep and seem to be emotionally healthy. Not everyone needs to feel creative in order to be mentally healthy. I also wonder, if we are too emotionally healthy, whether it makes us rather self-satisfied and smug. It keeps us in our 'comfort' zone, rather than moving us into our discomfort/challenge zone. No challenges in life would make it a bit dull, and certainly not encourage much new learning.

Figure 6.2 in Chapter 6 represents a theory of change, which suggests that change managers – which teachers are – need to move people/children out of their comfort zone into their challenge zone, in order for learning and change to take place. The good change manager/teacher manages to do this without moving them into a stress zone. There are, of course, huge differences in how learners cope with challenges, and there is not a great deal of practical evidence about how we can measure this accurately enough, in any one point in time, to be fully confident that we are 'challenging, rather than stressing' children.

Emotional intelligence

Daniel Goleman (1996) identified the following components of what he called 'emotional intelligence':

- *Self-awareness.* Knowing what we are feeling at the moment, and using those preferences to guide our decision making. This includes having a realistic assessment of our abilities and a well-grounded sense of self-confidence.
- *Self-regulation.* Handling our emotions so that they facilitate rather than interfere with the task in hand; being conscientious and delaying gratification to pursue goals and recovering well from emotional distress.
- *Motivation.* Using our deepest preferences to move and guide us towards our goals, to help us take the initiative and strive to improve, and to persevere in the face of setbacks and frustrations.
- *Empathy.* Sensing what people are feeling, being able to take their perspective and cultivating rapport with a broad diversity of people. This is sometimes described as having the ability to 'walk in another person's moccasins'.
- *Social skills.* Handling emotions in relationships well, and being able to read social situations, interacting smoothly and, at a higher level, being able to use these skills to persuade and lead, negotiate and settle disputes for co-operation and team work.

(Adapted from LEP, Module 4 of the *Learning
Mentor Training Handbook*)

One aspect of the teacher's role is therefore to be able to support learners in developing these characteristics and identifying those who may need particular help.

Effective communication

Effective communication is obviously a key aspect to social competence in our society. It has been divided into a four-level process that covers:

1   *Self-disclosure* – being able to say what you think, want and need. Teachers often need to teach children the language with which to do this. It may also be that some teachers and allied professionals need help themselves in this area.
2   *Assertiveness* – this means standing up for your own ideas, beliefs and opinions. It differs from being aggressive because it acknowledges that others have other ideas and that these ideas need respect. There are, of course, difficulties with 'respecting' other people's ideas when you believe that they are morally wrong, e.g. the circumcision of girls.
3   *Listening* – this involves hearing other people's verbal and non-verbal messages, and in this way understand what that person is really saying.
4   *Facilitating* – helping others to communicate what they want to say and making sure that you are communicating in the best way possible for understanding.

Emotional literacy

Greenhalgh (2001) gives the following definition:

> Emotional Literacy (also known as EI, Emotional Intelligence and EQ, Emotional Quotient) may be defined as the ability to recognise, understand and appropriately express emotions. It matters because it enables individuals to achieve their best and make a greater contribution to society. Emotional Literacy is more important than IQ for predicting lifelong success in work and personal relationships.

He gives this definition and then goes on to provide three steps towards helping a learning organisation, such as a school, achieve greater emotional literacy.

Step 1   has to be starting with oneself – looking at how emotionally literate/healthy we are and then moving from ourselves to the people with whom we work. This should ensure a more collective and societal change for the better.
Step 2   involves looking at the learners and the learning experiences offered. He points out that successful learning is dependent on healthy emotional well-being, where the learner feels safe from physical and emotional harm; feels valued as an individual; feels empowered by belonging to a caring community; experiences challenging but achievable learning tasks and succeeds. This fits in quite easily to Maslow's basic hierarchy of needs pyramid (see Figure 8.1).
Step 3   looks at the learning organisation itself. You can perhaps think of some ways in which nurseries, schools and other learning organisations can promote good emotional well-being. Some of these might involve having an effective, positive behaviour policy; promoting the values of a listening school; having a well-planned PSHE curriculum and a supportive pastoral system. Learning institutions with good inclusion strategies and active and effective anti-bullying policies are also more effective in promoting emotional literacy/health/intelligence.

Of course, emotional health and well-being is not a new idea. As far back as 1920 Thorndike identified it as 'social intelligence' and Gardner called it personal intelligence. There are several instruments of emotional measurement on the market aimed at the school population. At least one Merseyside LA has managed to find one that neatly identifies and classifies emotional levels all the way through from foundation to KS4. I was not happy with this when I looked at it, and this was not just linked to the fact that I think that children are tested and inspected far too much as it is.

Hierarchy of basic needs

Figure 8.1 shows Maslow's hierarchy of basic needs and is probably familiar to you. It is fairly self-explanatory and works from the base of the pyramid.

If we look at this in a school context, it is fairly obvious. Learners in schools who have physiological needs, such as being hungry and thirsty are not in the sort of relaxed, positive state that non-hungry/thirsty learners are. Many primary schools now provide some form of breakfast or snack for learners first thing in the morning, and most schools have ready access to water in classrooms. At the next two stages of the pyramid, we would all recognise the need for children to feel safe and loved, and belong to the community in which they

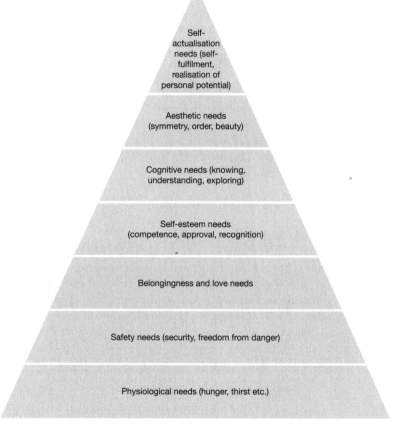

Figure 8.1 Maslow's basic hierarchy of needs

are living. Children operate within many communities so this basic need of 'belongingness' obviously applies outside as well as inside schools, and the development of multi-agency working is designed to build up the partnerships between those working in schools with children in their role as pupils and those who can gain access to children in some of their other roles. The growth of Internet chat sites for people of all ages, indicates the ways in which we are now able to define other groups to which they belong and seek to communicate, frequently with complete strangers. This can often be really positive, but as we are all too aware can lead to some challenging issues of safety.

It would be useful for you to identify the parallels between Maslow's model and the other definitions you have just read. I think they are all quite similar, with some additions, some rewording and a slightly different emphasis; but the message is much the same. Emotional competency is a basic need and until children reach a particular level in terms of achievement of their basic need, they will not be as ready for learning within a school situation. The role of the school is to try and get them into a better position for learning.

Attributes for healthy learners

One of the outcomes of a more integrated approach to children's services is that educationalists are listening to specialisms in other areas. The Mental Health Foundation (MHF), for example, which would once have been seen purely in its 'health' silo, provides some useful attributes for emotionally healthy learners, which I think has a slightly more comprehensive approach than some of the strictly educational ones:

- ability to make positive relationships;
- good self-esteem;
- resilience;
- ability to develop appropriate conflict resolution skills;
- ability to face setbacks, cope and learn from them;
- desire to learn and reach their full potential;
- sense of belonging and wish to be involved;
- develop psychologically, emotionally, creatively;
- use and enjoy solitude;
- become aware of others and empathise with them;
- play and learn;
- develop a sense of right and wrong.

This list sounds very much like a blueprint for many good nurseries I visit; except for the 'use and enjoy solitude'. Using and enjoying solitude is a very real asset, but often children who appear to enjoy solitude are deemed as loners who need pulling into things. Perhaps 'using and enjoying solitude' is an area that could do with more attention, and in particular setting up activities in pre-school environments that actually promote this.

Like Smith's work, the MHF acknowledge that life does throw up challenges and it is the ability to work through these that makes us emotionally healthy. They also acknowledge that there are circumstances that are impossible to work through and for which children – and adults – need help. These can include clinical depression; sudden death of a beloved family member; escape from a war-torn region; torture at the hands of so-called carers, etc.

Some classroom strategies to support emotional health in schools

General strategies

- recognising that this is an important issue that has a subject knowledge and skills base that need to be investigated;
- circle time;
- providing a stimulating classroom;
- setting appropriate tasks;
- encouraging co-operation and group responsibility;
- development of social skills and self-esteem;
- acting as a good role model – this may mean self reviewing and individual development both for the teacher and other colleagues;
- seeking out good resources, activities and reading around the area;
- working with, or ensuring that other adults work with, individual children on:
  - understanding their emotions
  - handling their emotions
  - anger management
  - handling relationships
  - bullying.

The role of other adults in supporting emotional health for learners in school

It is worth noting here that as the role of the teacher changes, the roles of other adults employed by the school has become far more crucial. There are an increasing number of children with emotional and behavioural difficulties in our schools and a glance through the national figures for exclusions and suspensions in primary schools shows that the numbers have risen rapidly in recent years. Learning mentors, who act as the 'children's advocate' have specialised training and often work with individual pupils as well as with small groups. Appropriate trained and experienced teaching assistants working with small groups can often make a real difference to the ability of individual learners to respond positively to school life. Mentors may run nurture groups in specialised rooms or units. Learning mentors often take responsibility for running Schools Councils, where specific whole school issues, e.g. bullying, are addressed and individual council members develop important social skills. These provide a heavily supportive environment. I have seen some excellent examples of nurture groups in very socially and emotionally deprived areas that are essentially doing amazing things to give back to children some of their lost childhood. This is specialist work.

Planning a structural behavioural programme

Fox (1998) suggests twelve different steps in planning a structural behaviour programme for children whose emotional difficulties are resulting in inappropriate learning behaviours. Fox advocates this as a good use of additional adult support, such as learning support assistants (LSAs).

Activity/Thinking Task 2

The first two unwanted behaviours have been linked with the behaviour wanted. Have a go at completing the next five in Table 8.2.

Circle time

Most of the classroom strategies outlined above are good practice. Jenny Mosley has produced a number of excellent practical books on the use of circle time in nurseries, primary and secondary schools. She has a specific approach to working with children's personal, social and emotional development; it relates to developmental work in groups based on the following points:

1   The group should meet regularly at a set time of the school day. This may be a class group, but it can also be a specific group set up with particular emotional needs.
2   It meets in a circle so that members can all see one another; it is easier to speak in a circle than in a rows; collective responsibility is taught and the circle group is a group of which you are part.
3   Initially a circle group can be intimidating if the learner is not used to such as setting, but it is always possible to opt out of rounds or activities the circle is undertaking.

Circle time generally runs to a particular pattern and most learners welcome this. It usually follows this process:

*   opening games and depending on previous activities some energisers (see Chapter 13);
*   a quick reminder of rules, in particular that of confidentiality;
*   a self-disclosure activity – something that allows the group to know more about one another and to personalise the experience. This is obviously more important when learners from different classes meet in a group, than a whole-class circle time;
*   an activity that relates to personal, social, health, emotional issues. This is also an area in which citizenship can be developed;
*   a closing round.

Incidentally, Jenny Mosley is also a wonderful speaker and it is well worth going to listen to her if you have an opportunity. Her website provides some ideas about the sorts of resource that can be used for different types of circle time.

In the previous chapter we looked at a planning framework for mind-friendly learning and this is also an essential element of encouraging good emotional health for pupils. Setting appropriate tasks is important. As we identified earlier in this chapter, if children and young people become stressed about tasks set they will react in survival mode.

Emotional health for all

Most primary schools and nurseries have policies and strategies outlining what all adults in the school should be doing in terms of promoting a positive learning ethos and enhancing mental health. These policies may sometimes miss out the key element of ensuring that the positive ethos for the children is also converted into good employment practices for

Table 8.2 Planning a structural behaviour programme

Step 1: Record unwanted and wanted behaviours	
Unwanted behaviours	*Desired behaviours*
Shouting out	Listening and working quietly
Getting out of the seat	Staying in the seat
Pencil tapping	
Frequent crying	
Constant talking, giggling	
Swearing or shouting	
Throwing equipment	
Step 2: Observation sheet	
Do a half-hour observation of the child	
Name: .... Lesson:	

Time	Shouts out	Out of seat	'On task'
10.00 – 10.05	3	2	3 mins
10.05 – 10.10	2	0	2 mins
10.10 – 10.15	2	1	1 min
etc.			

Step 3: Review

Review the observed and recorded behaviour and compare this to the list in Step 1. Decide which behaviour you are going to encourage, e.g. staying in seat.

Step 4: Environmental analysis

Identify ways in which this behaviour could be prevented in the first place, e.g. change seating, proximity to the teacher, peer group, task, child's physical and/or emotional state, in order to eliminate or reduce unwanted behaviour.

Step 5: Teach new skills

staff. Initiatives such as Improving Working Lives and Investors in People can help, but a few primary schools do have real challenges in this area as it is impossible to regulate for the amount of stress in employee's lives. There are, however, many strategies that can be used to help them cope with these and, hopefully, the ICS workforce will access many of the very good practices set up for other LA workers, such as aromatherapy, cheap access to sports centres, reflexology, etc. Teacher support network (www.teachersupport.info) provides independent support for staff in the education sector, as do teaching unions.

Anger management

Activity/Thinking Task 3

It is important that we understand our own emotions and how we mange them. Be honest with the response to these questions:

- How do you know you are angry?
- What gets you going?
- Do you feel you are good at managing your anger?
- Does managing your anger vary? Why?
- Discuss with someone else how you handle anger.

The five areas identified here are only a starting point. Each of them is at least worth a day's course and such courses on understanding emotions, handling emotions, anger management, handling relationships and bullying are all available. Ironically, when visiting a prison earlier this year, the prison education manager identified several of these areas as ones in which the prison education service worked. Anger management courses are also often offered to parents in parenting courses, and bullying courses to employees who feel they are being bullied in their work situation.

If you are uncomfortable about identifying when you get angry, you need to think carefully why that is. As I get older, I find I get less angry than I used to, but I sometimes think that some of that anger was quite useful. It made me get up and do something.

> **Serenity prayer**
> God grant me the serenity to accept the things we cannot change
> Courage to change the things we can
> And wisdom to know the difference.

Strategies for children

Strategies to teach could include – getting the child to explain to an adult how they feel; learning to walk away by shrugging shoulders and saying that it does not matter; asking why not and accepting the response; finding something else to do; counting up to ten, then walking away. There are some excellent books that raise these issues in the abstract and enable children to then discuss this situation. You can also, with the relevant permissions, take photographs of children acting out a situation; e.g. being ignored by their best friend for no apparent reason. The photographs can then be used to discuss what this feels like and how to deal with it. All these strategies need dealing with when the child is not angry.

Activity/Thinking Task 3

Draw up a list of ways in which children might be able to control their own anger. You should have at least five strategies on your list. In recording this you should write down the age of the child. For example: Thomas, aged five, does not get what he wants from another child and starts to shout and scream. He has learnt that this strategy usually works because he gets attention and often gets what it is he wants – particularly outside school in a crowded shop.

Helping children like Thomas – and indeed adults – to manage their anger is important. Some of the programmes on television about 'super nannies' prove that most anger can be managed if dealt with appropriately. However, super nannies are not managing 20+ children, all at the same time, in a relatively small space!

Some strategies for anger management

These strategies include:

- conflict mediation
- choosing stories
- nutrition
- relaxation training
- 'anchoring' positive states
- refuge – e.g. a quiet chair, a nurture base
- breathing – shallow breathing, intercostals breathing and abdominal breathing
- communication – this may involve teaching the language of anger and reconciliation
- warning lists
- trigger lists
- distraction
- relocation
- reframing
- do something different
- humour
- self-talk/self-calming.

Anger is often a secondary emotion. There is usually another strong feeling that underlies anger. We discussed earlier how fear about a set task could cause some children to become angry and disruptive. Other emotions such as inadequacy, worry, stress and hurt can also cause anger. There are also a number of medical conditions that can cause anger, for example high blood pressure. There is plenty of evidence that particular foods and fizzy drinks can distort emotions.

'Anchoring' positive states means teaching yourself – or others – to think about a particularly nice, pleasant situation when they are feeling angry and then 'position or anchor' themselves in that to avoid anger.

Small classrooms and learning areas often make it very difficult for children and young people to have effective 'time out', but a period of cooling down can reverse the arousal and give time for changing perspectives.

Risk factors for emotional well-being

Here are some of the potential risk factors for emotional well-being:

- peer rejection
- bullying
- school failure
- poor attachment to school
- being male
- belonging to a minority – being 'different'
- bereavement and loss
- period of upheaval
- obesity.

The gender issue is a complex one and although little research backs it up, I am still convinced that the fact that nearly all early childhood education is carried out by women must have some influence on boys feeling 'outsiders' in early care centres, nurseries and primary schools. It is possible for boys to go all through pre-school and primary school without meeting a male carer or teacher – only sixteen per cent of all primary teachers are men. I wonder what would be the result of a complete reversal of this; if girls only came across a female carer in secondary school. Certainly, I enter some early years settings and classrooms that I think are quite aggressively girly in terms of colours used, display, choice of resources and manner of relating to the children.

Any emotional health programme that seeks to support emotional growth can be divided into four practical steps:

1   activities that increase general awareness – of self, of choices, of others;
2   activities that promote self-control, including relaxation techniques;
3   activities that enhance feelings of positive emotional health – hope, self-esteem and positive thinking;
4   activities that involve levels of awareness of the social world of the individual and their capacity to interact in it appropriately.

Activity/Thinking Task 4

Try this on yourself, or with a child you know well.

More about me

I feel happy when . . .
I hate . . .
I wish that I was . . .
I worry about . . .
The thing that makes me angry is . . .
When people shout at me I feel . . .
The best thing that happened to me is . . .
The most important thing in my life is . . .
I feel successful when . . .

---

9 Behaviour management and discipline

QTS Standards

2, 3, 10, 21, 30, 31

Learning objectives

- to develop skill in observing effective behaviour management and discipline strategies in schools;
- to identify, research and evaluate some of the relevant research in the field;
- to internalise and use strategies drawn from this research and school-based observations to establish a clear framework for classroom discipline and management;
- to recognise that some children have specific needs in relation to behaviour management.

Behaviour that interferes with learning

Student concerns

This is the area that probably concerns student teachers more than anything else, particularly when they are first put in charge of a group or class of children. Will there be a riot when I am in charge? How do I develop strategies to prevent misbehaviour? How can I help to motivate children, so that they want to learn? What help can the school itself provide? If I could supply all the right answers to these and other similar questions, I'd be a multi-millionaire. There are a number of travelling behaviour management gurus who do move through the country, indeed the world, with 'the answer'. The truth is that there is no simple answer, but there are certainly strategies that can be used and learning/behaviour management theories that can be put into place. All schools have policies, guidance and practical help to support and manage learners' behaviour constructively. You are not alone and however hard it is, try to remember that it is the behaviour that is not acceptable, not the child.

Activity/Thinking Task 1

Spend five minutes recording what concerns you most about class management in relation to children's behaviour.

The responses I have had over the years from student teachers are things such as: fighting and shouting out; children being violent with either the student teacher or each other; repercussions from parents after a child has been spoken to; bullying, aggressive and defiant children who will not settle and cause disruption, or egg on other children who then cause disruption; children who constantly move about during the lesson, particularly difficult if this is the introduction; being ignored after correcting bad behaviour; being made a fool of; how to deal with children without physically handling them; losing control by reacting badly; not being taken seriously.

These comments can be sorted into different categories. Several relate to self-worth, and how child misbehaviour challenges this. Another category touches on legal issues, e.g. a handling policy for violent or disruptive children. The final category is really the search for strategies with which to cope. Did you find that you'd focused on a particular area?

Some behaviour problems that interfere with children's learning are:

- poor self image;
- physical and/or verbal fighting;
- insensitivity;
- lack of self-discipline;
- inattentiveness, poor listening skills, lack of sustained concentration;
- disregard for own, other children's or school property;
- stealing;
- failure to put things away and clean up after themselves;
- doing only what they want to do;
- constant socialising;
- depression, withdrawal, boredom, apathy;
- constant demands for their rights.

Behavioural problems are those that interfere with children's learning. They interfere with classroom life and, if severe, destroy a purposeful working environment. A great deal of research has gone into this area and educational psychology texts both paper and online can give you more details. Many findings show that disruptive children are often suffering from poor self-image. I am not so sure that this can be taken for granted in today's primary schools. It is more complex, and I have – sadly – met some primary children whose self-image is actually enhanced by being anti-school. Certainly secondary schools have had to deal with this particular issue for many years.

Avoiding misbehaviour

Much of this chapter looks at strategies to avoid misbehaviour, because this is really the key strategy to behaviour management. We have already looked, in previous chapters, at several strategies that come into this category. This includes establishing a purposeful learning environment; understanding the complexities of how children learn and a mind-friendly framework for planning for this; and looking at emotional health and ways in which this can be enhanced. Indeed, by this stage you already know quite a bit about behaviour management, and your classroom observations will have given you experiences of both effective and less effective practice. Unfortunately, some of the most effective behaviour management specialists are so good at classroom management, it is often difficult to identify how they achieve such good results.

Here are some factors that have been identified as being key to their success:

1   They present themselves as caring professionals.
2   They have high expectations for all children.
3   They motivate their learners into wanting to learn and behave.
4   They have procedures for handling potentially disruptive situations.
5   There are established rules for how children are expected to behave.
6   They convince their class or group that it is necessary to comply with these rules as well as the other 2Rs – routines and regulations.
7   If difficulties do occur, they have strategies to resolve most behaviour problems on a class and school basis.

Caring educational professionals

Caring teachers and other professionals

- Dress appropriately for respect; credibility; acceptance; authority; and as a role model. You never get a second chance to make a first impression!
- Value themselves as professionals.
- Are willing to share themselves – this does not mean sharing intimate information such as 'Do you have a boy/girl friend?' Do you like Miss/Mr . . .? Short professional pieces of information, such as where you found a particular item, your weekend visit to the art gallery, local park, the names of your children/pet, etc. Favourite football team can be a bit risky in some areas, where loyalties are very divided!
- Keep a sense of proportion as well as a sense of humour.
- Have a clear understanding of the school policies and strategies.
- Demonstrate that they are also learners – the teacher and colleagues as the 'lead learner'.
- Are tough when they need to be.
- Reward effort.
- Do not over praise and ensure that the praise identifies why the child is receiving it.
- See 'invisible' children.

As the author Pearl Buck once said 'Only the brave should teach. Only those who love the young should teach. Teaching is a vocation.' Teachers and other professionals in school have to care and show that they care. Particularly important is the use of praise – it has to be sincere and spontaneous; delivered privately; directed to noteworthy accomplishment; be specific and be focused on individual improvement and not with comparisons with other pupils.

Having high expectations for all children

Research (Hoskyn & Swanson, 2000; Rogers, 2006) shows that low achievers are:

- less likely to be asked to contribute;
- less likely to receive praise from their teachers and have less eye contact and general interaction;
- more likely to have conduct emphasised, rather than academic achievement;
- more likely to be at the receiving end of rudeness, lack of interest and inattentiveness from adults;
- more likely to be physically separated from the rest of the class.

Expectations can be raised by:

- valuing diversity and being culturally responsive;
- offering praise that is sincere and specific;
- calling equally on all children;
- giving children at least five seconds to answer;
- making eye contact when children speak and listening to what they have to say;
- grouping children in different ways for other activities, if ability grouped for maths and English;
- showing an interest in children's lives;
- modelling the respect and courtesy expected;
- encouraging children to set goals for learning.

Activity/Thinking Task 2

You might find it useful at this stage to repeat the twenty-minute activity monitoring sheet on a particular child whose behaviour is concerning you; or if you are working as the teacher, ask another educational professional in the classroom to do so.

In one very challenging school I visit, a trained teaching assistant spends half or a whole morning a week in each class and in the foundation stage, monitoring the behaviour of a group of named children where particular aspects of their behaviour are seen as an issue. The results of the observation provide some solid data about what is going on and what sort of potential disruptions may be linked with concentration; misunderstanding; other children 'setting up' the disruptive child, etc.

If you are confident you might ask a colleague to monitor your teaching in terms of raising expectations through responses and interactions with different children.

Valuing diversity

This needs to be integrated throughout the school and not just an 'add-on'. If you are fortunate enough to work in a culturally diverse school, you need to ensure that you know something about where the pupils come from, why the different communities have come to this part of the country and for how long they have been here. Do not make assumptions, avoid stereotyping either with a deficit or 'super hero' stereotype and avoid concentrating on one particular aspect, e.g. faith.

Children whose families have only recently entered the UK may have been moved around a lot. Sensitive issues include:

- culture shock;
- identity conflicts between home and school expectations;
- language and teaching style differences;
- previous educational experiences;
- conflicting demands – particularly if the child in your class is the only English speaker in their household and needs to be available to interpret for others;
- impoverished living conditions;
- prejudice;
- racism and bullying on the streets, playground and classroom.

What is so heart-warming is how many schools have very rich inclusive policies and practice, so that children feel that they are a welcomed part of a school community where there is authentic interest in their lives and achievement. These schools learn about and build on the many strengths their diverse communities have to offer and often act as a key focus for the local community. At the time of writing, this is particularly important as global disputes are reflected in some local communities and children bring them with them into school. Teachers are in the front line.

Research on behaviour management

There are hundreds of different websites that look at behaviour management and discipline and many of these specialise in particular strategies. The Bibliography provides some examples. DCSF services website when I accessed it transferred me to teachernet, but neither site was particularly helpful because the emphasis was on attendance. A good site is www.teachers.tv/ and the material is often changed. Sometimes there is a great touch of reality, as when the NQT finds after her first week in school, that not only does she have a challenging class, but she also has nits. Incidentally, one strategy to avoid nits is to ensure that you don't get too close to a child's head. Touch wood, in the thirty years I've been in primary schools I haven't had them yet. For a generic search on the web, use 'classroom management' for more practical strategies.

The generic educational psychology texts, available in any public library, will provide you with a good overview about how children learn to behave. Many of them will also show how you can link the theory into effective practice. I have suggested books by Jean Robb and Hilary Letts because I have witnessed at first hand the wonderful work they have done through their Successful Learning Centre for disengaged children and young people. They often work with families, rather than individuals, and are passionate about the need not to be drugging children with Ritalin and its equivalents. Their books are aimed at parents, rather than teachers, but the strategies are just as useful. The Network Continuum Press website will give you details about many good references. Many teachers have found Alistair Smith's work on accelerated learning in primary schools particularly useful and the Alite website updates its research pages regularly.

Ayres and Gray: an overview

Ayres and Gray, in their 1998 book, *Classroom Management*, identified six different theoretical approaches to classroom management: counselling; democratic; behavioural; research-based empirical; social cognitive theory; and assertive discipline.

The counselling approach

The best currently known proponent of this approach in terms of schools is Bill Rogers. Rogers has written several very easy to read practical guides and is an international guru on behaviour management. Certainly his UK courses get fully booked very quickly. The counselling approach links in closely to the social cognitive view of learning. One example of his theories into action is that of the identification of five distinct 'tricky personalities'. You should be able to recognise some of these from the classrooms and early years settings you have observed. You might even recognise yourself! His work is important because he does not just label children, he suggests practical strategies to 'counsel' them.

THE CHATTERBOX

- Give positive direction, e.g. 'Face this way Jane', followed by 'thanks'. He finds that using 'thanks' rather than 'please' communicates the expectation that the child will comply.
- Give a strategic pause after identifying the child – this communicates the expectation that the child will look towards you and listen. This can just be a slight pause after using a pupil's name.
- Don't get drawn into secondary issues – singled-out children may sulk or argue; acknowledge their feelings but return the focus back to the primary issue. If the child says 'We were talking about work' the response needs to acknowledge this, but you should redirect the focus, e.g. 'Maybe you were, but I want you to face the front and listen, thanks'.

THE CLINGER

- Start tactically ignoring, keep the focus on the lesson and reward non-clinging behaviour.
- Establish alternative routines – the card system described earlier, where children have an index card folded and taped into a pyramid; the 'ask three' strategy, where the child must ask three children before asking the teacher.

THE BOYCOTTER

- Offer a choice, or apparent choice, with consequences attached: 'If you choose not to work now, you will need to do it during your free time.' This lets children know that they have control over their own behaviour. It is their responsibility.
- Give time – if you turn away and respond to another child, the boycotter has the chance to comply without losing face.
- Re-establish the relationship with the child as soon as possible. This can be done after the child has complied with a smile or comment.

THE DEBATER

- As with the chatterbox, focus on the primary behaviour and do not get drawn into the debate.
- Avoid overreacting, which will only extend the conflict.
- Avoid power struggles.

THE SULKER

- Again focus on primary behaviour not secondary. A private discussion after the lesson can help the child understand that the behaviour is not acceptable. The earlier in the year, or teaching practice, that this can be done, the better. Time the invitation carefully, so that it comes just before the discussion. This avoids a prolonged discussion/ sulk on 'What have I done?'.
- Be positive and explain how such behaviour affects the working relationships. Be pleasant so that the relationship can be repaired.

The democratic approach

The major proponent of the democratic approach is Rudolf (1989). The democratic teacher helps and redirects children to develop self-discipline and self-motivation. This contrasts with the autocratic teacher, who dominates children and inflicts punitive consequences for rule-breaking. This is closely linked to the social cognitive view of learning and has certainly been used very successfully in some alternative schooling systems. Brophy and Evertson's (1976) research identified four teacher qualities that were important for good child behaviour – self-confidence; positive attitudes; high expectations; and authoritative leadership.

- *Self-confidence.* You need to play at acting the self-confidence at first, if you do not feel you have it. A former colleague of mine used to advise students to look into the mirror every morning and say aloud 'that is the face of a good teacher'. This is what you are selling yourself as. Children test student teachers: 'We've done this before'; 'This is boring'. You need self-confidence to evaluate the value of the comments and react accordingly. Most importantly you need to know the purpose of the activity. This is why having a clear learning objective is so important.

- *Positive attitudes.* Children, like adults, respond best to teachers who show that they like them and respect them. This involves getting to know the children and it takes time to build up this professional relationship. Make sure that you build positive relationships with all the children and avoid accusations of creating 'teacher's pets'.

- *High expectations.* If you expect children to be able and responsible, they are more likely to act that way.

- *Authoritative leadership.* Brophy and Evertson found that effective teachers seek feedback and consensus on decisions and make sure that children understand their decisions. They found authoritative leadership is more effective than either authoritarian rule or laissez-faire leadership.

The behavioural approach

The major proponents of the behavioural approach are Pavlov and Skinner. Their ideas have been developed to provide simple, practical and effective approaches to behaviour management that can be powerful agents of change. The behavioural approach has often had a bad press because the approach implies humans can be trained like Pavlov's dogs. Indeed, a recent television series reinforced this view by helping wives to train a dog and then transfer the knowledge to working with their husbands – with some mixed results! The behavioural approach is still a popular approach in schools because it is easy to learn, straightforward to apply and embodies a systematic approach to assessment and target setting in terms of behaviour management.

The behavioural approach to learning assumes that behaviour is primarily a response to observable events. A child might not like another child, but behaviour modification can at least stop them hitting the other child. The attitude may not have changed, but at least the behaviour has. The behavioural approach is determined by its consequence and because it is learnt it can be unlearnt, i.e. inappropriate behaviour can be unlearnt and replace by the appropriate behaviour. The practical aspect of this theory is that it provides a systematic methodology for behaviour assessment because it provides for a baseline to be established, which can later be examined after behaviour has been modified. This database collection is exactly what the teaching assistant was collecting in the example given above. She spent time in specific classrooms, monitoring behaviour so that the initial baseline could be assessed as strategies were put into place.

Empirical approach

Kounin's work (1970) is a good example of the empirical approach. His work was based on looking at what was going on in classrooms. It was not based on any particular psychological or educational theory, which means it can be related very directly to the needs of a particular school community. Kounin found that expert teachers had three key characteristics that helped them to 'nip problems in the bud', i.e. prevention, rather than cure. These teachers had what he called 'with-it-ness', overlapping, and pacing:

1 *'With-it-ness'* – this simply means that teachers let children know that they are aware of what is happening all the time. They regularly scan and monitor the classroom and position themselves where they can see all the children. Student teachers often find this skill very difficult, particularly after they have spent time working with small groups with the class teacher taking responsibility for the whole class. Make sure you are aware of what else is going on in the classroom. If a child from outside your group is misbehaving, make sure that you take action if the teacher has not seen what is going on. If you ignore it, they will learn that you accept misbehaviour.
2 *Over-lapping* – this means that good class managers can multi-task without disrupting the class. They can work with individuals or a small group and still deal with other children who have questions. This involves making sure that children have routines for seeking help and teaching them to discern which questions warrant your immediate attention.
3 *Pacing* is essential. Effective teachers can keep attention on instruction and not on mis-behaving children. This is done by avoiding extended reprimands or overreactions and ignoring minor inattentions. Serious behaviour is promptly attended to in non-

disruptive ways, e.g. eye contact, a brief comment, a question directed at the miscreant. This keeps the lesson momentum.

Kounin also identified four common mistakes that teachers can make during transitions from one activity to another. He calls these thrusts, dangles, flip–flops and fragmentations.

1 *Thrusts* – This happens when the teacher – or more likely the student teacher – interrupts an activity with no warning 'Everyone stop working now', 'Time's up', 'Tidy up'. Like most of us, children do like some sort of warning before being told to end what they are doing. This is particularly true if they are enjoying doing it and want to finish. They may delay finishing and then start less enthusiastically on the next activity.

2 *Dangles* – This is when learners are left 'dangling' while the teacher gets involved in setting up materials, reviewing a lesson plan, speaking with a specific group of pupils or dealing with an interruption from a classroom visitor. Learners have nothing to do except be patient and of course, for some pupils, this is virtually impossible to do without getting into trouble.

3 *Flip-flops* – this happens after a lesson starts and the teacher suddenly returns to another separate activity to report back on it. Basically, pupils may be working on some mathematics problems, the teacher stops the whole class or a small group and draws their attention to another completely separate activity before asking them to return to the mathematics. This stops the momentum of the activity and can make it very difficult for some learners to get back on track. It often happens for the best of intentions, the teacher finds a small group who has forgotten what they are supposed to be doing. The teacher assumes that this may apply to most of the class, stops them all and reminds them of the original task. For those who did listen, understand and started on the task, they are forced to stop, listen again, and then carry on where they left off – if they can remember.

4 *Fragmentations* – this happens when the teacher, or other educational professional, starts one group off with a piece of work, explains what they are to do and then lets them move into doing it. Meanwhile the rest of the class is patiently waiting for their group to be assigned a task. This is sometimes inevitable, but can be avoided if the transition is planned through carefully.

Activity/Thinking Task 3

What strategies would you use to avoid some of the situations listed in Table 9.1?

Social cognitive theory

Albert Bandura is one of the main proponents of the social cognitive approach to behaviour management. Initially, his work grew from a behaviourist approach to managing the aggressive behaviour of very young children. This was most famously linked to a Bobo doll experiment with kindergarten (US-based) children. Essentially, a rather unethical experiment in today's terms, he had a film session and a real-life session of someone hitting, hammering and shouting at a Bobo doll (life-sized plastic clown). After the children had

Table 9.1 Managing situations

Ineffective transition strategy	Effective management technique
Punishing slow workers for not finishing by keeping them in at playtime and lunchtime	
Traffic jams when learners need to get materials from storage areas	
Requiring learners to continue an activity they cannot either do/or concentrate on	
Getting fast finishers to wait while the rest of the group or class finish	
Long transitions while each group of pupils is set off to do their tasks	
Ending an activity abruptly without warning	

seen this, they were taken to a room with toys and initially not allowed to play with them, i.e. they were deliberately frustrated. Later in play, they modelled the aggressive behaviour they had seen and the Bobo doll in the playroom was hit and hammered as modelled by the adult in the previous session. The key break with behaviourism was that it looked as if the modelling of this aggressive behaviour was repeated without promises of reward or punishment.

Many other observational learning experiments have been repeated since then and Bandura's work has informed hypotheses about how aggressive behaviour is learnt, as well as strategies in which it can be 'unlearnt'. There are, of course, direct links made between modelled aggressive behaviour seen on the television, playstations and computer games. The effects of these on children and adults have been debated for some time (Palmer, 2006). Of course, there are several well-known court cases where defending barristers have argued that it was violence seen in the media that had resulted in the defendant imitating what had been watched.

Bandura looked at the ways in which our cognitive processes influence the ways in which we learn through observational learning if four components are present:

- attention
- retention
- motor reproduction (actually being able to imitate the behaviour observed)
- motivation.

These four components translate into the classroom, because what happens there is not only recognising negative observational learning, but also being able to effectively model preferred behaviour. This is sometimes forgotten by student teachers who assume just a verbal statement will be enough.

This may initially seem a rather depressing scenario when even very young children are presented with violent images on an almost daily basis via the television; but Bandura's work has been developed to show how factors such as self-image, self-esteem, attitudes and imaginings can be used to promote positive observational learning. Practical strategies include teaching self-motivation, identifying and clarifying beliefs, counteracting distorted beliefs and modelling good behaviours.

Assertive discipline approach

The main proponents of the assertive discipline approach are an American team, Lee and Marlene Canter, as set out in *Assertive Discipline* (1992) and other publications. This is another very popular theory that has influenced behaviour management in many primary schools. It owes a great deal of its success to the missionary work of the Canters themselves and is based on the belief that both teachers and children have both rights and duties. Children need and respond to limits set by teachers. Teachers therefore have to set those limits and establish them with support from the parents and school management. A classroom discipline plan includes rules, positive recognition and consequences. Children can be involved in drawing this up themselves. Assertive discipline aims to achieve a safe classroom environment; it enables teachers to teach effectively and facilitates pupils' learning.

When it first came into the UK it was particularly popular with educational psychologists, but did concern some teachers because it appeared to focus on negative, rather than positive, behaviour. Initially, the Canters suggested that children who misbehaved should have their names placed on the board. Each time the name appeared on the board, it resulted in a specific punishment. Any child whose name appeared three times would know that a letter would go home to their parents/carers. Later they withdrew this recommendation because it appeared to reward negative behaviour, on which some learners seemed to thrive. Today they suggest a three-point strategy:

1   Teach specific behaviours – don't assume children know what you want; describe, discuss, model and practice the behaviour you want.
2   Use positive repetition – if children perform an activity as you want, comment on it, e.g. 'Thank you, Sam, you have worked hard today'.
3   Use negative consequences – children need to know what will happen if their behaviour falls out of line.

Several LAs invested in the assertive discipline approach and certainly, as a whole-school approach, it has had some very positive results. Good in-service assertive discipline that followed the recommendations of the Canters, involved a staff meeting over a period of time with a trained and experienced trainer. At one time the training materials could only be circulated by specifically trained people. This had real advantages because it acknowledged that specialist understanding and experience was necessary. The school drew up a whole-school approach together and made considered plans for reviewing and evaluating it. The major problem with assertive discipline was that once initial training was over it could degenerate quickly. Student teachers and newly appointed staff picked up bits, such as writing miscreants' names on the board without having oversight of the overall philosophy.

A side product of the assertiveness discipline approach was the positive discipline approach, which many of the behaviour management strategists recommend. This means rewarding appropriate behaviours and 'disarming' misbehaviour by refusing to give it status, e.g. if a child starts demanding attention, the teacher ignores him or her, looks elsewhere and only rewards the child with attention when he or she continues with the task. This, of course, is easier in theory than practice, and for this reason the following steps may be useful:

* *Define a goal.* What do you want children to know and value?
* *Recognise positive steps.* Practise recognising and rewarding the attitudes, action and skills that help children, e.g. do they concentrate on their work? Can they appreciate another viewpoint?
* *Reinforce positives.* Help children to notice their own accomplishments and recognise small steps forward.
* *Be positive.* And appreciate progress, remembering the starting point.

Positive discipline is very much about teaching and practising the behaviour expected. When you are in a class, either at the beginning of the school year, or when a new teacher arrives, you will find that the most effective practitioners say what they expect and then practise it with the children. For example, 'When I raise my hand, I want you all to stop what you are doing and look at me. Now let's have a go at doing that.' This sort of thing should become so automatic that it is not necessary to provide extrinsic rewards such as team points, marbles, raffle tickets, etc. Sweets, of course, are off the reward menu now because of the healthy schools initiatives.

Overall, it is important that these different approaches are not seen as independent from each other, and schools use a variety of different strategies in practice. The biggest controversy is really between the type of counselling approach proposed by practitioners such as Bill Rogers and behaviourists such as the assertive discipline gurus, Lee and Marlene Cantor. This is largely a difference between intrinsic and extrinsic motivation. And this is something we shall look at elsewhere.

Activity/Thinking Task 4

Choose two approaches to behaviour management and discipline. Research both of them and identify similarities and differences between them. Where possible, try to provide examples of the different approaches from practice you have seen in school, or indeed you remember from your own schooling.

Sociology and behaviour

Much of the research work about behaviour management and discipline has come from educational psychology; but educational sociology has some important insights and in the following section we look at two aspects of children's lives that are likely to affect learning and may influence behaviour – basic needs theory and the national figures on neglect. They are often overlapping aspects of some children's lives.

Basic needs

In the previous chapter we looked at Maslow's hierarchy of basic needs and this showed how learners have wide ranging and complex needs. The hierarchy is a useful framework because it shows why some needs have greater immediacy for children than others and will influence learning and behaviour more directly.

Activity/Thinking Task 5

Return to Maslow's hierarchy of needs (see Figure 8.1) and think of any child in your class at the moment who may be at, or near the base of this pyramid, i.e. does not have the very basic requirement for food, sleep and adequate shelter, feels unsafe and/or not part of any community. What effect may this have on their behaviour? If you do not know the class well, you should ask the class teacher and other educational professionals who work in the classroom. Many of these children are not attention seekers and may be invisible. It is also useful for you to know which children are on the 'at risk' register. They are certainly near the bottom of this pyramid and some are extremely effective at making sure they do not draw attention to themselves. This is a learnt strategy for surviving in abusive and violent households.

Sadly, children lacking Maslow's very basic needs are far more common in our class-rooms than we might expect. When children's basic needs are not being met, their ability to settle down and learn will be severely restricted. Some schools recognise this and offer a simple breakfast when children arrive in the morning. If you look carefully in the media, schools have often supported families who have been made homeless or have had their refugee status taken from them and been threatened with expulsion. Of course, it is not the 'school' that does this. It is individuals, the head teacher, the governors, the teachers, the parents and children within the schools who take a stand on potentially very difficult and controversial issues. Looking at children's needs in this way raises issues about the need for schools to have a much more holistic approach. A holistic programme would cover 'the whole child' – social, emotional, physical, academic, intellectual, psychological and ethical. Indeed, all those aspects covered by the ECM agenda. Good class management is about helping children to feel safe and wanted in school. Children should feel that school is a place where someone will look after them and others will not be allowed to bully or intimidate them. For some children, school may be the only place where this happens. School may also be the only place where they are accepted and have a feeling of belonging. When we look at children's needs in this way, it is clear that teachers have a huge responsibility. It is one shared with colleagues and enshrined within the mission statements of many schools. The working through of the mission statement are testaments to the professionalism of the vast majority of those working in schools.

Neglect

Figure 9.1 comes from a 2004 ECM document. It is sadly titled 'the neglect pyramid' and the figures, even in 2004 were an understatement. The numbers of looked-after children, for example, is steadily rising and in 2007 were up to about 80,000.

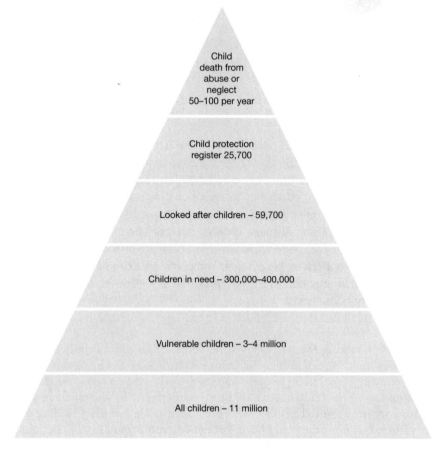

Child
death from
abuse or
neglect
50–100 per year

Child protection
register 25,700

Looked after children – 59,700

Children in need – 300,000–400,000

Vulnerable children – 3–4 million

All children – 11 million

Figure 9.1 The neglect pyramid

As a former social worker, I feel very passionate about the need to recognise that a significant number of children in our schools have basic needs that are not being met and suffer from neglect, which prevents them from learning and also may result in them acting through behaviours that disrupt both their own and other children's learning. Both the Maslow hierarchy and this neglect pyramid should make all of us think before condemning children whose personal circumstances are unknown to us and may be horrendous.

Tips from teachers

Here are just a few tips from teachers about classroom management. Many teachers start at the beginning of the school year by drawing up with the children a list of positive behaviours. For example 'we raise our hands when we want to speak.' Children often write these out, so that they have visual ownership of them. For younger children, teachers often take photographs of the positive behaviour, and children put the caption underneath. If they are still at the emergent writing stage, the photograph provides the message. Teachers speaking to post-graduate and undergraduate trainee teachers at Liverpool Hope have advised:

- Know and follow school procedures – this is vitally important, particularly in challenging schools, where all staff need to be seen working together. It avoids children manipulating different adults.
- Give the child time out in another class or another part of the room. This should not be for very long as children tend to forget why they are sitting elsewhere. It is better to have the time out with a younger aged class to reinforce the idea that the behaviour shown is not suitable for their age.
- Ensure the child knows what they have done wrong.
- Don't humiliate children.
- Don't use school work as a disciplinary measure.
- Don't punish when you feel angry.
- Don't punish the whole class when it is individual.
- Have a staggered approach.
- Removal of an in-school privilege such as part of 'golden time' on a Friday afternoon.
- Removal of a home privilege – this requires working closely with parents or carers.
- Avoid keeping children in at break time and lunch times because it means they need supervision and you miss your own much needed break from them. It also means that they may be resentful when all the other children return. In some cases, children may misbehave to avoid going out to play.
- Rewards linked to work, e.g. notepads, non-school rubbers, etc. rather than sweets.
- Asking for help from more experienced and/or skilled colleagues.

You might like to identify the directly behaviourist rewards in this list!

Teachers advised supporting self-esteem through:

- showing that you care;
- giving children responsibility;
- using words and phrases that build up self-esteem and avoiding those that hurt;
- defining limits and rules clearly;
- rewarding clearly, but do not over-reward, emphasise the positive;
- helping children develop tolerance towards those with different values, backgrounds and ideas;
- discussing problem behaviour in terms of the behaviour, not the child;
- taking children's emotions, feelings and ideas seriously;
- being a good role model;
- having high, but reasonable expectations;
- being available;
- showing children that what they do is important to you.

Activity/Thinking Task 5

- See if you can think of another five ways to help children feel good about themselves.

- Compare your list with someone else.

- Observe carefully in school and identify anything else which good teachers and other educational professionals do to promote self-esteem.

Table 9.2 Behaviour, sanctions, comments

Stage	Behaviour	Sanctions	Comments
1	AGGRAVATIONS Wandering about; calling out; interrupting teacher when talking to whole class; interrupting other children; ignoring minor instructions; talking with other children; making silly noises; pushing in line	NAME WRITTEN ON WHITEBOARD Minimal contact – eye; frowns; placing self near child; reminders; change of seating	Not recorded; after several repetitions within a certain time period, e.g. three incidents in a morning, a warning is given that the next time it will change to Stage 2 and will be recorded
2	LESS SERIOUS Eating sweets; not responding to teacher's requests to work; being more disruptive; deliberately creating a disturbance; accidental damage through carelessness; dallying; cheek, off-hand comments; minor challenge to authority; swearing; annoying other children	Separation from the rest of the class/group Writing a letter of apology Withdrawal of privileges, e.g. playtime Child to fill in a consequences report to go into class behaviour file	Reminder that the incident is recorded in the behaviour file
3	Deliberately throwing small objects with the intention of breaking them; harming someone; damaging school or pupils' property; leaving class without permission; repeated refusal to do set tasks; continued or more serious cheek/challenge to authority; harmful/offensive name-calling; bullying	Detention at break time; mention to deputy/head; contact made with parents	Use of a designated teacher
4	VERY SERIOUS Repeatedly leaving classroom without permission; fighting and intentional physical harm to other children; throwing large, dangerous objects; serious challenge to authority; verbal abuse to any staff; vandalism; stealing; persistent bullying	Head to be involved Head contacts parents	Possible involvement of outside agencies
5	EXTREMELY SERIOUS Extreme danger or violence; very serious challenge to authority; verbal/physical abuse to any staff; running out of school	Probably means immediate exclusion; fixed term – up to . . . days	Parallel procedures for official out-of-school activities

Whole school management of behaviour and discipline

It is vital that you are aware of school policies and procedures. Some are extremely useful and give important support to student teachers, supply teachers and teachers who have newly arrived in the school. You should make sure that you can identify the different types of psychological theory involved – particularly how much is linked to behaviourism.

Activity/Thinking Task 6

Obtain a copy of any policy relating to behaviour, e.g. behaviour policy; anti-bullying; anti-racist; home/school contract; restraint policy. Most of these will be LA approved and all will have been approved by the governing body. They should all have a regular review date as behaviour policies date in the same way as most policies.

- Identify the main points of the policy.
- Evaluate how useful this would be to you as a student teacher in the school.
- Discuss and compare policies with someone else from another school.
- Try to identify which specific psychological theories are embedded with the policy statement.

Note: Some schools have a website that provides examples of policy statements.

Table 9.2 (on the facing page) outlines some useful strategies from one school.

10 Special children and inclusion

QTS Standards

3a,b, 5, 6, 20, 21

Learning objectives

- to develop skills in identifying children with SEN;
- to understand the role of the SENCO/manager;
- to be able to set high expectations for children with SEN and establish appropriate targets for them;
- to know the *Code of Practice on the Identification and Assessment of Special Educational Needs* (DfES, 2001);
- to recognise skills involved in establishing effective working relationships with specialist staff supporting children with SEN;
- to develop skills in identifying able and gifted children and knowledge of strategies to support, extend and challenge them across the curriculum.

If a child does not keep pace with their peers, perhaps it is because they hear a different drummer.

(Adapted from Henry David Thoreaux)

This chapter is divided into three strands. One looks at the formal background to two areas that are often put together as if they were much the same thing – inclusion and special needs. The second strand uses practice I have observed in several different schools. This is because practice is very different and there is no one best blueprint. The third strand looks very briefly at just a few of the most common special needs you will find in schools and I am very grateful to Wendy Hall, at Liverpool Hope, who has a very extensive collection of materials and experience in supporting special needs teaching in primary schools.

Official definitions: National Curriculum and guidance for the early years foundation stage

National Curriculum – inclusion and special needs

Provision for SEN comes under the heading 'inclusion' in the front of the much forgotten and ignored National Curriculum Handbook (DfEE, 1999). It covers three principles for inclusion – setting suitable learning challenges; responding to pupils' diverse learning needs; and overcoming potential barriers to learning and assessment. Under this third principle are included two groups: pupils with SEN and pupils with disabilities. The important point is made that not all pupils with disabilities will necessarily have SEN.

The government has used the term 'educational inclusion' to indicate its commitment to providing equal opportunities for all pupils 'regardless of age, gender, ethnicity, background and attainment, including special needs and disability'.

Evaluating Educational Inclusion (Ofsted, 2002) suggests that educational inclusion is 'more than a concern about any one group of pupils such as those pupils who have been or are likely to be excluded from school'. It should be about particular attention being paid to the provision made for and achievement of different groups of pupils within the school. This term covers:

- girls and boys;
- minority and ethnic and faith groups, travellers, asylum seekers and refugees;
- pupils who need support to learn English as an additional language;
- pupils with SEN;
- gifted and talented pupils;
- children 'looked after' by the LA;
- other children, such as sick children; young carers; those children from families under stress; pregnant schoolgirls and teenage mothers; and
- any pupils who are at risk of disaffection and exclusion.

Activity/Thinking Task 1

1   Why you do think both boys and girls are identified by Ofsted as being 'at risk' of not achieving their potential?

2   What groups do you feel are missed out by Ofsted?

3   Use the DCSF or Ofsted website to find out about at least one nationally funded initiative that tries to address any one of these issues.

The guidance for the EYFS

The guidance for EYFS also covers inclusion under a heading of meeting the diverse needs of children, and points out that meeting the individual needs of all children lies at the heart of the EYFS, because practitioners should be delivering personalised learning, development and care to 'help children get the best possible start in life'. There is an exhortation to focus on 'removing or helping to counter under-achievement and overcoming barriers for children where these already exist . . . Identify and respond early to needs which could lead to the development of learning difficulties . . . appropriate challenges for gifted and talented children'.

Code of Practice

The DfES (2002) Code of Practice for SEN outlines five fundamental principles:

1   A child with SEN should have his/her needs met.
2   The SEN of children will normally be met in mainstream schools or early education settings.
3   The views of the child should be sought and taken into account.
4   Parents have a vital role to play in supporting their children's education.
5   Children with SEN should be offered full access to a broad, balanced and relevant education, including an appropriate curriculum for the foundation stage and the national curriculum.

LAs must:

1   Identify, access and provide for children with SEN.
2   Audit, plan, monitor and review SEN provision.
3   Support pupils with SEN through School Action and School Action Plus.
4   Secure training, advice and support for staff working in SEN.
5   Review and update the policy and development plans on a regular basis.

At this stage the writing and monitoring of individual education plans (IEPs) remained a key feature of the Code. The vast majority of these plans, at school level, identified language-related targets for pupils. Class teachers were responsible for working with SEN children on a daily basis and for planning and 'delivering' the IEP. For nearly every child in any of the three Key Stages – foundation, KS1 and KS2 – this has major implications.

Sadly, this Code of Practice led to an inordinate amount of paperwork, and in primary schools particularly, it meant that the SENCO was often spending the small allocated special needs time doing paperwork, rather than supporting colleagues. In 2007, a central government scrutiny issued a report to examine ways in which schools and LAs could fulfil their legal obligations in supporting children with SEN, and cut down on paperwork and bureaucracy. This resulted in some significant changes in the original legislation:

1   Schools no longer have to write and review IEPs.
2   LAs no longer have a statutory obligation to ask schools to provide information which has been previously provided, where a school can confirm it remains valid.
3   LAs can combine planning, funding, delivery and accountability processes in order to maximise the range, quality and relevance of local provision while reducing unnecessary bureaucracy.

This will, of course, produce different practice between LAs and it is likely that the practice adopted will depend to some extent on the way in which Ofsted interprets it at both school and LA level.

Further legislation

2007 disability equality duty

Implementing the Disability and Discrimination Act in schools and early years settings involved the introduction of guidance materials to explain how the disability equality duty (DED) should be implemented by schools. It covered among other things accessibility, which for some primary schools is a major issue and certainly several schools have internally appointed an accessibility officer.

Defining special needs through measuring achievement

All of us are special and of course all children are special. So this is a good example of a word that when used in an educational context has a particular meaning. In essence 'special' in terms of educational needs is defined through measuring achievement. In the UK, and indeed in most of the world, an individual's academic achievement is measured in terms of their English and mathematics. In England, the government have further defined it for primary schools as through the acquisition of specific levels in SATs. Children who do not have a Level 4 or 5 in both English and mathematics at the end of KS2 are seen to be underachieving in relation to the 'national average'. The overall scores from a cohort of children are then used as a measure for the standard of education in the school. This, in turn, is put with other schools in the same LA and used as a measure of the performance of that LA. When schools and LAs are inspected by Ofsted, these SAT results are seen as important indicators of the success of the school and LA. Indeed, lower than average scores in any one year are likely to trigger a school inspection – either by the LA or Ofsted or both.

Activity/Thinking Task 2

Try to think of at least five reasons why measuring school success through the SATs may have serious weaknesses. You may like to look at the statistical evidence as well as the more sociometric data.

Now look at the SATs results of a school known to you. They can be found in any school prospectus. You can also find them in the summary Ofsted reports for the school. Compare the school results with the national results, which, by law, must also be included. Is the school in line with other schools nationally, or is it above or below? Can you think of reasons why this might be the case. As with the NHS, why might schooling also be linked to a lottery postcode situation?

Schools analyse and evaluate their SATs results and this is also done nationally. One pattern that has emerged from this analysis is the general under-achievement of primary boys in all the core areas. Schools have been looking at this gender difference for a long time. In the 1970s and 1980s they looked at lower and fewer A-level scores for girls in science and mathematics. Nationally, the government has been looking to raise boys' achievement, particularly in English and has recommended specific targets to improve performance. What does the pattern look like in a school known to you? Can you think of reasons for it? Setting high expectations in terms of behaviour, concentration and appropriate learning strategies may be an important element in raising attainment.

Most LAs cluster particular schools together, so that comparisons can be made with similar schools. There are several different ways of doing this, but one of the most common is that of FSMs. The percentage of children taking free school dinners in a school is seen as a measurement of the economic deprivation within its catchment area. The national average for FSMs is 19 per cent. Other indicators used by Ofsted teams when inspecting a school and deciding whether it is giving value for money include the number of children on the special needs register and the numbers speaking English as an additional language. Can you think of any factors that might make FSMs a questionable measure of economic deprivation? If you are interested in local statistics for schools in a specific area they are now freely available from the general government website http://neighbourhood.statistics.gov.uk/NeighbourhoodProfile. Comparisons are made between local figures, e.g. percentage of households renting, and national figures and the summary provides a generic statement about local deprivation covering health, education, housing, life expectancy, income, employment, crime and living environment.

School definitions of SEN through attainment

Schools use three basic methods of measuring a child's performance and SEN are often a product of these figures. The figures commonly used by schools are:

1   supplied online by the government (Raiseonline);
2   using measurement by textbook or scheme of work;
3   using a variety of standardised testing instruments, both online and paper.

Use of national curriculum data

Raiseonline (reporting and analysis for improvement through school self-evaluation) replaced the more kindly named PANDA (performance and assessment data) and supplies all schools with what is described as an 'independent and factual set of data by which a school's performance can be judged'. It provides contextual information about FSMs, EAL, stability, a deprivation indicator and level of attendance and matches all these against a national average. It looks at the SATs results and also has a CVA measure that looks at the KS1 SATs of the pupils who have just taken KS2 and attempts to identify the academic value the school has added. Again, these are measured against national averages. It is these figures that are used by Ofsted prior to inspection. This is done together with the short commentary reviews against all the figures. All schools of course look much further at these government figures to determine which of their children are 'vulnerable/of concern/have special needs'. They collect their own data (see below) and analyse it carefully. One of the key players in this data analysis is the Fischer Family Trust, who provide data analysis linked to likely attainment.

Measurement of attainment by textbook and scheme

This is far less common than it used to be, largely because the Primary National Strategy materials are used as schemes of work and many schools feel obliged to teach through them to a specific time frame. Away from central government schemes, English and mathematics schemes that contain textbooks and workbooks generally arrange them into notional age ranges, so Book 1 is for Year 1, Book 2 for Year 2, etc. This makes good commercial sense as schools purchase fifteen or thirty copies for each class. Teachers make very different use of such texts, but generally children are ability grouped when working through them. Some children are identified early because they cannot cope with the text at all. Others are identified only as they struggle with it and others as they work through at a slower pace than others. By the end of Y3, it is usually possible to see that children who are still on the Y1 or Y2 texts (or their equivalent) have been identified as having particular learning difficulties.

Standardised testing

An increasing number of schools are using standardised tests to identify those children who have learning difficulties and those who are very able. Sometimes this indicates a concern about the validity of the SATs as an objective form of measurement, but often schools use these in addition to the SATs. One of the best sources of information about the range of standardised tests available is the National Foundation for Educational Research (NFER) catalogue. The NFER has a huge bank of tests covering many areas of learning, but schools will often use reading and maths tests from other sources as well. These tests are 'standardised' against a norm, i.e. they have been given to a large number of children of a specific age. This enables a distribution curve to be drawn up and children can be identified as being on the norm (average), below the norm and above the norm. Children who fall into the bottom sixth are generally those considered to be at risk. This does perhaps deflect attention away from children who may be underperforming, but are on the norm or above. An increasing number of schools are using standardised tests to identify under-achievement amongst children who seem to be performing satisfactorily in class. PIPS (performance indicators in primary schools) tests are used fairly widely by primary schools for early literacy and numeracy skills.

It is perhaps worth mentioning at this stage that much of the controversy about using standardised tests is that they have been used to label children and place them in particular programmes. Test developers argue strongly that a child's test scores should be just one of many different pieces of information contributing to placement and performance setting. They should never replace informed teacher judgement, although ironically they may be most useful when they disagree with such judgements.

Interpreting scores requires some understanding of statistics. Results are reported in different ways, including composite scores, scores in major skills areas, individual item analysis, etc. Some are more appropriate and useful than others. The test manuals are full of useful information and should be read and referred to before using the test. Test scores can reveal important discrepancies, and differences in average scores between certain groups of children may reveal differences in opportunities to learn. Standardised tests are not all equally valid and reliable, i.e. measuring what they claim to measure and providing individual scores that remain consistent over multiple tries. Their increasing use suggests that more time should be spent during ITT on their use and ways in which children can be supported in learning how to take such tests. And of course we all know that some areas are very much easier to test than others. Remember Gardner's theories of multiple intelligences. It is obvious that the SATs and many other standardised tests only measure logical-mathematical and verbal-linguistic intelligences. This means that children who have strengths in other areas – musical, spatial, kinaesthetic, interpersonal, intrapersonal, naturalistic, existentialist, spiritual and moral – are unable to demonstrate their achievement formally through the SATs.

Identification of children with SEN

Example of use of concerns registers

Many schools set up a concerns register in the nursery and record on this any 'deviant', i.e. not average, behaviour or learning. This covers all areas of learning, but tends to concentrate on social, emotional, intellectual and developmental dimensions. This is reviewed and updated throughout the year and continues when children move into the reception class. It is often not resourced because of a lack of funds, but also because it is acknowledged that children mature at different rates. Indeed, many of the children who are identified as having indications of special needs on their initial entry into the nursery are later removed from this informal register. Date of birth is often a key issue, as children born between May and August have had less time to mature before entering school.

In Y1, many schools have more formal reviews of all children. Children's intellectual development may be measured, using the levelling process in the national curriculum. They may be asked to produce free writing, read their reading book and use early mathematics skills. A general decision is often made that if children are not working at Level 1 of the national curriculum, they are put on to a special programme. There are many national programmes now available for literacy and numeracy. This will probably involve working in groups, which are particularly carefully monitored. In Y2, this national curriculum levelling process is used to identify children who are only working in English at the 2c level or below. A child gaining Level 2 in English can do it at different points 2a, 2b and 2c. It is now generally agreed that the 2c is a very low level and children reaching this are 'at risk' because they are unlikely to be able to reach Level 4 by the time they have finished in primary school. The children most at risk are the older children in the Y2 class.

Use of checklists for identification

A checklist approach is often used, such as the one below:

Social

- poor attendance and/or punctuality;
- frequent moves of school;
- nursery attendance;
- socialisation problems;
- chooses younger children to play with or prefers playing by themself.

Physical

- visual – near- or far-sighted, wearing inappropriate glasses, failure to wear glasses, seated in poor position to see;
- auditory – temporary (glue ear), permanent – with or without hearing aid;
- kinaesthetic – mobility, medical conditions, including those involving medication that may make the child drowsy.

Intellectual

- discrepancy between overall intelligence and achievement or performance;
- difficulty with speaking, reading, writing and maths;

- difficulty with perceptions of time and space;
- poor hand–eye co-ordination;
- low self-esteem;
- poor organisation;
- weak short-term memory;
- concentration and attention problems;
- overreaction to noise and/or changes in routines;
- inability to follow instructions;
- hyperactivity;
- poor emotional control;
- weak listening skills.

Poor attendance and/or punctuality may be a very simple explanation for a discrepancy between overall intelligence and achievement or performance. Many schools spend a great deal of time encouraging reluctant attendees to make an appearance. This problem often starts in the nursery, when patterns of attendance are erratic.

Learning mentors are often charged with this as a whole school responsibility and work with the family as well as the children who are poor attendees. Attendance is monitored closely by schools, education welfare officers (EWOs) attached to clusters of schools, LAs and Ofsted. Attendance that is lower than national levels is often another trigger for inspection.

Activity/Thinking Task 3

- How does a primary school you know encourage attendance? Schools with challenging attendance figures often have a number of imaginative initiatives, try to find at least five different ways in which such schools do this.

- Even schools with very good attendance figures may have a couple of children whose attendance gives them concern. For what sort of reasons might children be kept off school on a regular basis?

One school's response to inclusion and identifying vulnerable groups

It is often easier to see how this works out in practice if we look at a particular school. So I am very grateful to Prescot CP School in Knowsley, for permission to use part of their whole school evaluation of special needs within the school. They do call this inclusion – the provision for and the achievement of all groups of learners. Like most schools, procedures change and develop, so what is set out below is likely to be reviewed, adapted and developed over time.

Step 1

First, the school uses its comprehensive data collection to identify vulnerable groups, with one set of data tracking the whole school and the others tracking KS1, lower KS2 and upper KS2. Put together these were, at the time of writing:

Table 10.1 Tracking inclusion – exemplar of section of document

Our information tells us that this group . . .	To support this group we will . . .	Things working particularly well are . . .	As a result . . .	Emerging priorities to improve further still
Children with disability				
• Can be disadvantaged or marginalized and excluded unless correct provision and support is planned	• Place the child on the medical register if appropriate • Involve parents to discuss programme of support and individual needs • Make appropriate provision • Closely monitor academic and social progress	• Attitudes of peers and acceptance • Role models – teachers • Appropriate provision planned for	• Children are fully involved in all areas of the curriculum • Outcomes evidenced in inclusion team tracking records	• Resources • Teaching assistant support • Adaptation of the environment
Looked-after children				
• Are vulnerable and are less likely to make good academic progress and achieve well unless they are given support • Tracking and monitoring essential	• Ensure whole school systems for LAC/CPR/attendance are cohesive and useful • Create personal educational plans • Discuss needs weekly in inclusion team meetings • Network with other agencies • Ensure close working relationships with parents/carers	• Dramatic improvement in physical appearance/health of children on register • Social, emotional and academic achievements • Links to 'stay safe' from ECM outcomes	• Academic progress in median to upper quartile for named children • LAC in our school achieve well above national benchmarks for LAC from the DfES • Evidence in KS2 outcomes 2006	• To look at children who are cared for by grandparents (two identified children)
Ethnic minority				
• Form a small group of learners in our school, which is predominantly white	• Tailor the PSHE curriculum to support the group of learners • Ensure that racist behaviour	• Active teaching of anti-racist education through PSHE curriculum	• CVA profiles evidence that ethnic minority children make good or very good progress (Jenny in upper	• Further celebrate diversity in our locality and region • Ensure this is

• May have EAL and practise a different faith to the majority of learners in our school • May have recently moved to Britain (two families) and therefore need additional support	is monitored and dealt with robustly in line with clear whole school systems • Survey learners to ensure that racist bullying is not taking place • Liaise closely with parents	• Surveying of foundation parents with adaptation of curriculum as a result of outcomes	quartile+ in 2006 profile) • Ethnic minority children make excellent progress in foundation (evidence FS profiles and electronic child-profile base) • Reduced incidents of racist comments/bullying evidence in parental concern file and outcomes of anonymous pupil surveys)	embedded as integral part of the curriculum, not a bolt-on extra

EAL

• More often start school as new inwardly mobile learners in KS1 or KS2 having missed our foundation stage/KS1 • Often start as mid-year transfer • Can leave the country and return later	• Quickly obtain information about the child using inwardly mobile assessment procedures • Involve EAL support from the LA for assessment and programme of support • Identify EAL children in the inclusion file and monitor weekly in inclusion team meetings • Termly tracking and rigorous scrutiny of CVA for this group of learners • TA support when necessary • Adapt information and letters to parents with EAL	• Positive home/school links • The environment/curriculum encourages good relationships and is language-based	• Progress made by EAL children is good • See foundation child profiles	• Consider support programme for EAL gifted and talented child in Y5 from September 2006 • Have a support programme in place for identified children who leave and return to Britain frequently • Identify children who have made less progress and assess further

- children with disabilities;
- looked-after children;
- ethnic minority;
- EAL;
- hearing impaired;
- those children attending afternoon nursery;
- low attenders;
- low baseline results/outcomes – in particular literacy/phonic skills;
- sick children;
- children living in poverty;
- passive girls;
- disaffected children;
- bullying – victims and perpetrators;
- children frequently changing schools;
- children who frequently take holidays or have extended holidays;
- children with challenging behaviour that can create barriers to learning for themselves and others;
- children under-achieving in literacy/with barriers to learning in literacy;
- gifted and talented;
- numeracy – children who are in lower quartile progression;
- emerging gender issues (this year);
- families with barriers to learning/access to school events/education.

Step 2

This initial identification of vulnerable groups is then looked at under five categories and indicates an ongoing process to give specialised, informed support for learning:

1 Our information tells us that this group . . .
2 To support this group we . . .
3 Things working particularly well are . . .
4 As a result . . .
5 Emerging priorities to improve further still are . . .

This is most easily seen in the examples from the school's inclusion documentation shown in Table 10.1.

The role of the SENCO

Table 10.2 shows an adapted version of a job description for a SENCO from Devon County Council. Table 10.3 shows how an inclusion team was structured in one Merseyside school with a particularly challenging catchment area.

Individual education plan

Exemplar

Table 10.4 provides an exemplar of an IEP. There is specific IEP writing software, which is used by many schools.

Table 10.2 Specimen job description for a primary school SENCO

Job description	SENCO
Responsible to	SMT/Head
Principal purpose	The SENCO with the support of the SMT and colleagues, seeks to develop effective ways of overcoming barriers to learning and sustaining effective teaching through the analysis and assessment of children's needs, by monitoring the quality of teaching and standards of pupils' achievements, and by setting targets for improvement. The SENCO should collaborate with curriculum co-ordinators so that learning for all children is given equal priority, and available resources are used to maximum effect.

Key responsibilities

1 To co-ordinate provision for pupils with SEN – Overseeing the day-to-day operation of the school's SEN policy.

2 To contribute to the strategic planning for SEN within the school.

3 To liaise within and outside school – liaising with: fellow teachers, parents of children with special educational needs in co-operation with the class teacher; external agencies, including other schools, the LAs support and educational psychology services, health and social services and voluntary bodies; other SENCOs.

4 To promote staff development in relation to SEN – this includes keeping abreast of latest research; assessing the needs for, contributing to and teaching, where appropriate, the in-service training of staff.

5 To manage SEN resources – accumulating and promoting the use of special needs resource materials; responsibility for spending and monitoring the SEN budget within agreed guidelines, and in line with priorities established in the school development plan; supporting teachers with the management of teaching assistants; teaching individuals, small groups or classes as appropriate, including team teaching or support teaching.

6 To maintain and oversee records on all pupils with SEN.

Source: Adapted from Devon County Council.

Activity/Thinking Task 4

Informally and sensitively interview the SENCO in the school in which you are working. If this is difficult, interview a SENCO from any mainstream primary school. Increasingly, SENCOs are being appointed from educational professionals within the school who have special expertise, so you may be interviewing an HLTA or a teaching assistant. If possible, look at their job description, but more importantly discuss the sort of work they do, the time allowed for this and their expectations of other educational professionals in the school. In some schools the number of SEN children is so high that there is a team, rather than one individual. It might be interesting to see whether the 2007 legislation regarding not having to draw up IEPs has influenced their role.

Table 10.3 Exemplar of an inclusion team, when the primary school has a much higher than average percentage of learners with SEN

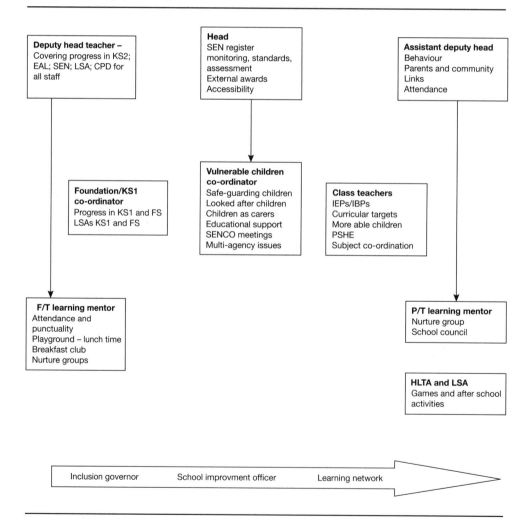

Table 10.4 Exemplar of an IEP

School (primary): **Mill Street CP**	INDIVIDUAL EDUCATION PLAN (IEP)			**School Action/Action Plus**
Name: Brittany Williams	**Date of birth:** 18.9.00	**Year group:** 3	**Classteacher:** Emma Carson	**SENCO:** Ian Jones
IEP start date: 1.9..08	**Review date:** *to be agreed*		**Signed:**	**Signed:** ....

Strengths
Good at maths. Relates well with peers. Enjoys swimming.

Areas to be developed
(each area should have a corresponding target):
Literacy – fluency when reading; spelling phonetically regular words; handwriting formation.

Targets	Strategies	Provision	Success criteria	Achieved
1 To be able to read additional high frequency words in isolation and in context: 'said', 'what', 'come', 'about', 'they'	• Multi-sensory approach using alphabet letters • 'Key into Key Words' pockets and games, make sentences, make books using targeted words	• TA withdraw five min daily • Peer to check words • Complete in literacy hour independent work	• Look, trace, make and read 5/5 • Read 5/5 consecutive occasions • Complete and read 4/5	
2 To form correctly all the ascending letters in joined script	• Verbalise the letter formation and write on tactile surfaces • Proofread and correct formation and position of letters • Peer check and colour chart	• Wipe-clean board, different surfaces • Lined paper • Motivation chart to colour	• All ascending letters to be correctly positioned and formed 9/10 in a piece of writing	
3 To be able to spell phonically regular words containing 'ch'	• Read words containing 'ch' – initial and final phoneme • Look, say, trace, make, write in spelling log – highlight 'ch' • Games and ICT reinforcement	• 'PM' alphabet books introduced by TA • Spelling log • Time and materials available in literacy hour	• To spell correctly all targeted words learned in spelling log	

Additional information
To have eyes re-checked and hearing tested

Parent/carer involvement
To support in learning high frequency words. To read and find targeted words as reads

Pupil's view
Wants to achieve targets and read with Dad at home

Evaluation and future action
To add to the high frequency words learning but change partners. To repeat writing strategies and target descending letters. To spell 'sh' words. Glasses not needed, hearing still to be checked

Activity/Thinking Task 5

Look through IEPs (if available) for a class with which you have been involved. What sort of guidance has been used to draw up the IEP? Devise a guidance template for yourself after having read through several of the school IEPs.

Points for target setting within IEPs

- Targets need to be addressed in an appropriate specified time.
- They need to be SMART (specific, measurable, achievable, realistic, time-related) and easily negotiated, particularly with the learner concerned.
- They should usually begin with easily comprehensible verbs – 'to know', 'to be able', 'to produce'.

Policies for special needs in mainstream schools

LAs and schools all have policies related to SEN and most schools follow the LA guidelines. Many LAs produce additional guidance for parents. These will be attractively presented, easy to follow and freely available. You may be able to find them in the local library as well as in school.

School policies are comprehensive and will explain the code of practice and distinct school procedures for ensuring compliance with it. Most policies will cover:

- a policy statement showing how the philosophy of the school is linked with its special needs policy and the requirements of the Code of Practice;
- the name of the SENCO;
- procedures for initial identification of special needs and the responsibilities of the class teacher for this identification;
- assessment, monitoring and review arrangements;
- a description of the different stages in the Code. Some LAs have a slightly different staged process, but the school policy will make it clear what happens at each stage;
- copies of forms to be filled in;
- referral and review procedures;
- roles and responsibilities – LA, governors, head teacher, SENCO, class teachers, subject co-ordinators, support teachers and assistants, outside agencies;
- details of parental involvement;
- resources;
- descriptions of different types of special needs;
- suggested targets and teaching strategies;
- bibliography.

Staffing

Working with a LSA or SNA

Children may have additional adult support provided as part of the provision for their needs. Indeed, if we looked at the growth of teaching assistants in school, one of the major factors was the closing of special schools to ensure that mainstream schools had a much more inclusive community of learners. Many pupils who fifteen years ago would have been in a special school are now in mainstream, often with paid and volunteer adult help. These adults are often known as LSAs or SNAs. They are usually well trained and often work with the child alongside a group of other children. In these circumstances it may be difficult, as a visiting adult, to identify the 'special' child. This is a great testament to the work of the LSAs, many of whom have worked with a particular child for several years. The 2001 Code of Practice states different kinds of special need that may require additional learning support.

- mild learning difficulties;
- moderate learning difficulties;
- specific learning difficulties (e.g. dyslexia, dyspraxia);
- severe learning difficulties;
- profound and multiple learning difficulties;
- physical disability;
- sensory impairment (visual, auditory or kinaesthetic);
- language impairment;
- communication impairment, including different levels of autism and Asperger's syndrome;
- emotional and behavioural difficulties, including attention deficit (hyperactivity) disorder (ADD/ADHD).

There are different patterns of organising this additional support. One of the most common is to place the child in a group of other children who have learning difficulties, but not necessarily IEPs. The additional adult is then used to support the whole group and ensure that the child to whom they are attached is part of the class and has an opportunity to take part in group and collaborative activities. This works with varying degrees of success. It is certainly better than the child and their adult support working in isolation outside the classroom in a corridor, but some children with SEN can be very isolated, even if they appear at first sight to be an integral part of the class. Playtimes and lunchtimes are key times to identify such isolation and then work to effect strategies that provide genuine inclusion. Charitable organisations related to SEN are becoming more involved in 'selling schools' their expertise. This can be trained personnel as well as more paper- and electronic-based resources. There are potential conflicts sometimes, between the desire of the charity to demonstrate their support and the danger involved in labelling a child over the long term.

Activity/Thinking Task 6

Your school may or may not have a policy for special needs, but certainly there will be some policies that cover this area, although they may have different titles. It is important to familiarise yourself with them and identify what you feel are key points for anyone coming into the school for the first time – either as a parent with a child with special needs or as an educational professional. Note down any two issues for each of these interested bodies.

Staff development

Many LAs have excellent training programmes for staff involved with SEN, and student teachers and other colleagues can learn a lot from LSAs. The ECM agenda, with its attached workforce reform model has resulted in many personnel taking extensive training in special needs, which far exceed that undertaken in teacher training courses. They may already have degrees with special needs as a main subject or be in the process of undertaking such degrees, for example doing special needs foundation degrees with top-up qualifications in learning and teaching. In addition many of the professionals working with children with special needs have formal qualifications prior to being appointed. These may be nursery nursing, GNVQ, early childhood studies degrees, as well as degrees in subjects such as childhood studies. Many are attracted into special needs through having experience with members of their own family with special needs and often have a lifetime experience of working with very special children.

Any adult working in the classroom with special needs children should:

- Have an effective job description *even if they are not paid for the support work they are doing*. This should cover their role in relation to the child, teacher and school.
- Be clear about their roles and responsibilities.
- Already have expertise in the field of special needs or be undertaking it.
- Have good knowledge of the specific form of special needs with which they are working.
- Have confident knowledge about strategies to be used to extend the child's learning and raise expectations.
- Be valued as part of the learning support team.
- Be given regular opportunities for planning with the rest of the classroom team.
- Be clear about learning objectives and resources available.
- Be deployed efficiently, effectively and flexibly.
- Be given ongoing opportunities for training and development.

Activity/Thinking Task 7

Interview – informally – an adult who is working alongside a child or children with SEN in a mainstream classroom. Find out sensitively what form of training has been made available to them and how they are involved in planning.

Common classroom learning difficulties

Hall (2007) defines a special needs child as 'a child who is not making progress and not reaching the expected attainment of other children of the same age'; and special needs provision as 'provision that is extra to and additional to the normal differentiated activities that would be expected in any class. Special needs requires differentiation by outcome; task; support; enrichment; extension and time'.

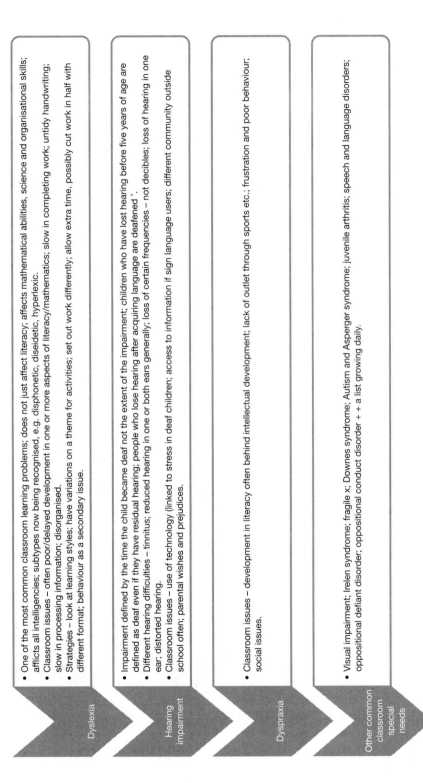

Figure 10.1 Common classroom learning difficulties

Dyslexia

- One of the most common classroom learning problems; does not just affect literacy; affects mathematical abilities, science and organisational skills; afflicts all intelligencies; subtypes now being recognised, e.g. disphonetic, diseidetic, hyperlexic.
- Classroom issues – often poor/delayed development in one or more aspects of literacy/mathematics; slow in completing work; untidy handwriting; slow in processing information; disorganised.
- Strategies – look at learning styles; have variations on a theme for activities; set out work differently; allow extra time, possibly cut work in half with different format; behaviour as a secondary issue.

Hearing impairment

- Impairment defined by the time the child became deaf not the extent of the impairment; children who have lost hearing before five years of age are defined as deaf even if they have residual hearing; people who lose hearing after acquiring language are deafened '.
- Different hearing difficulties – tinnitus; reduced hearing in one or both ears generally; loss of certain frequencies – not decibles; loss of hearing in one ear; distorted hearing.
- Classroom issues – use of technology (linked to stress in deaf children; access to information if sign language users; different community outside school often; parental wishes and prejudices.

Dyspraxia

- Classroom issues – development in literacy often behind intellectual development; lack of outlet through sports etc.; frustration and poor behaviour; social issues.

Other common classroom special needs

- Visual impairment; Irelen syndrome; fragile x; Downes syndrome; Autism and Asperger syndrome; juvenile arthritis; speech and language disorders; oppositional defiant disorder; oppositional conduct disorder + + a list growing daily.

Dyslexia, hearing impairment and dyspraxia

Figure 10.1 outlines some common classroom learning difficulties – dyslexia, hearing impairment and dyspraxia.

ADD and ADHD

This is probably one of the most controversial of all categories of SEN. It is now the most frequently diagnosed learning need in the USA and this pattern is likely to be repeated here. At the time of writing five per cent of the English school population are identified with ADHD. This comes to a total of 366,000 learners. Children who are diagnosed with ADD and ADHD are seen to display specific behaviour such as those shown in Table 10.5.

Teachers spend more time coping with misbehaviour and less time on teaching, and the ADHD child continually receives negative messages from everyone, including (generally) his or her peer group.

The disorder is often treated with a drug called Ritalin, or similar types of drugs such as Concerta and Equasym. These are used to stimulate the central nervous system and help the learner to become more responsive to feedback from his or her social and physical environment. It is claimed that a drug such as Ritalin has a 70 to 75 per cent 'success' rate; that it reduces disruptive behaviour and helps to improve relationships with parents, teachers and peers. It also helps the child to concentrate long enough to complete academic work, thus improving achievement. It is generally given alongside a programme to teach the child acceptable behaviour, and he or she is kept on it from two to seven years. Anyone who has seen the difference between a child before and after taking Ritalin can understand why it is seen as some sort of solution to severe behavioural problems and it is not surprising that there was a 156 per cent rise in the prescription of these drugs between 2001 and 2007 in the UK. But it is extremely controversial. There are negative side-effects, such as sleeping problems and weight loss. It is also claimed that at least nine children have died in the UK from its use and there is currently a push from the medical profession for it to have a 'Black Box' warning.

The idea of drugging children into compliance is disturbing and there is little evidence about the long-term effects of such treatment. Robb and Letts work with children identified as having ADHD and their book *Creating Kids Who Can Concentrate* (1997), is an excellent read for anyone concerned about finding proven strategies for beating ADHD

Table 10.5 Suggested characteristics of ADD and ADHD

ADD	ADHD
• Distracted by everything	• Fidgets with hands or feet
• Lack of concentration	• Leaves seat often
• Disorganised	• Inappropriately active behaviour
• Forgetful	• Talks excessively
• Seems not to listen	• Difficulty in waiting turn
• Fidgety	• Intrudes on others
	• Blurts out answers

Source: With thanks to Wendy Hall.

without drugs. It is a comprehensive guide that shows how lack of concentration has become a medical condition. It then moves into do-it-yourself mode and uses children with whom the authors have worked as case studies to suggest solutions. The final section shows how adults, in particular parents living with the child on a daily basis, in helping such children can help themselves. This includes using relaxation to 'give you a tranquil moment as you work your way through the book'. Medical, nutritional and educational experts have suggested that the disorder is a psycho-social issue that should be treated without drugs, for instance by changing the child's diet or environment.

It is also worth noting that there may be a financial incentive for some parents to register their child as having a special need involving ADHD. And there is evidence that the drug has been used as a mood enhancer for adults, including students who have taken it to enhance examination performance.

Able children and giftedness

The definitions of able and gifted children are very vague, so this section looks at children who are at the opposite end of the 'learning difficulties' spectrum. Anyone who has been a parent of a very able child knows that such children have their own special needs and are frequently overlooked in school if their behaviour is satisfactory. They may be part of that very useful 'sub-teachers' group mentioned earlier; but they may also be isolated and quietly unhappy. The distinction between a gifted and a very able child is a difficult one to make. 'Gifted' tends to be used to describe very exceptional children, such as musical and mathematical prodigies. This has the advantage of making them relatively rare! The federal government in the USA offers a much broader definition of the gifted child as one who 'gives evidence of high performance capability in areas such as intellectual, creative, artistic, leadership capacity or specific academic fields, and who requires services or activities not ordinarily provided by the school in order to fully develop such capabilities.' Most of our very able children in England would come into this category.

Lee-Corbin and Denicolo (1998), in their work on recognising and supporting able children in primary schools examined key research on able children; looked at the educational provision for them; explored case studies of achieving and underachieving able children; and looked at ways in which teachers can be more responsive to their needs. They note that teachers have different concepts about the very able – some defining them as those children who are excellent all-rounders, while others move toward the definition of seeing them as gifted in a particular area.

One workable definition of the intellectually very able child is that the child:

- can think much faster than other children;
- can identify and solve more complex problems;
- thinks in unusual and diverse ways;
- exhibits profound insights.

In the old days of IQ testing, the very able child would be seen as one who had an IQ of 135 and over. Research on the human brain has demonstrated that such children are biologically different; but as we shall see later this sort of 'advanced brain function' appears to result from both genetics and inheritance and environmental opportunities.

Special programmes for the very able/gifted tend to be low-key, as selectors of participants disagree over the definition of these terms. Saturday morning clubs for very able primary children held in Liverpool over thirty years ago attracted a wide range of children, including the siblings of those initially identified. There is also the fear of elitism and a general distrust of using scarce resources for the very able. In most schools, scarce resources are used to support those with learning difficulties because their needs are seen as being greater. There is also the belief that very able children can get by themselves. If we are concerned about all children receiving a challenging education, then academically very able children cannot be left out. Gifted/very able athletes do tend to get more resources with extracurricular clubs, leisure clubs and club provision; but even in this area the UK lags behind many other countries.

Sadly, intellectually very able children walk into our classrooms and nurseries every day knowing 90 per cent of the content before they start. There are three types of programmed intervention that can be found in schools in the UK:

1   *Enrichment.* Classroom work can be extended, either by using more in-depth material or adding topics to study. Enrichment programmes often build on the child's own interests and involve either the individual or small groups. They are often built into homework and after-school projects, e.g. foreign language teaching. Programmes may be general enrichment to extend the children's interests; special skills programmes to help children pursue an area of interest; and self-selected projects that will make a contribution to the school or community.
2   *Acceleration.* This offers content at an earlier age so that the child can complete school-ing in less time. Technically, this can be done by early entrance to school, skipping classes, or moving through the curriculum at a more rapid rate. The private sector tends to be much more flexible about acceleration and it is rare to find children in the state sector in non-age-related classes. The increasing use of cross-age ability group-ing for mathematics and English can provide the younger able child with opportunities for acceleration.
3   *Affective programmes.* These address social and emotional needs and focus on the special problems and concerns of very able children. Again, they tend to be found in the private sector in the UK and are often linked to small educational consultancies.

Specific support strategies for the able and gifted

The six strategies below are simply good practice and are not elitist. Their use for very able children involves using teaching methods that sustain the momentum of their work by stimulating intellectual curiosity, matching approaches to the children being taught and exploiting opportunities to contribute to the quality of pupils' wider educational development. All these form part of the standards for QTS. Teachers need to have high expectations for the very able and this is a challenging as well as a humbling task. Most of us meet children in our teaching careers who we know are intellectually more able than ourselves, but they still need our support.

1   Give children opportunities to make choices – about what they learn, how they learn and how they demonstrate their learning. Encourage self-directed behaviour. This is actually becoming less difficult as the curriculum is becoming less proscribed than it has been since 1998, and with the help of the literacy and numeracy initiatives. Some subject areas and curriculum designs lend themselves more easily to different teaching strategies.

2   Facilitate opportunities to enable high-ability children to work with other high-ability children. Co-operative learning situations that continually group very able children with less able can lead to frustration. 'Sub-teaching' can be a useful learning device for the 'sub-teacher' but over a period of time children can become frustrated in this role.

3   Provide materials and resources that challenge children. If able children are never given such challenges they have trouble developing good study skills and learning how to learn. This is particularly true for those children who do not learn study skills at home and who are entirely dependent on school for their intellectual challenges.

4   Matching learning outcomes to children's needs. Give very able children credit for what they already know and can do. It is still possible to see young able readers plodding through a reading and/or phonic scheme that offers little challenge or interest and then see them happily reading far more complex texts when they have a choice.

5   Allow and plan for independent study projects. These may be after-school or homework projects, as well as projects within the prescribed curriculum. Areas such as history, geography, religious education and ICE (information, communication and entertainment) are particularly good for this type of study project because they harness literacy skills as well as extending children's investigative, study and IT skills.

6   Provide opportunities to practise divergent and critical thinking. Many of the newer initiatives, such as outdoor education, developmental education, global citizenship, environmental education and modern foreign languages have produced some excellent materials and resources for primary pupils (and teachers) that challenge children's thinking and encourage varied learning strategies. Many of these initiatives are informed by people who are not qualified teachers, but have a particular passion and enterprise to inspire and support children.

The National Association for Gifted Children (NAGC) provides good guidance on its website. They provide a checklist, drawn up from information supplied by parents. The child:

- has a wide vocabulary and talked early;
- asks lots of questions and learns more quickly than others;
- has a very retentive memory;
- is extremely curious and can concentrate for long periods on subjects of interest;
- has a wide general knowledge and interest in the world;
- enjoys problem-solving, often missing out the intermediate stages in an argument and making original connections;
- has an unusual and vivid imagination;
- could read from an early age;
- shows strong feelings and opinions and has an odd sense of humour;
- sets high standards and is a perfectionist;
- loses interest when asked to do more of the same.

These are very much language-related, but children may be gifted in other ways, e.g. musically, and yet be very average linguistically. Giftedness in one area may be linked with difficulties in another area. NAGC suggest that many gifted children may also have Aspergers Syndrome, ADHD, dyslexia and dyspraxia.

There is a wealth of material in this area, although take care with some of the websites on specific disorders, they may have their own agenda, rather than providing authenticated data.

11 Planning

QTS Standards

3, 10, 17, 22, 23, 24, 25, 26b

Learning objectives

- to review changes in the school planning process for Key Stages 1 and 2;
- to look at ways in which schools drew up curriculum plans;
- to examine types of planning: long-, medium- and short-term, daily, lesson;
- to identify core skills needed to permeate through planning.

Whole school planning

Influences on planning

Figue 11.1 sets out just some of the influences on planning in primary schools, you may be able to think of some others. This figure makes it appear as if all schools have the same. If this were the case all schools would have exactly the same planning. Fortunately, because all schools have different communities, there are some fairly large differences between the ways in which they plan. And as curriculum planning is a dynamic process, so we should not expect it to remain static. The ECM agenda and the Excellence and Enjoyment papers and support materials (DfES, 2003, 2004, 2007) also provided some ongoing encouragement for schools seeking to be more creative in their planning.

School curriculum planning

Ideally, the schools aims and objectives and/or its mission statement drive school planning, and some schools have a curriculum statement that looks at this process. Indeed, a model is provided later in this chapter. More realistically, government pressures in the form of league tables, target setting, SATs and inspections drive the school planning process.

Figure 11.1 Influences on curriculum planning

The following paragraphs describe the five key educational focuses for curriculum planning.

Subject-based

In some primary schools subjects are taught in distinctive subject areas, and each curriculum area has its clear subject-related knowledge, skills and understandings. These then have to be worked through. This is a very traditional format and one that appeals to many parents because they recognise it from their own schooling.

Key skills

In schools where 'key skills' are used as starting points for the curriculum, planning will be informed through this. Key skills in primary schools are generally identified as: communication; the application of number; information technology; working with others; improving own learning and performance; and problem solving. You might be able to identify some gaps here in key skills. One of the most practical guides to skills planning can be found in Chris Quigley's (2004) *Key Skills for An Excellent and Enjoyable Curriculum*. In this he takes each subject area and shows how the key skills can be woven through them.

Themed planning

Key skills planning is often linked with what is sometimes called 'themed' planning. This involves different subject areas being linked together when the subject areas are appropriate. This is effectively what has nearly always happened in the foundation, and used to happen in many primary schools in the 1960s and 1970s. It was then known as topic work and fell into disrepute because it was unclear whether pupils were gaining a broad curriculum. Themed planning in today's schools is very much tighter and individual children more closely tracked. Some schools like to keep their dedicated mathematics and English teaching outside of the themed planning and teach these in the morning, leaving the themed planning work covering science and the foundation subjects to the afternoon. Obviously, core subjects do permeate the themed planning, so are reinforced.

School self-evaluation

At the time of writing the SEF (self-evaluation form) is informing school planning towards a much broader format than has been required in the past. As the term SEF implies, this means that school planning must be informed by self-evaluation. This should result in a different, more unique form of curriculum. Some schools arrive at this through a process of consultation, where teachers look at the needs of their learners and then other stakeholders such as parents, governors and the local community are also consulted. Results from these sorts of consultation can be surprising, for example in one of the schools where I am a governor, parents with children in the nursery and reception classes were asked what they wanted for their children in the curriculum. They raised concerns such as drugs, rail links, racism, health and heart disease. The school then looked at what they were going to do about it.

In the end each school does have its own unique working curriculum, although the written ones may look quite similar.

Activity/Thinking Task 1

Find the aims and/or objectives for a primary school you know. If possible ask about the processes that went into deciding what they should be; it may be that staff do not know, but ideally staff, parents and pupils 'sign up' for them. Parents often do this via the home/school contract. What implications do their aims and/or objectives have for curriculum planning? Many local libraries contain school prospectuses and there are certainly plenty to be found on the Internet. You might find it useful to make comparisons.

School vision into action

Good schools have visions about how they want to enhance the lives of children. These are often set up as aims and objectives, sometimes within a mission statement. The task then is to convert the vision into action via planning.

Here are the aims and objectives for one church school (not the one whose planning we are going to look at).

OUR MISSION STATEMENT

- to promote the highest standards in all respects of the curriculum by ensuring that all pupils develop their best potential;
- to encourage learning by providing a welcoming, friendly and supportive environment in which Christian values are central to the ethos of the school and its teaching;
- to show concern and care, through a strong sense of Christian values, for all members of the school community;
- to nurture links between school, home, parish and local community; in providing an awareness and experience;
- in the Christian faith we further endeavour to cultivate the foundations of mutual respect and responsibility;
- to use the financial resources at our disposal to provide good accommodation and surroundings and the highest possible level of staffing and equipment;
- to support all staff by providing opportunities for their professional development.

Our aims are:

- to establish a very happy, secure, well ordered and stimulating environment for staff and children to work within;
- to promote respect for others and their property and to promote good working habits, and encourage an enquiring mind and self-discipline;
- to encourage children to take a pride in what they do;
- to offer the children a broad and stimulating curriculum so that each child will, to the best of their ability:

  - learn to use language effectively and develop a love of books/literature;
  - develop a knowledge and understanding of mathematical concepts and operations;
  - learn to investigate the environment in a scientific way and take an interest in caring for the environment;
  - acquire and develop a knowledge and understanding of geography, history and religion;
  - be encouraged to enjoy and communicate through aesthetic and physical activities such as art, craft, drama, movement, music and physical education.

- to give support and encouragement when difficulties arise;
- to recognise the role of parents as partners in the learning process;
- to encourage a positive relationship between home, school and the community;
- to promote the international dimension in the school;
- to ensure equal access and opportunity for all pupils.

Long-, medium-, short-term, daily and lesson/activity planning

Long-term planning

Long-term planning is generally carried out as a one- or two-year rolling programme. Traditional examples of long-term planning for Y1 and Y5/6 can be found in Tables 11.1 and 11.2.

Table 11.1 Traditional long-term planning – Y1

	Term 1	Term 2	Term 3
English	Genres of literature Personal narrative Taking turns Listening to others	Traditional stories/ rhymes Collaborative writing Role play	Poetry Narrative writing Formal speaking
Maths	Shape	Graphs Fractions	Money Measure – length, time, capacity
Science	Sound	Light	Growth Lifecycles
Technology	Cutting Joining	Moving joints	Design proposals, individual and pairs
History		Famous people	Family to grandparents
Geography	Weather	Journeys	Local study
Art	Colour – mixing tones, shades Application – roller, blow painting, various artists	Landscapes – different techniques, painting oils/pastels, collage- textured landscapes Artists – Breughel, Constable	3-D paper sculpture, clay, salt dough, plasticine
Music	Dynamics Tempo	Duration Timbre	Pitch Texture
PE	Gymnastics Dance	Small apparatus Team work Dance	Outdoor games Gymnastics
RE	Friends	Famous people who helped others	Family
IT	Mouse and keyboard skills Communicating information	Communicating information and handling information	Control Word processing Communicating information

Table 11.2 Traditional long-term planning – Y5/6

	Term 1	Term 2	Term 3
English Set 1	Writing styles Spelling Handwriting	Information retrieval Poetry Reading skills	Author study Drama and role play Punctuation
Set 2	Listening skills Reading skills Writing – narrative Vocabulary and punctuation	Speaking skills Reading skills Non-narrative writing Grammar	Discussion Information retrieval Dialogue Author study
Set 3	Writing narrative Spelling Handwriting Grammar Listen/reading skills	Continue Vocabulary and punctuation	Poetry Author study Non-narrative
Maths All sets at own level	Place value Addition/subtraction Negative numbers Probability Co-ordinates Flow charts	Multiplication Division Fractions Decimals 2-D and 3-D shape Length, area, angles Symmetry	Problem solving Revision – four rules Investigations Mass Weight
Science	The universe and solar system	Evolution of animals	Reproduction and sex education
Technology	3-D modelling linked to science	3-D modelling linked to history and science	Home technology Surveys/question-naires
History	Britain 1900–1930 First World War	Britain 1930–1950 Second World War	Britain 1950 to present
Geography	Map work	Contrasting UK locality	Rivers
Art	Observational drawing 3-D modelling	Colour Painting e.g. Blitz, propaganda posters	Collage Modern fashion and artists
Music	Creative music Timbre	Structure and dynamics	Pitch
PE	Gymnastics Games skills	Gymnastics Six weeks of creative dance per term Folk dancing	Athletics Basketball Problem solving
RE	Creation stories	Continued	Myths and legends Comparative religions
IT	Control information	Data handling Control information processing	Data handling

This form of long-term planning ensures:
- Coverage of all the subject orders/areas of learning and RE across the whole Key Stage.
- Progression in each subject area across the whole Key Stage.
- Balance within and across subjects in each year of the Key Stage.
- Appropriate allocations of time.
- Continuity between Key Stages.

In this school at this time, the long-term planning for the nursery, reception and Y1 and Y2 took the form of a one-year plan because they had single age-groups. Years 3/4 and Y5/6 were in mixed aged groups and therefore had a two-year plan. These long-term planning sheets are informed by a scheme of work – which traditionally would cover a particular subject area.

Scheme of work

A broad definition of a scheme of work is a unit of curriculum that includes:

- *Aims*. These are more generic than objectives, identifying the destination to be reached by the end of the sequence of lessons.
- *Objectives/intended learning/learning outcomes*. These are more specific and translate the general aims into practice. Chapter 7 went into this in much more detail and provided some suggestions for the type of language to use. It is important to remember that scheme objectives are less precise than lesson objectives because many of them are designed to be achieved over a sequence of lessons. A very rough guide is that a scheme of work will need to contain what you want children to know (knowledge) and to be able to do (skills). They also cover concepts to be explored and these are often subject-specific – for example, in the medium-term history scheme on princes and princesses (see the following section, 'Medium-term planning') we would want to explore children's understandings of what a prince or princess was. This is more than knowledge because it is ongoing and much harder to assess.
- *A clear sequence of lessons*. This is intended to maintain pace, motivation and challenge for children.
- *Assessment details*. The QCA exemplar provides a section headed 'Expectations at the end of this unit'. This differentiates between what most children will know, what some children who have not made so much progress will know and what some children who have progressed further will know. Most of the expectations are in terms of knowledge and skill and form the basis for assessing individual children's progress as well as providing the starting point for planning the next part of the scheme of work.

Medium-term planning: termly or half-termly

When the National Curriculum was first introduced in 1988, there were no detailed government guidelines for planning. Schools devised their own medium-term plans, based on the school's scheme of work for each subject area.

Table 11.3. shows an example of this traditional type of planning. When detailed medium-term planning guidelines became available from QCA and the DfEE/DfES/DCSF many schools used the termly planning sheets provided, followed LA guidelines or purchased commercial schemes. The Primary Strategy documents for both literacy and numeracy were very distinctive medium-term planning sheets and although only guidelines, schools initially had to justify themselves if they chose not to follow them.

Central government control over this area of planning can be quite invasive. The long-running phonics debate (at least seventy years in the UK) has been resolved by 'advising' schools to follow a specific strategy and directing them to particular publishing initiatives that adopt these techniques; as well as supplying a great deal of resource material via central government publications.

Table 11.3 Traditional medium-term planning

Y1: Spring term: history – princesses/princes, past and present				
Activity	*Learning objective*	*Organisation/differentiation*	*Resources*	*Assessment*
To match objects to two people from contrasting periods of time – today and in the past	Adult support	Worksheet	Children should give simple explanations for their choice	
Looking at evidence – clues *The Happy Princess* – fact *The Happy Princess* – fiction Illustration of what the word 'princess' evokes	To consider evidence and make decisions about the two stories	Questioning	*The Happy Princess* Fictional princess story	Children should be able to tell whether or not a story or book is fact or fiction
Queens – fact or fiction Sorting activity	To look for clues that may inform us, tell us what we want to know	Giving written explanations	Worksheet	Children's ability to sort successfully
Princess Elizabeth – watch video – write story	To illustrate how we can find out about the past	Picture clues Oral clues	Video and worksheet	

This form of medium–term planning develops the KS plan for a particular term into a detailed sequence of subject-specific and linked units of work. This often makes use of national documents, such as those produced under the auspices of the Primary Strategy, the Excellence and Enjoyment documentation and the QCA schemes of work. It provides – particularly at KS2 – a detailed specification for each unit of work to be taught within the term, setting out specific learning objectives; emphasis, priorities and depth of treatment; resource requirements; links and references to other units of work; the nature of the child's tasks and activities; suggested teaching strategies and child groupings; strategies for differentiating work; assessment opportunities.

Short-term planning

Short-term planning is carried out by individual teachers and other colleagues, but if the school has more than one form of entry, it is likely that teachers and colleagues will plan together. Short-term planning sheets are usually weekly sheets and are most commonly found for mathematics and literacy. These are very comprehensive and are particularly useful to ensure consistency between classes in schools with two or more form entries. They also help to ease the planning load for teachers and colleagues and can utilize specialist expertise more effectively.

Local government initiatives seem to be geared more at providing often quite detailed short-term planning advice – basically using information from central government briefings and working them into local medium- and short-term planning structures. Schools are then advised to follow these, often with more challenging schools having additional advice on how they should be adopted, and often including some degree of compulsion if the authority is concerned about standards within the school. In Chapter 7 we discussed the increased complexity of having to document objectives/outcomes/success criteria. The Primary Strategy in 2004 suggested writing the success criteria on the board to provide a visual prompt for children and teachers. Individual LA consultants sometimes advised copying this out. As with any copying, some children may take so long copying the success criteria that their final ultimate success may be only to have written it down!

Daily planning

Daily planning is most commonly found in early years settings, see Table 11.4, and for student teachers. Well done, these daily planning sheets can really build on the previous day's experience to build up learners' confidence and expertise. They can be flexible in terms of the employment of other adult professionals including volunteers, students and work-experience personnel.

Lesson/activity plans

Student teachers and other educational professionals in training are expected to provide detailed lesson plans, even when the weekly planning sheets for subjects such as English and mathematics may be quite comprehensive. The mind-friendly planning framework, described in Chapter 7 covers this, and all ITT institutions have their own preferred templates. This is often complicated by having slightly different templates for different subject or focus areas. Student teachers and other students working in school are always asked to prepare daily planning schedules, including lesson plans. When Ofsted inspections lasted almost a week, many head teachers asked for daily plans so that teachers and colleagues could familiarise themselves again with preparing at this level. Fortunately, the shorter Ofsted inspections have taken some of this paperwork pressure away, but there has been a steep rise in the number of internal observations of staff and this usually requires a lesson or activity plan. Table 11.5 provides a useful example of a lesson plan, with the lesson taught being later identified as outstanding by Ofsted!

It is generally accepted that the large A3 weekly planning sheets in numeracy and literacy are detailed enough for experienced teachers, but student teachers are usually expected to provide a detailed plan as well. Publishing software companies have been keen to move in with expansive lesson plans for each subject area, which reinforces the idea that teaching

Table 11.4 Daily planning

	SAMPLE DAILY PLAN FOR TAs (TEACHING ASSISTANTS) IN THE NURSERY		
Activity	*Special notes*	*Key questions/observations*	*Assessment from TAs*
Welcome circle: Play 'Drum Outdoors'. Give each child a wooden beater and go outside. Encourage the children to make music by banging on beaters on different objects – railings, door, upturned pots etc.	Wooden beaters from music room, various subjects suitable – pipes, railings doors, pots, create, etc.	'What was your favourite sound you made?' 'Shall we all play together in our band'	Am – Chn. Loved this Rosie would not join in – target her participation
Extension: Ask the children to choose their favourite sound and then all play together as though in a band with the adult as conductor (P) (Sabba 10.00–10.15/Sarah 1.45–2.00)	Letters and sounds – Aspect 1 Environmental Studies P9		
Outdoor play: Sarah 10.15–11.15/ Sabba 2.00–3.00			
Creative: Children to have a pretend tea party for their favourite teddy or doll that they have brought in to school	Various role play prompts – picnic blanket, tea set, play food, etc.	Encourage all children to take part in small groups 'What does your teddy like to eat?' 'Shall we have a picnic today?' 'Where shall we go and what shall we take?'	Am – only half did this – re-do tomorrow? Thursday?
Extension: Use imagination in role-play and recreate scenes that are familiar to them Sabba 10.15–11.15/Ann 2.00–3.00	Please note mini-observations for profiles		
Kyle Marsden duty: Yvonne 9.00–10.00 Sarah 10.00–10.30 Sabba 10.30–11.30	Follow Kyle's interests and remind him of nursery rules and routines so that he will be able to play independently	Please engage in lots of conversational language with Kyle	Absent
Sarah: Prepare snack 9.00–9.15 Work with Miah-Rae 9.30–10.00 Work with Kyle 10.05–10.30 *Final Circle:* Sing 'Say Hello' from *Music Express* CD and also Track 2 *Extension:* Children to sing 'Hello' to different friends and respond to the action in Track 2 (Ann 11.15–11.25)/Ann 3.10	Encourage Miah to use both sides of her body in play *Music Express* CD Tracks 1 & 2 Track 3 – bounce teddy Observation sheet – multiple ones	Conversational language	AM to Track 3. Chn good at keeping beat Oliver needs more opportunity to turn take in small groups PM Sam small group to foster relationships, confidence, language

Table 11.5 Detailed lesson plan: lesson observation cycle

SUBJECT Mathematics	TEACHER DM	YEAR GROUP 6	DATE Wednesday 22nd	OBSERVED BY ....

ASSESSMENT THAT HAS INFORMED THIS LESSON   Previous two lessons have been on 'time'.

Lesson 1: Focus was on reading and writing time and answering questions involving time days, weeks, months or years. Id. four groups from assessing responses to reading and writing time questions. See attached Excel table for assessment notes.

Lesson 2: Focus was on answer questions on time from previous year's SATs questions on time.

Intervention sessions 40 minutes Monday 20th Nov. in new classroom with all 6H children identified as a 1 or 2 above. All children given input on reading time. Children identified as group 1 children to work on Teaching Time on Apple Computers. Focus on "Stop the Clock Game" for Year 3 & 4 move onto Year 5 (24 hour clock). Spent most of 20 minutes doing input and quick fire questions to group 2 children – very little time to consolidate. Consolidate learning on Wed. during whole class input on Word problem involving time.

Assessment of intervention to be done by redoing assessment sheets on reading and writing time (as a homework). Children to self assess against answer sheet on Wed. and discuss progress with peers and have group discuss way forward with teacher for each individual.

MAIN ACTIVITY OBJECTIVES – HOW LEARNING IS SHARED WITH THE CHILDREN

Display objectives on chalk board

Objective to solve a time based word puzzle

Success criteria on interactive whiteboard

Success criteria:

- can identify the key facts needed to solve the problem;
- can determine what the question really means;
- can organise the information to answer the problem;
- can add time (e.g. 10:50 + 20 mins does not equal 10.70 but 11.10 instead).

MAIN TEACHING ACTIVITY (DIFFERENTIATED)

Introduction: Group 2 children to get laptop each and work through the Time games list in handout. Any question regarding IT (finding Games etc) seek peer support before asking me. Continue with Test base sheets from last week when finished
(Teacher support every 5 minutes)

All group 1 & 2 children to work through CDPS (Can Do Problem Solving). Time problems (The Airport) 15 minutes

USE OF ICT IN THE LESSON

Interactive whiteboard, CDPS (Can Do Problem Solving)
Whiteboard 5 software. Pre-prepared Smartboard document with success criteria established

Laptop trolley with Teaching Time Package installed

PLENARY

Reflect on and discuss progress made against success criteria for those who did this activity
Discuss extension task, could you do it? Would you need to develop/practise other skills first? If so what?
A few group 2 children to outline what they did and progress made and where to next for them

---

DEPLOYMENT OF TA's GROUP OBJECTIVES AND FOCUS

No TA. All group O identified children to begin worksheet The Bus Station (A). Extend on to Bus Station (C) if time allows

Focus to solve practical word problem involving time by adding on time and creating a timetable of events

Group 1 children to self assess progress on reading and writing time. Through peer and teacher led discussion evaluate and decide on whether more consolidation or move on to task. If good progress move on to The Bus Station (B). If feel more support needed then discuss probs. And will need further support (possibly provide by using Time games or further consolidation and practise outside of lesson time with worksheets)

ANY INCLUSION ISSUES

Passive group (Monday a.m. teach with group from 6S)
Sam P, Connor, Bethany, Jessica, Sam W, Rachel, Doug, Ella, Lauren, Sam Y, Melissa

Make sure these children do not take the back seat in group based discussion around the main activity. Targeted questioning of these individuals and praise their ideas and contributions
SEN Group (Time)
John, Manuel, Zoe, Sam P
This SEN group have difficulties reading and writing time

FOCUS FOR ASSESSMENT IN THIS LESSON

Group 0 Have they meet success criteria? Where to next?
Group 1 Have they consolidated their individual skills around reading and writing time? If yes, how have they progressed against the success criteria? If no, what needs to be done next to best consolidate reading and writing time for them? (More home-based activities from worksheets? More access at home/school (if no home Internet) for use of Teaching Time games and activities?)
Group 2 What can you do now that you felt unsure of earlier today, last week, when we first started time?

can only be effective if it is backed up by its own little rain-forest. There are also government plans available on the Internet. However you start to devise lesson plans you cannot just lift lesson plans from other sources – including colleagues in the same school. You need to customise them for your school, your class or group and for individual children. And never ask children to do anything you have not tried yourself – including something as obvious as a worksheet!

Planning can be a time-consuming business. The danger is that this leaves no time or energy for more creative activities, such as making games and researching and trying out new teaching approaches. Or even having some sort of life outside school.

One school's planning story

This is a story of how one primary school's planning has changed over the past ten years. This is to show planning as a dynamic process, influenced by changes in particular factors such as those outlined in Figure 11.1 (see p. 161). This school was chosen because it has consistently had good Ofsted reports, the latest one, a few weeks ago at the time of writing, recorded it 'outstanding' across the board. The school has an above-average FSN intake.

Phase 1

Ten years ago, the school had a new head and deputy and the time seemed right for a reassessment of its previous model. The starting point was a weekend away to agree school values: this involved all 'stakeholders', as the terminology was at that time; all educational professionals (teachers, teaching assistants, welfare staff, etc.); parents; and governors. This was eventually finalised into a curriculum model, Figure 11.2. Out of this curriculum planning model came the long-, medium- and short-term planning sheets. Extracts from these can be found in Tables 11.1 to 11.3.

Phase 2

Prescot CP now plans differently, although you will find many examples of the form of planning they were using. The initial desire for change was brought about by greater experience with the planning process; some long-term dissatisfaction with some of the government schemes of work by both staff and pupils; change of personnel; broadening of central government's willingness to allow schools more freedom for long- and medium-term curriculum planning; the ECM agenda; and the SEF.

Prescot wanted to start again from basic values looking at long-term planning in terms of:

- the characteristics of the locality in which the school is placed; and
- the needs of the children.

It had a relatively long-term history of seeking out the views of its learners, parents/carers and other stakeholders, through a variety of formal as well as informal means. These included questionnaires, interviews, briefings, meetings, conferences, professional development, etc. and took place regularly during the course of the school year. Reviewing school values involved additional meetings and conferences so that these groups all had the opportunity to identify the specific features of the locality and the needs of its children.

Curriculum planning model

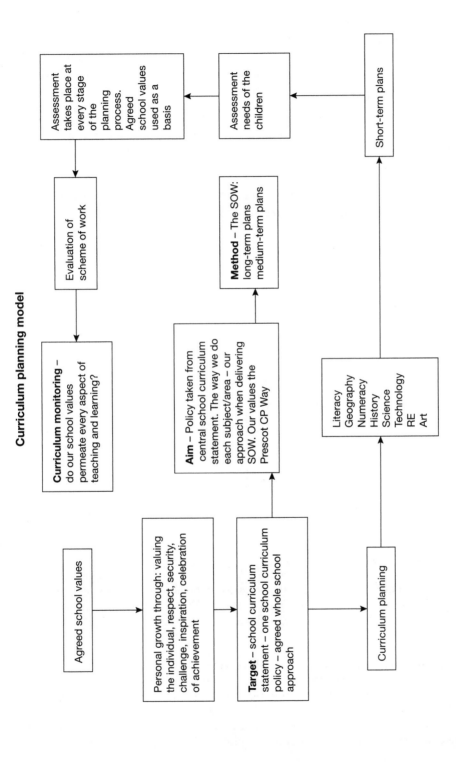

Figure 11.2 Curriculum planning model: Prescot County Primary

There was also an acknowledgment that the school had an increasing number of children who were not in its immediate catchment area.

The result can be seen in the long-term planning shown in Table 11.6, which essentially opens up the planning within clear focus areas of the SEF.

Activity/Thinking Task 2

Table 11.7 (see facing page) may look very unfamiliar to you, but it is based on the move to encourage schools to make their curriculum 'lively and engaging for pupils'. This is done through meeting the needs and opportunities presented by pupil, school vision and locality.

If you work in a school, use as the starting point the question 'What is distinctive about the work of our school?' and try completing Table 11.6 below.

Table 11.6 What is distinctive about our school?

Feature of our school	*So what? (Our distinctive work)*
Our pupils and their parents	
Our vision	
Our location	

Source: Adapted from Quigley, 2004.

Cause and effect – teaching and learning

One of the outcomes of this curriculum review for the school was reviewing their internal lesson observation criteria for teaching and learning. In Table 11.8 you can see how the long-term focus area plan feeds into the observation schedule.

Assessment and evaluation of planning

We will look at assessment in more detail later on, but at this stage it is essential to recognise that assessment and planning are closely related and assessment of a lesson or a sequence of lessons informs the next stage of planning. Evaluation of the scheme of work, a sequence of lessons, or just one lesson, takes place in two ways.

Table 11.7 Long-term planning based on identified focus areas

---

Long-term planning for focus area

Characteristics of Prescot County Primary School as a provider
- We will develop a unique curriculum for Prescot County Primary School.
- We will use the distinct character of our locality to inform teaching and learning.
- We will become a centre of excellence with a distinct character.

Gathering the views of learners, parents and other stakeholders
- Systems will be further developed and improved upon to gather the views of parents, learners and other stakeholders.
- The views of learners, parents and other stakeholders will be respected and valued.
- Outcomes will be used to inform school self-evaluation and will influence strategic planning and school improvement whenever appropriate.

Achievement and standards
- Develop language skills with a focus on speaking and listening.
- Alter the curriculum to enhance foundation subjects.
- Establish learning lunchtimes.
- Network with other institutions, e.g. higher education.
- Specialist teaching support will raise standards across the curriculum.
- Develop use of peer learning.
- Continue to promote CPD for all staff including team teaching, networking and use of sabbaticals.
- Further enhance support and resources for children with additional educational needs.

Quality of provision
- We will develop MFL across the school.
- We will plan from children's interests.
- Learners will have the freedom to explore.
- Free the curriculum!
- We will foster a love of books and a culture of reading.
- Best practice from 'Excellence and Enjoyment' will be implemented to raise standards across the curriculum.

Learner's personal development and well-being
- We will further develop pupil voice.
- We will provide rich opportunities for all learners to develop general knowledge and experience new things
- The whole school community will be involved in school self-evaluation and developmental planning: staff, parents, children, governors and ex pupils.
- Learners will have time to explore and reflect.
- Involvement of the wider community and parents will be maximised.
- Children will be encouraged to become more independent and to take responsibility.
- Crèche and childcare facilities will enhance pre-school provision.
- A quiet room will be established.

Quality of leadership and management
- Sustain and build upon high standards and expectations across the curriculum.
- Develop the outdoor environment to enhance learning and leisure time for children and adults.
- Develop international links.
- Provide and promote choice of learning environments.
- Transform the learning environment for Foundation.
- Workforce remodelling: develop a more flexible workforce.

Overall effectiveness and efficiency
- Expand facilities for parents and toddlers with an outdoor area.
- Extend school hours.
- Use the wider community.
- Use experts and specialists to support innovation and school improvement.
- Expand the school.
- Grow tomorrow's leaders.

ECM – what it means to us!
- *Be healthy*: Through a holistic approach we will promote, provide and educate healthy lifestyle choices at Prescot County Primary School.
- *Stay safe*: Prescot County Primary will provide and support a secure, stable environment where every child is safe and cared for.
- *Enjoy and achieve*: We will encourage children to become aware of their whole well-being in order to develop confidence to achieve their full potential.
- *Make a positive contribution*: We will prepare our children at Prescot County Primary to make positive social, emotional and personal choices. All children will have the skills and attitude to make a positive contribution to community and environment.
- *Achieve economic well-being*: We will encourage all learners, adults and children, to be confident and fulfilled; to achieve aspirations and look forward to a secure future.

Table 11.8 Cause and effect

PRESCOT COUNTY PRIMARY SCHOOL

'PUTTING THE LEARNER FIRST'

CAUSE AND EFFECT – TEACHING AND LEARNING – DEVELOPMENT OF INTERNAL LESSON OBSERVATION
CRITERIA TO FOCUS ON LEARNING AND PUPIL RESPONSE/ACTIONS/EXPERIENCE

CAUSE / INPUT / TEACHING	EFFECT / IMPACT / LEARNING
Structure and pace of lesson	If the lesson has a good structure and pace the children will be focused, motivated to learn, appropriately challenged and will make progress or consolidate
Achievement of lesson objective?	If the children have achieved the lesson objective they will feel confident and positive about their learning and eager to focus on what comes next
Effective use of demonstration and modeling	If there is effective demonstration and modelling, children will be aware of the expectations and understand what the outcome/process should be. They will be inspired and more able to work independently
Creativity and inspiration	If there is creativity and inspiration the children will be enthusiastic, excited and more confident to take ownership of their own learning
Inclusion – provision for all groups of children	All have achieved to their own levels Children are active and on task – challenged but not stressed Children using resources effectively to complement their learning style
Presentation of work: adults and children	Pride in work High standards throughout books Modelled work reflected in children's work
Active listening skills: adults and children	Children respond to ideas of others including but not solely the teacher Children answer and ask relevant questions Adult responds to children's relevant ideas rather than following unswerving path
Celebration of achievement	Pride in work (increase in self esteem) Positive behaviour impact Enjoyment of learning

	Progress made within the lesson
Thorough planning due to AFL and children being aware of their targets and success criteria for achieving them	
Sound teacher subject knowledge and levels for each group of learners Children aware of success criteria for lesson outcomes Revisiting outcomes and targets	Standards achieved by children
Evidence of high expectations	Children 'Have a go'. Share targets and learning Children have high expectations of themselves and freely share these with each other
Use of assessment for learning	Children are extended and challenged. Targets and success criteria are achieved Children responding to marking and discussions
Use of marking/target setting	Children see progress and aware if achieved target. Children have high expectations because they can see work/structured play is valued Children in routine of reading and reflecting on targets and revisiting and responding next lesson
Verbal feedback/use of dialogue to elicit challenge	Using appropriate vocabulary/age appropriate they can talk about what they have learnt Challenge/celebrate each other on targets and success criteria of the lesson Celebrate each other's success and motivate each other to achieve high expectations
Clear and effective routines	A calm, secure, environment that develops positive behaviour facilitating confident, independent learning
Identification of potential barriers to learning	If potential barriers are identified all learners are enabled, all children have high expectations of themselves
Organization and management of the classroom and resources	An organized and well managed learning environment impacts on children's ability to organize and manage their learning
Effective use of ICT to support teaching *and* learning	ICT prepares all pupils to be motivated and engaged. Leading to learners being ready to participate in future society. Bring the outside world into the classroom!
Encouragement of independence in children: managers of their own learning	A well-resourced environment facilitates children to make appropriate choices as to their next step in learning
Curriculum design and planning	A flexible, unique curriculum will broaden children's horizons leading to more effective learning

Informal

Teachers and other colleagues are constantly undertaking informal evaluation of their planning, either by themselves, in conversation with colleagues and of course observing the responses of pupils. This informal evaluation is linked to assessment of children's learning as an outcome of planning and an evaluation of their own teaching. The importance of this informal assessment and evaluation is often missed, just because it is informal. It might involve a short conversation with the additional adult supporter(s) in the classroom; someone in the corridor, a longer discussion at lunchtime; listening to children in the playground; a statement at a school based in-service, or even waking up in the middle of the night thinking how something could be planned better next time!

Formal

This provides a written or electronic record of how successful planning has been in achieving the desired learning outcomes for children. The planning sheets above identify assessment of children's learning in different ways. The QCA schemes of work used suggest that progress and assessment were checked by matching the expectations to achievement at the end of the year. The medium short-term planning sheet for Y1 history in the spring term is similar to the QCA exemplar schemes as it has an assessment column which records what children are expected to learn at the end of the unit. This is all done prior to teaching the scheme.

In weekly planning sheets assessment and ways forward are often identified, although in practice space is often at a premium. Daily lesson or activity plans, which students must complete, are evaluated at the end of each day. In Table 11.5, for example, learning was evaluated through a numerical system where zero stood for no problems, one for more practice, two for more teacher input, and three very limited understanding. A record was also kept of pupils without watches because obviously that influences their ability to tell and record time.

Teachers assess children's learning formally on these sheets. The comments made here are generic, so individual assessment records are kept elsewhere, although sometimes children's names do appear. Most schools have workable assessment records for each child in the core subjects and increasingly these are electronic. In most schools I visit, foundation subjects are more likely to be assessed through content completion. Children's learning is assessed in terms of the progress they make through the scheme or unit of work and the attainment levels they reach.

School planning reviews

As we noted above, schools have to review their policy documents and schemes of work on a regular basis. And we have already looked at some of the reasons why this has to be a dynamic and honest process. Other points influencing reviews are:

- Assessment of children's learning as an outcome of the lessons and sequence of lessons planned for that subject area. For example, when geography was identified as being an unpopular subject in one school, one of the ways of improving its attraction to the children was to change to another, closer locality.
- Changes in government requirements – how quickly schools jump depends heavily on the confidence and insight of the head teacher and senior management team. And

there are huge differences within LAs as well as between authorities about central announcements regarding change. Experienced and/or insightful heads can often determine early on whether this is change that will happen, or whether it will die a quiet death. Growth of the neighbour learning networks has aided this process with far more collaborative planning and informed leadership support from fellow headteachers and members of SRTs.

- Changes in staffing and staffing expertise. One of the most obvious changes in recent years is the advent of MFLs and the varying opportunities different schools have to use expertise from staff who are fluent speakers in more than one language.
- Use of new technology, e.g. computer networks, digital developments, etc. I have watched reluctant adult IT users become wonderfully enthusiastic and skilful when they watch eight-year-olds devising their own websites, blogging, filming, etc.
- Changes in school organisation or grouping within classes. Failing and rising school populations often result in a complete review of existing curriculum planning.

Trainee teachers and planning reviews

Plans

Student teachers are required to monitor, assess and record their own planning evaluations and then use the information from this to improve their effectiveness. Most students start their planning evaluations in terms of class management. Here they record their ability to maintain a purposeful working atmosphere, establish a safe environment and monitor behaviour. Later, as these essentials become well established and taken for granted, they move on to the planning implications for other teaching and class-management standards, such as planning to provide learning objectives that challenge children of differing abilities and interests, and looking at ways in which a sequence of lessons can be planned to maintain pace, motivation and challenge.

Lesson evaluations

The success of individual lessons and therefore the overall scheme should be evaluated. The chapter on mind-friendly planning provided a couple of different templates in which this could be done quite simply. You need to cover: the response of the children; the quality of the children's oral work and recording; the level of activities (too high? too low?); a critical analysis of your own performance in classroom management and organisation.

Assessment of children's learning

This should focus on the intended learning for the lesson. How will you find out if children have learned what you intended? – e.g. through observing the pupils; listening and talking to children and marking their work. How also do you know whether learning has taken place as a result of your effective teaching?; or they already knew about what you were teaching.

Curriculum entitlement and breadth of study

The primary curriculum has been under constant review since the Plowden Report. One of the major issues, then and now, has been the balance between 'the basics' – English and mathematics and other subject areas, i.e. science and the foundation subjects. At one time, in the fairly recent past schools have been required to identify the hours given to different subject areas and recommendations have been made by central government on how to do this. ICT now forms an increasingly important role and joins English and mathematics as being basic to a child's curriculum entitlement. This is particularly important, where children do not have access to the appropriate IT at home.

We have mentioned Gardner's multiple intelligences theories earlier and, although I am sceptical about them, it is obvious that they raise issues about curriculum entitlement to subject matter that utilises and develops intelligences in other areas outside mathematics and English. Do our children have good access to music, art and design, physical education, drama, outdoor education, interpersonal and intrapersonal skills, spiritual and moral education? Increasingly, schools are asked to supply emergency patches to areas of children's lives which are seen to be deficit – citizenship, healthy eating, social enterprise, service learning and of course spiritual, moral, social and cultural development.

Activity/Thinking Task 3

Review the weekly timetable for a class known to you and write down the percentage of time spent on each subject area. If your school follows a more thematic approach, try making a rough estimate. Look at ways in which spiritual, moral, social and cultural development is planned.

Most schools have responded pragmatically to the measurement of standards through the SATs in English and mathematics. They have cut down the times for other curriculum areas and given additional support (often in both time and personnel) to those areas. Target setting has increased the pressure on schools to raise the levels of their SATs results, and looking through SATs results for the previous three years will give you an idea of how effectively your school has done this. After-school and lunchtime clubs can increase coverage of other curriculum areas, particularly sport, music, drama and art. As these tend to be free-choice activities, it means that some children can effectively cut themselves off from the opportunity to extend their experience in areas where they may be less proficient. Extended school provision is slightly different from this and may not help to support quality provision of subjects missing from mainstream classes.

12 Assessment for learning

QTS Standards

3a and b, 11, 12, 13, 26a, b, 27, 28

Learning objectives

- to explore what is currently understood about the meaning of the term assessment for learning (AfL);
- to examine the relationships between planning, monitoring, marking, assessment and target setting;
- to recognise the relationship between national systems for assessment and recording and those at local level;
- to know some of the requirements concerning reporting formally to parents/carers.

Assessment for learning

The definition of AfL

AfL has been defined and redefined in several different ways over the past few years. It seems to have extended its brief well beyond the fairly simple definition provided by the Assessment Reform Group (ARG) in 2002. AfL, stated the ARG, is the process of 'seeking and interpreting evidence for use by learners and their teachers to decide where the learners are in their learning, where they need to go, and how best to get there.' The focus of assessment is then on its use by learners, and its purpose is to improve learning and raise achievement. Behind this is a philosophy about assessment that goes back twenty years or more, when pupils were more heavily involved in self- and peer-assessment. The rapid growth of electronic software has changed the medium, but not the message. Most permanent recording now takes place digitally, and teachers, colleagues and children can have immediate access to such systems as they move round the classroom or early years settings.

Ten principles of AfL

The ARG's definition and its findings were adopted by the then DfES, Ofsted, National Strategies and QCA. The ten principles for AfL are identified in Figure 12.1 and there is nothing that comes over as transformational. In Activity/Thinking Task 1 we ask you to demonstrate how five points of the general guidance to these principles can be used as a checklist. You will find many schools have a self-evaluation grid for AfL.

Activity/Thinking Task 1

Think of an activity that you have planned and then assessed. Did your assessment involve pupils showing any of the following:

- changes in their attitudes to learning and in their motivation, self-esteem, independence, initiative and confidence
- changes in their responses to questions, in contributions to plenary sessions, and in explanations and descriptions
- improvement in their attainment
- an ability to ask relevant questions
- active involvement in formative assessment processes, e.g. setting targets, peer or self-assessment, recognising progress in their written work, skills, knowledge and understanding.

I would expect the answer to Task 1 is a positive one, even if you cannot assess for learning each particular point for each child. This is assessment over a longer period of time. A learner who is afraid to ask questions, may take time to trust both the adult and peers. Indeed, many adult learners are also afraid to ask questions for exactly the same reason. It is worth remembering that the final feature of the mind-friendly lesson planning cycle, was exactly the last point made here – a child's ability to reflect on their learning process.

Obviously to assess effectively, a number of other conditions need to be met, some of which are quite difficult if you are a student teacher, a supply teacher or another educational professional who does not often teach a particular group or class. The assessor needs to:

- know their pupils well, know why pupils make mistakes, and be able to make judgements about next steps or interventions;
- share learning intentions with pupils and use them to mark work or give feedback or rewards;
- build in review time for themselves and their pupils;
- encourage pupils to take responsibility for their learning by providing opportunities for them to describe their response to learning intentions or targets, the strategies they use and the judgements they make in relation to their progress;
- give pupils examples of a variety of skills, attitudes, standards and qualities to aim for;
- analyse pupils' performance in tests and use the information for future learning plans;
- feel confident and secure in classroom practice.

Figure 12.1 Assessment for learning – principles

And as we have already seen planning needs to:

- place emphasis on learning intentions and on sharing them with pupils and other adults in the classroom;
- embed assessment criteria for feedback and marking, peer and self-assessment;
- where appropriate acknowledge differentiated classroom groups;
- build-in review time and flexibility;
- record pupils who need additional or consolidation work;
- make time for guided group sessions for explicit formative assessment opportunities;
- record when adjustments have been made and what did or did not work and why.

AfL and whole-school planning

Again, as we noted with the planning, effective assessment needs to be part of a whole-school ethos that:

- values attitudes to learning and promotes trusting relationships;
- encourages and builds self-esteem;

- believes that all pupils can improve and measures individuals against their own previous attainment instead of against other pupils;
- uses value-added data;
- provides support, guidance and appropriate training for teachers, students and other professionals who work with children in school;
- manages change well and includes maintenance systems;
- encourages review and self-evaluation at individual, subject and school level.

Hopefully, you are in a school where all these comments are self-evident. The school has a clear learning and teaching policy where 'all' staff have worked together to create it; where staff discussion has enabled a shared philosophy and a shared language and where ideas are developed that raise achievement by enabling learners to take greater responsibility for their learning. It does not mean that assessment is absolutely perfect, it means that staff are 'working towards' and continuing to learn.

Learning to monitor pupil learning

Monitoring learning

The word 'monitor' is a typical example of a word that within the education sector has a very specific meaning. When student teachers first start working in a classroom, the word 'monitor' often seems to mean to them 'monitor for good behaviour', i.e. monitor the children so that they behave. It is far more complex than that. Monitoring shows learning and teaching in all its complexity and involves very high order skills. It is best to start with small groups and follow school practice:

- Monitor clearly defined learning objectives – with some children these may not be curriculum centred.
- Identify children for whom the learning objectives are inappropriate.
- Identify individual learning patterns and ways to improve them.
- Listen carefully to pupils, analyse responses and move learning forward.
- Identify misconceptions and help to remedy them.
- Record observations systematically and link them with learning targets.
- Establish a firm database to report on children's progress to themselves, their carers, other teachers and adults working in the classroom, governing bodies, LA and government departments. The growth of multi-agency work, means that marking evidence, like attendance, may need to be used to complete the CAF.
- Be flexible to children's learning so that children continue to be treated as individuals and are not pigeon-holed into learning categories to make monitoring and marking easier.
- Ensure that any adult working with a group of pupils is involved with monitoring and assessment and understands the purpose of the activity, the intended outcome for the individual/group and is able to respond appropriately.

Monitoring by questioning

Ideally, questions should try to avoid the obvious teacher question that asks a question for which the teacher knows the reply. This is harder than it seems, particularly when looking for some quick affirmation that something has been learnt. However, you will have opportunities to observe skilled teachers and other professionals use other types of questioning. They may do this by:

1 framing a question that explores issues central to pupils' understanding;
2 extending the wait-time to allow longer, better developed answers – rather than the quick, expected answer;
3 putting across the message that what is wanted is a thoughtful response, rather than the first right answer;
4 allowing pupils opportunities to discuss thinking in pairs/groups, so that one person can speak on behalf of others;
5 expecting all pupils to contribute to answers (one, quite controversial, suggestion was made that the teacher should decide on a 'no hands-up' policy in order to draw all pupils into thinking rather than those whose hands go up first);
6 training pupils themselves to pose questions: use the 'who', 'why', 'what', 'when', 'where', 'how' strategy, getting pupils to ask questions using one of these words as a starting point – it makes a useful ten-minute time filler.

Apparent confusions held by children may be deeply held misconceptions, which need to be addressed carefully over a period of time. 'Wrong answers' may well be right answers but in the wrong place! One of the great advantages of small-group working is being able to ask pupils for clarification about ideas. And it is amazing the number of children who can give a 'right' answer for the 'wrong' reasons. This is why it is important, where and when possible, to ask children how they arrived at a particular answer. The numeracy strategy was particularly strong on this and it provides a good example of 'metacognition'. Many pupils need the language to be able to do this and the teacher to model it for them. It is always worth remembering that for many questions there is no one right answer. In fact, it is often only in very simple closed questions that there is the 'one right answer'. Be flexible and encourage your pupils to be flexible too.

One example of a misconception was provided to me by a colleague teaching 'Earth and beyond' in science. Children had been asked to draw what they thought happened at night-time when the sun went down. One child produced a beautiful drawing to illustrate exactly that. Basically the sun came up in the morning, moved across the sky and then went down at night-time. It went down, deep down into the Earth and came through on the other side of the world, so that it could shine there. This produced sunny Australia while England slept. The whole procedure was then followed again. This child's 'misconception' forms an Ancient Greek myth about the chariot of the god Helios moving across the sky. Pretty good for an eight-year-old.

Marking

Marking from a child's perspective

Marking is the most visual method of monitoring pupils' work during the course of a lesson and when work is sent home. It provides feedback to both the children and parents. Ideally, marking should take place alongside the child, so that it becomes a teaching tool, rather than a summative assessment. The Derby City Primary Strategy team in a presentation pointed out that their research had shown that despite all good intentions,

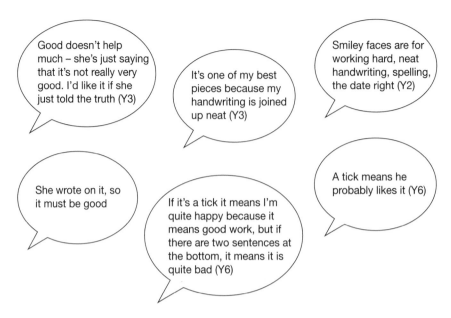

Figure 12.2 Some pupil interpretations of written feedback from Derby City Primary Team

children believed the purpose of marking is for the teacher or teaching assistant to find out what they have got right or wrong, rather than being a developmental process. The team also suggested that:

- Children are rarely given time to reading marking comments.
- Children often cannot understand or even read the teacher's handwriting or comments.
- Children are rarely given time to make any improvement on their work.

Figure 12.2 shows a very easy way to do your own assessment of children's understanding of marking – just ask them.

School marking policies

Marking is generally the first experience student teachers and teaching assistants have of formally assessing children's work. Most schools have very clear marking policies and try to make their marking criteria clear to learners, parents and other educational professionals. Marking, as we are all aware, should evidence monitoring of learning; celebrate achievement; identify areas of improvement; and should focus on the learning objective(s). There is little point in focusing on neat presentation, for example, when the lesson objective and success criteria were to provide accurate measurements of centimetre lines. I have heard the 'Neat work, well done' comment described as a 'nag' target, where 'nag' targets are always ongoing. Other 'nag' targets might result in comments such as 'This is not enough. You can do better'; 'Check your spellings'; and the old favourite 'You have tried hard today, keep it up'.

Activity/Thinking Task 2

Collect information about marking from a primary school. Draw up a grid for yourself and evaluate how useful this would be for you as a new member of staff. Suggest – to yourself! – anything else that could be added to help make it easier for anyone coming into the school, for example a supply teacher.

Effective marking policies

- The assessment criteria used for marking should be clear to children, parents and teachers.
- Assessment criteria should not be a secret and it is useful to discuss with children their understanding of the marking system.
- Marking should show children that someone is taking an interest in their work.
- Marking shows parents and other interested parties that children's work is being monitored.
- Marking celebrates children's achievements and identifies areas for improvement.
- Marking should be focused on the learning objective or target.

Marking for the student teacher is made much easier when a marking policy is in place, but there are also other factors to take into account:

- Ensure that children know what sorts of standards you expected. A change from one teacher to another is often confusing for children as they no longer know what is expected. Looking through children's previous work helps to gauge what they can do. Some children try especially hard for a different teacher; others may have a 'wait and see' strategy.
- Help children to understand that both effort and attainment are rewarded and making it clear which is which.
- Tell children what they need to do to improve. This needs to be very clear and is very skilful. You have to be quite clear in your own mind what you want. Avoid asking the question 'Do you understand now?'. We often do not know whether we understand something or not. Better to ask whether the child knows what to do.
- Make sure that marking is not just being done for the sake of it – because the words look better corrected than not corrected.

Student teachers should also note the following by looking at how their class teacher marks work:

- when and how the teacher marks in different subject or themed areas;
- the style of handwriting used to mark work;
- the use made of different-coloured pens;
- the use made of marking in terms of individual achievement (e.g. is it recorded anywhere else?);
- how marking is linked/or not linked to individual and group target setting;
- if a response is expected from the child (dialogue marking).

Where possible mark as you monitor. It gives instant feedback for both you and the child and saves marking later! This is often difficult if your school favours the detailed guided session; where the rest of the class must work unsupported unless there is additional adult support.

Assessment

Purposes of assessment

- *diagnosis*: to identify strengths and weaknesses in order to monitor progress;
- *guidance*: to aid decision-making;
- *selection*: placing pupils in the most appropriate situation (set/group);
- *prediction*: potential of the pupils for future achievement;
- *evaluation*: effectiveness of learning and teaching;
- *accountability*: quality of teaching and effectiveness of the school.

Assessment can be:

- norm-referenced, i.e. compared to that of their peers;
- criteria-referenced, i.e. compared to a set of predetermined criteria;
- ipsative, i.e. compared to child's past performance.

Different forms of assessment

As you know, assessment is carried out formally and informally. Both are an integral part of teaching. The original NNF had a very useful overview of assessment. It looked at short-, medium- and long-term assessments and passing on information about pupils' attainment and progress.

Informal assessment

This takes place all the time and is linked closely to monitoring. It involves looking at what children are doing, assessing what they need and responding to this. Informal assessment can involve non-verbal communication, such as a nod, smile, frown or movement of the head. It also involves explanations, questions, and words of praise or admonishment. It is carried out 'on the hoof' and forms the basis of the interaction between the teacher and the class and the teacher and individual child.

Formal assessment

This is planned for in advance and is an integral part of monitoring both learning and teaching. Below we look at different types of formal assessment as well as identify its four main purposes.

1   *Formative*. This identifies achievements in children's learning in order to move it forward. This area of assessment involves the student teacher as soon as he or she enters the classroom. This is very much linked with a definition of assessment *for* learning, which sees practice as the process of seeking and interpreting evidence for

use by learners and their teachers to decide where the learners are in their learning, where they need to go and how best to get there.

2   *Summative*. This is assessment *of* learning and looks at learning over a period of time. Traditionally, end-of-year tests did this. The SATs can be seen as summative assessments of children's learning at a specific point in time. The optional SATs are often used in the same way.

3   *Diagnostic*. This is used to identify specific learning difficulties for which there are known strategies to improve learning. Miscue analysis for reading is one diagnostic test, which provides a detailed analysis of the type of problems that children might have. Diagnostic testing is closely linked to specific teaching strategies to improve performance. The Reading Recovery programme is an example of this process in action.

4   *Evaluative*. This means evaluating learning outcomes in terms of overall success. Schools are encouraged to evaluate new initiatives in terms of their overall success in raising standards over a period of time. Sadly, in our rapidly changing society, this period is often quite small and does not give initiatives time to 'bed in'. As the psychologists among you will know, the Taylor effect described when some change was made that appeared in the short term to have a very good effect. This then faded. Researchers identified that the attention given to the innovation, rather than the innovation itself, was what was causing the improvement. As soon as the attention went, so did the improvement.

The distinctions between these four different assessment purposes are less clear cut in practice. Practice SATs papers, for example, are used diagnostically to identify areas for improvement as well as provide practice for children.

Instruments of assessment

This sounds like some form of torture, but is just a useful term to differentiate between different types of assessment. Nearly all of the instruments have built-in recording methods. They include:

1   *Records of achievement/personal portfolio assessments*. This is less popular/fashionable than it used to be, but I suspect many of you reading this were involved with this type of assessment when you were in school. One of the most comprehensive prior to the literacy strategy was the 'primary language record', drawn up by London teachers and used all over the country. It was particularly good at looking at the language strengths of children who had English as an additional language.

2   *Standardised tests* (includes the SATs, as well as commercial tests). Standardised achievement tests are potentially powerful tools for teaching. They are the most objective and scientific measures we have. But they still make many people uncomfortable, particularly when used with primary-aged pupils. The memories of the 11-plus fade slowly and of course in some areas of the country still exist. These memories are linked with denied opportunities, unfair tracking policies, negative labelling of 11-plus failures, intellectual and cultural bias and political machinations. Looking at reactions of parents to school reports outlining SATs results, I am not convinced that this has changed very much. The seven-year-old with a set of Level 3s is given much more positive feedback than one with less, for example a friend's Y2 child received a bike from her grandparents because of the row of 3s she had received.

3 *Scheme checklists*. Whether commercial or school-created, these examine what progress has been made over a specific period of time, such as over half a term or at the end of a unit of work. As online testing schemes become easier for teachers to devise this is a likely area of growth.

4 *Assessment through learning continuums*. Programmes such as the Australia-based 'First steps language programme' provide learning continuums in different areas – e.g. reading, writing, spelling and oracy. The continuums are based on learning indicators shown by children at different stages. Children are assessed by watching their learning behaviour and then placing them on the relevant point on the continuum. One of the most powerful aspects of this form of assessment is that it provides teaching strategies to move children from one stage to another. Table 12.1 illustrates this. One of the major advantages of these 'learning continuums' is that they are developmental, rather than age-related. The levels for the national curriculum are age-related and as anyone involved with levelling knows, are not particularly accurate without far more detail.

5 *Foundation profile assessment/e-profile*. Since 1988, it has been a legal requirement that schools conduct an approved baseline assessment procedure to measure children's attainment on entry to statutory schooling, i.e. on entry to KS1. This has been adapted several times and is now a summative foundation profile assessment that covers 'each child's level of development against the thirteen assessment scales derived from the early learning goals'. Early years settings are generally very quick to do their own child-profile assessments when children first arrive. This provides a useful and necessary baseline for looking at both under-fives and under-threes. The under-fives, and particularly the under-threes, are likely to be an important growth area for more formal testing, however disguised.

Table 12.1 Extract from 'First steps' spelling continuum

Phase 2: Semi-phonetic spelling	**Phase 3: Phonetic spelling**
In this phase children show developing understanding of sound-symbol relationships. Their spelling attempts show . . .	In this phase writers are able to provide an almost perfect match between letters and . . . sounds. Letters are chosen on the basis . . .
[EXAMPLE OF CHILD'S WRITING SHOWN]	[EXAMPLE OF CHILD'S WRITING SHOWN]
Key indicators • uses left to right and top to bottom orientation of print . . . etc.	*Key indicators* • chooses letters on the basis of sound without regard for conventional spelling patterns . . . etc.
Major teaching emphases Semi-phonetic spellers need to be exposed to print in natural and meaningful contexts . . . etc.	*Major teaching emphases* Phonetic spellers should be exposed to a wide variety of printed materials to provide data . . . etc.

6 *IEPs.* These are teaching and learning plans for children identified as having SEN, and are no longer mandatory. The guidelines for IEPs are set out in the revised Special Needs Code of Practice (2001). An IEP is drawn up by the school's SENCO, working with the child's teacher, LSA and anyone else who may be working with the child. This is now fairly multi-agency and as well as covering the child's carers may also involve advisory teachers, the educational psychology service, educational social worker, lead professional, etc. Ideally, the child should be involved.

7 *CAF.* This came out of the ECM agenda and requires an input from primary schools, if the child or young person with additional needs is in primary school. The CAF is an attempt to cut down on all the different forms completed by different agencies involved with children and their families. It is a 'simple pre-assessment checklist' and under the learning section requires information about understanding, reason and problem solving; learning, education and employment; progress and achievement in learning; and, finally, the child's aspirations – their ambition, their confidence, view of their own progress and motivation and perseverance.

8 *Observation checklists – paper and electronic.* Teachers and teaching assistants have used observation checklists for some time, so that they can target and assess particular learning performances such as working collaboratively, problem solving and finding information from non-fiction texts. Some of the most common commercial checklists are related to personal and social behaviour and to early reading strategies, e.g. holding a book correctly. Electronic observations are also becoming far more common.

9 *Record books – paper and electronic.* More and more information is now stored electronically as learning software becomes much more commonly used in schools. And there are still some of us who prefer reading from downloads, rather than on the screen, so even electronic assessment often translates into a hard copy format. Medium-term planning sheets in most schools involve identifying assessment opportunities, whoever is responsible for creating them. Short-term planning involves assessing children after teaching has taken place and documenting ways in which this assessment could be used for future planning. Teachers also keep subject record books to cover particular areas of the curriculum and records on the progress and attainment of individual children in specific subject areas. In subjects such as English and maths several different aspects of children's learning may be recorded. These may be linked to different attainment targets set out in the national curriculum documents. Schools devise common recording devices to identify different stages in the learning process, for example: no assessed learning;/partial learning; x understood. Records for many foundation subjects tend to be limited to curriculum coverage in order to keep assessment manageable.

10 *Performance assessments.* Many schools have experimented to find other methods of assessing children's learning, and both the literacy and numeracy strategies include sessions where children can 'perform their assessment'. Observation checklists and comment slips are used to record them. Performance assessments include:

- *electronic*: with 'approved' software on a growing expansion of hardware (e.g. laptops, tablets, PDAs, MP3 players); this includes films, blogs, creation of websites, photo-stories, PowerPoint presentations, etc.;
- *written products of various kinds*: journals, letters, discussion papers, diaries;
- *kinaesthetic products*: games, puzzles, sculpture, cakes, interactive displays;
- *visual*: role-play, drama, debates, oral reports.

The ICE aspect of this is potentially very exciting and hopefully will have a much more important role in assessment. I watched eight-year-olds recently, editing their own and others' blogs. This required individual children demonstrating how they could concentrate for considerably long periods of time, because they were involved in the learning. The quality of shared editing was very high. It can be argued that these performance assessments are more authentic than traditional assessment measures because the monitoring of learning and its assessment then become a learning experience in themselves. Children have to relate their learning to real-life situations and the teacher's role is to observe, rather than to instruct. Performance assessments encourage learning and teaching for performance, rather than measurement.

Another, very familiar example of a performance assessment can be seen in the oral mental arithmetic sessions recommended in the numeracy strategy. These are:

- teach children to perform their knowledge;
- establish clear performance targets, which move beyond simply covering curriculum content and working towards performances of understanding;
- publicise criteria and performance standards;
- provide models of excellence;
- teach strategies explicitly;
- enable ongoing assessments for feedback and forward curriculum planning;
- celebrate performance.

Out-of-school assessment

It is also worth remembering that most primary children also receive education outside school. Some faiths hold evening and weekend schools for their children and testing often takes place in these, so that children can move onto the next stage. Some parents/carers pay for additional schooling/tutoring and there are likely to be both formative and summative tests taking place here as well. In local supermarkets and chain bookstores there are many commercial schemes waiting for concerned parents and carers to buy them. These also contain testing papers. The Internet provides plenty of testing opportunities for primary pupils. Many of these are very didactic. Often forgotten by schools is all the testing and assessment that takes place in many 'leisure' activities that children undertake, for example: swimming badges, dance certificates, football trophies, gymnastic awards, selection for sports teams. Indeed, coaches from premier league teams send out scouts for five-year-old boys who 'show promise' and each football match can become a test in itself, with the potentially high celebratory salaries for parents to dream of and 'encourage' their children to attain. Out-of-school assessment may be far more important for some children than those taking place inside.

Activity/Thinking Task 2

Identify different 'instruments of assessment' you have seen used in school. Then evaluate two of them in terms of their use and manageability: (a) for the children; and (b) for the teachers and colleagues.

Target setting and school improvement

School

We have, hopefully, just completed a very astringent period of target setting, not only in education, but in all public services. Primary schools have become extremely competent in developing their own SMART targets and far more competent than in the past in negotiating LA targets. The major targets for primary schools over recent years have been the SATs results and attendance and retention of pupils. Targets within the SATs results have been refined considerably as contextual data is drawn in to compare results at KS1 with those of the same children at KS2. These variables for contextual detail include stability (mobility of school population), deprivation, and numbers of EAL, SEN and FSMs are also drawn into the measurements.

Raiseonline

Current data on performance is not only collected by the school but also by the government, and then submitted back to the school. Raiseonline examines context, attainment and CVA data. It explores hypotheses about pupil performance; analyses question level data for national, optional and progress tests; and, of course, sets and moderates pupil targets. Its summary sheet covers contextual information; attendance of learners; how well do learners achieve; how well learners make progress; how well learners with learning difficulties and disabilities make progress; KS1–KS2 CVA; the standards reached by learners, and then specific summary comments on KS1 and KS2. My own feelings about this is that it is not a scientific process, despite all the data collected. Some of the most challenging schools I visit have ended up with miserable summary statements such as 'learners make inadequate progress' and 'standards are low'. Words that state the obvious, but are based only on what is easily and narrowly measurable. It will be interesting to see how soon some of the health and social care statistics are incorporated into the contextual data, e.g. 25 per cent of the children in this school are witness to domestic violence; 75 per cent of the mothers smoked during pregnancy.

Target setting and the class teacher

The class teacher's role in this is clear, whatever the age of the children. They need to be able to set challenging and realistic targets to feed into school targets. Standardised tests are used to provide a range of information about child performance and much of the target setting is based on this. There are several excellent software packages that do this in the medium term, but there is a danger of using only these in the short term. We all know that working to a target set by someone else is very difficult. Our own life experiences tell us this. How many of us fail to keep to the targets we have been set – for losing weight, cutting down alcohol or giving up smoking. One of the reasons Weight Watchers are so successful is that targets are reached through rewards and peer support, rather than someone else setting them for us.

How teachers involve pupils varies. Some schools display common targets in classrooms and nurseries. Individual targets are often found in children's books or even on their desks. This very visible display has the advantage of informing parents as well as reminding the children. Although I am not sure I would welcome my individual targets being visible to everyone!

Unpicking the reason(s) why some children may not be making the necessary progress can often result in some unexpected target setting, which may not be included in an electronic database, or has only just started to happen. For example, in one class a small group of pupils had been identified as being very passive in many of the lessons and their progress appeared to be suffering as a result of this. As part of a carefully devised group activity, these children were sitting together with a teaching assistant. The whole class (mixed Y1 and Y2) were looking at friendship. This group shared the learning objectives with the whole class but also had individual targets linked to their own interaction. These included participation with adult support; participation independently; play/interact with one child; speak with an adult prompting; to let someone have a turn; to help other children join in.

Pupil tracking

If targets are not just about academic attainment neither is pupil tracking, although most of the features tracked, such as attendance and behaviour, have a huge impact on progress. A large amount of data is generated by efficient tracking but management information systems (MIS) have not kept pace with the data generated. Schools started with a number of different MIS, of which 'Sims' was the most commonly used one. A DfES web-based system was introduced in 2006 and this may make a difference, although some schools, with the relevant expertise, prefer to devise their own tracking systems as it allows them more flexibility. If this technical aspect of tracking interests you could look on the BECTA site for more information. BECTA is responsible for delivering the e-strategy that will enable personalised learning.

The *Making Great Progress in KS2 Report* (DfES 2007), noted that all the best-practice schools in their survey had in place tracking systems that were thorough, regular, individualised and well-maintained. Evidence was scrutinised regularly. This included folders of work, end-of-unit assignments, and one-to-one sessions with pupils. Tracking was reported usually at half term intervals, against specific criteria. This information was detailed enough to use in forward planning, to set targets and plan lessons. Interestingly, they noted that some schools shared judgements with parents, but perhaps more interesting is the fact that some of these very successful schools did not. Three other facts were noted as being key to the success of these schools – a senior management team that took a high-profile hands-on approach to assessment; gaps in evidence were identified and the numbers translated into action. The schools were all using national curriculum levels, with some sub-levelling as well.

Written reports to parents

Written reports

It is a legal requirement that teachers report upon the achievements of their children each year. Surprisingly, it was not until 1991 that reports had to be made to parents about the progress of their own children. This takes the form of a written report and must provide results of any national curriculum foundation subjects and other subjects and activities in the curriculum. Schools must provide information about pupils' general progress and arrangements for discussing the report with teachers. At the moment, schools have their own format for reports, many of which are very attractively presented. Most schools now

Table 12.2 Extract from Ben's report

CHILD'S RESULTS			
End of Key Stage 1 Teacher Assessment 20__			Ben JONES 2PW
ENGLISH	Teacher assessment results	Speaking and listening	2
		Reading	3
		Writing	2A
MATHEMATICS	Teacher assessment results	Mathematics	3
SCIENCE	Teacher assessment results	Science	3

School St. Edwards Primary School   *Class* Year 2

Name Ben Jones   *Date* Summer Term

English *Attitude and effort:* **A**	**Mathematics** *Attitude and effort:* **A**	**Science** *Attitude and effort:* **A**
Can • Become aware of authorship and publication • Write simple evaluations of books read and discussed giving reasons • Pose questions prior to reading non-fiction to find answers • Write non-chronological reports using appropriate language to present, sequence and categorise ideas • Turn statements into questions learning a range of 'wh' words to use to open questions • Write in clear sentences using capital letters and full stops accurately • Discriminate, spell and read the phonemes 'ear' and 'ea' • Use synonyms to extend and enhance writing	*Can* • Count forwards and backwards in ones or tens from any two digit number (e.g. 26, 36, 46, etc.) • Read and write numbers to 1,000 and know what each digit is worth • Use £.p appropriately • Understand simple divisions and the link with multiplication • Solve simple number problems and explain how to work them out • Use metres and centimetres • Read a simple scale • Use litres and millilitres • Describe position and direction using mathematical vocabulary	*Can* • Describe how to use pushes and pulls to make familiar objects speed up, slow down or change direction • Recognise that push and pull are forces • Recognise similarities between animals and plants and differences within these groups • Suggest questions relating to differences between living things and with help, record and interpret findings
Comments/Targets Ben is a keen reader with strong comprehension skills. He consistently produces writing of a high standard *Target*: handwriting	**Comments/Targets** Ben is working comfortably at Level 3. He is a quick learner and a methodical worker. Keep up the good work!	**Comments/Targets** Ben has shown an interest in all science topics. He makes intelligent contributions to class discussions

have specialised software to take the burden off report writing and to make comments more objective. There is a delicate balance between the brutal truth and a bland statement. Comments in the reports need to match the records of individual children, to be understandable, to set future learning targets and to match legal requirements. Table 12.2 provides a shortened example of this.

Student teachers are rarely involved in report writing, so that it is not surprising that when they become NQTs they often find the task difficult. The software available certainly helps and even when not used, schools generally adopt a school writing style so that parents get some idea of continuity in terms of reported progress and achievement. The schools also keep copies of reports, so it is possible to look back over how pupil progress has been recorded for any one child. The best way of finding out how to write reports is to examine reports from more than one school. Some schools prepare reports several times a year.

Activity/Thinking Task 3

Ask your school mentor if you can see examples of reports from each school year; or ask a couple of friends with children of school age if you can look at their children's reports. It is usually easier to get a good report this way! If you have children yourself re-examine their reports. How do such reports make you feel? How helpful are they? How much guidance do they give parents in terms of future target setting for their child? What meanings does the child get out of these reports?

If you are working in a school without the software, these hints from Reeves in *Reporting to Parents* may help.

1   *Keep notes during the year.* These should be systematic and useful. They need to include details of judgements you've made, information about specific achievements or difficulties, records of activities undertaken and particular discussions with parents.
2   *Don't spring surprises.* Written reports should not stand alone, but should be used alongside other ways of communicating with parents.
3   *Pay attention to language and style.* This is much easier to do now that reports are word processed.
4   *Pay attention to details.* Spelling the child's name, using the correct name (e.g. a nickname may be used in school, but hated by parents).
5   *Be concise.* Don't waffle and ensure that you are not using meaningless phrases.
6   *Make what you write useful to parents.* This involves being specific in what the child can and cannot do, and where parental support would be most useful.
7   *Avoid jargon.*
8   *Set the context.* It is easy to write a very positive report about a slow learner, without disclosing that the child is having learning difficulties. Parents need to know how their child's progress compares with other children's. Teaching is a caring profession and we don't like hurting or upsetting people, but parents need to know if something is wrong. This also needs to be linked with point 2, 'Don't spring surprises'. Parents of able children are often disappointed by the low levels expected of their child. Challenges for these children are also important.

9 *Be positive*. Remember Gardner's multiple intelligences. Try to ensure that you can report on areas where the child is successful as well as areas where there are problems.

Parents' evenings/open days

Schools have a procedure for these and generally plenty of advice. The points made by Reeves, above, also apply to how you deal with parents and are worth reading through again before an open evening. Remember to make notes on what is said if you think points made are particularly important. It also gives parents a sense that you care because you are noting down their comments and feelings.

E-mails

As we move into e-mailing of teachers direct, it is worth remembering all the very good advice and netiquette about writing and responding to e-mails. Ensure you know the school policy. Being old-fashioned, I always prefer standardised English and get concerned about mis-spellings. Delay all responses so that you have time to think them through, and save copies of everything.

13 Brain breaks and healthy schools

QTS Standards

5, 15, 18, 21a, b, 30, 31

Learning objectives

- to gain some knowledge of the healthy schools programme, including brain kinesiology;
- to recognise its intention to influence all four aspects of the curriculum – formal, hidden, experienced and observed;
- to evaluate it in terms of effectiveness through observation and interview.

Healthy schools

Determinants of health

So far in this section we have looked at planning the formal curriculum. In this chapter we look at the healthy schools programme, where the formal, hidden, observed and experienced curriculum overlap. This means it has – or should have – enormous implications for all those working in schools. This is because health is an overarching area of children's lives, influenced by factors well outside the school's formal remit (see Figure 13.1).

This can be an extremely depressing, deterministic view of the world. However, schools are about the business of making a difference, creating change and enhancing children's lives. The healthy schools initiative was born of the belief that this was possible.

Background

The healthy schools programme is a very ambitious attempt to educate the outside world from inside schools. It builds on the experience of health educational professionals who ran programmes such as the 'Child to Child' initiative. This went into specific classes

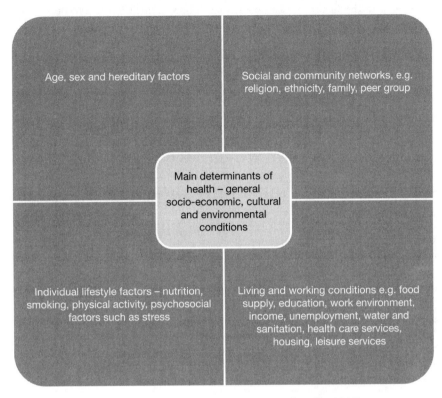

Age, sex and hereditary factors

Social and community networks, e.g. religion, ethnicity, family, peer group

Main determinants of health – general socio-economic, cultural and environmental conditions

Individual lifestyle factors – nutrition, smoking, physical activity, psychosocial factors such as stress

Living and working conditions e.g. food supply, education, work environment, income, unemployment, water and sanitation, health care services, housing, leisure services

Figure 13.1 Determinants of health (adapted from Naidoo and Wills, 2000)

and asked children what they felt were the local health issues. They then worked with the children and their teachers to provide an education programme for other children in the schools and the local community. As always when you ask children, you get issues you don't expect, e.g. the amount of dog dirt on open areas such as the school playing field.

It has long been recognised that the physical health of children is a critical element in creating a healthy and productive citizenship – or in the early 1900s was critical to the maintenance of the British Empire. School dinners were first introduced into the elementary/ Board schools in 1902, as a direct response to discovering that the majority of young men turning up to be recruited for the Boer War were unfit to serve. Victorian log books recorded well before this the appalling conditions of many children coming into school who were too tired and hungry to do any school work. In this book, we have already looked at Maslow's basic needs hierarchy, which places physical needs before any other. The implication of this, and indeed our own common sense and experience, suggests that hungry and poorly nourished children do not learn as effectively as those who are well fed. Surprisingly, research by the Food Standards Agency in 2006 on links between nutrition and children's performance concluded that eating better made you more healthy, but there was still not enough evidence to show that it meant the healthy-eating child did better educationally. However, all of us have watched the effect that fizzy drinks, sweets and crisps have on children's ability to concentrate and learn. So there is a long tradition of being interested in the health of primary school children, both inside and outside schools. And it has moved well beyond the nutritional aspects.

In October 1999, a national healthy schools programme was launched by the Department of Health (DH) and the DfES. This was followed by other school-related initiatives, such as the 2004 Healthy Living Blueprint for Schools, and the publication of the Children's National Service Framework. Jamie Oliver produced a very powerful television and practical campaign to improve school dinners and really captured a media interest in what children ate in schools. By the end of 2006, half of all schools had achieved healthy school status.

Organisation

At central government level the National Healthy Schools Programme is sponsored and managed through the DH and the DCSF (formerly DfES), with the overall aims of:

1   raising education achievement;
2   reducing health inequalities;
3   promoting social inclusion; and
4   supporting children and young people in developing healthy behaviours.

There is also a free booklet available from the DCSF that provides a short national guide for schools called, unsurprisingly, *National Healthy School Status* (www.healthyschools.gov. uk). Most LAs have a much more detailed guide for their schools.

Figure 13.2 shows not only how health across the school has to permeate not only across the formal curriculum, but also into areas of the hidden, observed and experienced curriculum, such as the physical environment of the school, health and welfare of staff and the organisation, ethos and climate. It also must involve links with the families and the community.

Activity/Thinking Task 1

Re-read the start of this chapter and identify some of the challenges in central government's overall aims for the Healthy School Programme. How will schools be able to demonstrate that their healthy schools programme has been responsible for raising achievement and promoting social inclusion? Most schools have more realistic aims and objectives linked to their programmes.

There are 150 local programmes and each LA has a healthy schools partnership that runs the programme. These partnerships have an accreditation process, with a national quality assurance programme of monitoring, support and training. The local healthy schools programme website will provide you with the name of the LA and the names of its health partner. This will be one or more primary care trust (PCT) and an initial contact person. Most of these contact people trained as teachers before moving into the healthy schools programmes. They are mainly from the secondary sector. But an increasing number of them do seem to be coming from other more specialist health areas. This may mean that primary teachers will need to become more closely involved in the medium as well as the message.

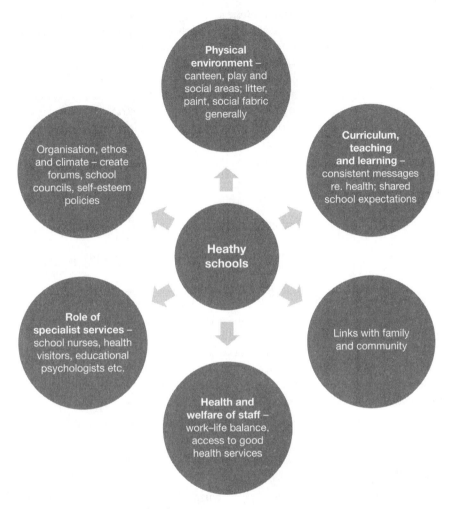

Figure 13.2 Health across the school

My experience of the healthy schools programmes in the north-west, is that they have been very good, even though I am not convinced that they can meet all the aims of the national programme. The LA healthy school guides are produced by people who know their areas, often because they have worked for many years with the same communities. They also have plenty of manageable, practical ideas. Examples of good practice have included:

- breakfast clubs;
- cooking clubs;
- growing clubs/nurture clubs;
- working with parents/carers;
- working with local health services;
- increasing physical activity;
- themed after-school work, not replacing the curriculum but complementing it.

Later we will follow a school-based illustration from one school in the north-west that illustrates very clearly how the school went through a clear process of audit, prioritise, target, plan, implement, monitor, evaluate, celebrate and improve.

Accreditation

In order to win healthy school status, schools have to demonstrate standards in the 'core themes' using a whole-school approach and involving the whole school community. These are:

1   PSHE – including sex and relationship education and drug education;
2   healthy eating;
3   physical activity;
4   emotional health and well-being.

Ironically, there is nothing about promoting the health of adults working in schools, which I have included in Figure 13.2. Many of us working in schools do have some not very healthy behaviours, so it might seem that a wider remit should cover all those working in schools – just as the Criminal Records Bureau (CRB) covers us all. It is, after all, difficult to encourage children into keeping fit, if our own practice is fairly abysmal – and it shows! The healthy schools programme did not initially cover the LA 'stand alone' nursery schools; although obviously the EYFS guidance does cover many of the aspects. Most schools do include their nurseries in their healthy school programme, through having a whole school approach, a healthy school process and by utilising a web of support from other professionals.

A case study: St Patrick's Catholic Primary School

Starting points

It is often more useful to look at how a particular school has gone through the process, rather than just look at the formal documentation. St Patrick's has a long history of being an excellent school, with imaginative, creative and forward thinking practice. Many of the aspects of the healthy schools programme were already embedded within the school, but the need to gain the National Healthy Schools Standard (NHSS) meant that it had to be organised and presented in a particular way. The school was also interested in gaining the standard because they recognised that it linked with other central government initiatives with which they were already heavily involved, largely by nature of their particularly challenging catchment area:

• ECM agenda, with its five strands: being healthy; staying safe; enjoying and achieving; making a positive contribution; and achieving economic well-being;
• Excellence and Enjoyment initiative;
• key skills and thinking skills;
• cross-curricular teaching (topics, themed work);
• CVA; and, of course,
• Ofsted inspections.

Adopting healthy lifestyles was seen as a priority for the school. The starting point was to look at the local data and report this in the SEF to provide a formal contextual account against which outcomes could later be measured. Then a working party of teachers, non-teaching staff, governors and parents was created with a senior member of staff taking overall responsibility for the initiative. It is worth remembering that in small primary schools the responsibility for the Healthy Schools Programme is often done by someone who has many other responsibilities. He or she cannot devote their attention to a single initiative or responsibility. The establishment of an effective working party resulted in an action plan and a subdivision of the working party into four smaller groups, each with responsibility for part of the healthy schools evidence grid. The immediate action after this was:

1   to draw up a PSHE self-evaluation document in consultation with all the staff;
2   to set up a School Council;
3   to set up ongoing consultation with all staff to provide evidence, where applicable for the healthy schools evidence grid.

Pupil-related issues

Figure 13.3 sets out the various steps linked with pupil-related issues.

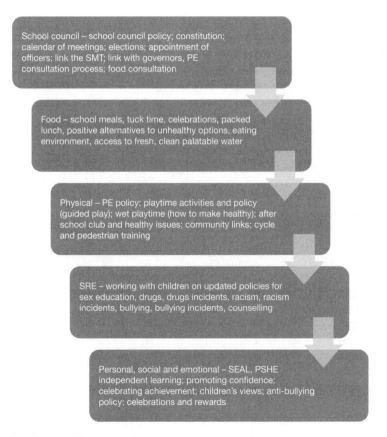

Figure 13.3 Pupil-related issues

Staff-related issues

For staff there were several issues, some probably unforeseen.

1   *Policy making and professional development.* Naturally, the policy making linked closely with what was already going on in the school, but the amount of time it takes from staff, pupils, teachers and governors should not be under-estimated. Policies are worthless if they arise without consultation and stay on the hard-drive of a computer awaiting inspection. These policies came out of consultation and involved all staff being made aware of them, a related staff handbook and induction policy and programme. Both the strategic and operational side of policy making required monitoring and evaluation. The inclusion and special needs policies for any school are an important element in the healthy schools programme. As we saw in Chapter 10, it involves identifying vulnerable children and certainly all five of the ECM strands are involved.

Policy making can provide useful professional development for staff and this was linked in with a wider understanding of outside agencies where children and their parents/carers could be referred. Staff also looked at that very difficult issue of work/life balance and care of the 'whole person'. Not only children in the school, but also the adults. This may be an issue that is more embedded within faith schools, as identifying personal beliefs are often an appointments issue. Staff development also involved looking again at the school learning and teaching policy, positive discipline, school development plan and the mission statement.

2   *Food.* Nationally healthy food policies and their outcomes have proved to be a far more problematic issue than expected. Numbers taking school dinners over the whole country fell, in response to parents being concerned that their children were no longer eating any lunch. There is no conclusive evidence that these figures have yet risen over the country. Indeed, looking at what most children come to school with in their packed lunches, we would want all children to have a hot school dinner. A few LAs (e.g. Hull) now offer every child a *free* hot school dinner. St Patrick's, like most schools, had had customs of birthday cake treats as a normal part of their practice. In the end this had to stay, although pushing sweets through the playground railings was stopped.

3   *Physical.* Staff promoted physical activity and extra-curricular physical activities. A school travel plan was drawn up to encourage walking to school and links made with schools sports clubs. A sports development team was created and parent volunteers drawn in.

Evaluation

This is very much a shortened version of what is a long and ongoing process. An evaluation to date shows that:

- everyone has to be involved;
- CPD continues to be needed as different contingencies arise;
- working in small teams ensures higher involvement;
- there have been changes in the dinner menu; water is available, as is fruit, healthy tuck and a Friday restaurant;
- there has been some opposition from parents, e.g. birthday treats, playtime snacks and lunch boxes;

- SRE has had a renewed programme of study;
- SEAL is used across the curriculum;
- the profile of PSHE programmes have been raised.

Accreditation took place through an informal visit by a local healthy schools team member to assess the school against the evidence grid. This was followed by a formal half-day accreditation visit where a development programme was agreed. This is reviewed every three years for ongoing accreditation.

Activity/Thinking Task 2

Interview someone who works in a primary school to ask them how their school is carrying out the healthy schools programme. If possible, without offending them, ask what training they have had in relation to the programme. Then ask yourself how much training you have had and what you think you might need in order to gain a greater understanding of the issues involved.

Healthy brains

The brain – the foundation for learning

One of the areas that healthy schools has been involved in is how to promote 'healthy learning'; and there have been close links made between educational kinesiology and mind-/brain-friendly learning. This has been a very controversial area as new scientific findings about how the brain works have been linked with less scientific (but frequently quite effective) strategies to improve children's learning by giving the brain more exercise. Perhaps one of the most exciting and revolutionary findings for me from the research evidence is that learning changes the physical structure of the brain. And this continues to happen throughout our lives. Sarah-Jayne Blakemore and Uta Frith's (2007) award-winning book *The Learning Brain* is a relatively easy to read book on brain research and how the workings of the brain shape both formal and informal learning. Another slightly heavier read, but accessible as a free e-book is the American National Research Council's (2000) *How People Learn*. Both texts are heavily evidence based, but are excellent reads. They are particularly optimistic about the continual development of the brain, and its ability to adapt and change with experience.

Neuroscientists study the anatomy, physiology, chemistry and molecular biology of the nervous system with particular interest in how the brain activity relates to behaviour and learning. They ask questions such as:

- How does the brain develop?
- Are there stages of brain development?
- Are there critical periods when certain things must happen for the brain to develop normally?
- How is information encoded in the developing and adult nervous systems?
- How does experience affect the brain?

Some of the findings have particular implications for learning and teaching:

1 The functional organisation of the brain and the mind depends on and benefits positively from experience.
2 Development of the brain is not merely a biologically driven unfolding process, but also an active process that derives essential information from experience.
3 Research shows that some experiences have the most powerful effects during specific sensitive periods, whereas others can affect the brain over a much longer time span.

The implications of these findings for those of us working with children and young people are very positive. First, it is tremendously important that experience makes a difference to the physical structure and functional organisation of the brain. This means that our young learners cannot be written off at any age because, for example, they come from specific catchment areas, speak different languages, have carers who do not fit the norms of the learning organisation, behave inappropriately, are disaffected, are too young or too old to learn, etc.

Second, it means that all those involved in multi-agency services have responsibility to respect children's rights and recognise that they themselves have a duty to ensure that they provide children with positive learning experiences. Basically, what we do in our work with children does make a difference to the physical structure and functional organisation of the brain. This is a huge responsibility and means that we have to look carefully at whether these experiences are enriching or impoverishing our children. The curriculum – formal, hidden, experienced and observed – is the visible means of expressing that responsibility. Now we turn to look as some of the ways in which this research has percolated into schools.

Educational kinesiology

Edu-kinesiology is an 'education movement based programme which uses simple movements to integrate the whole brain, senses and body, preparing the person with the physical skills they need to learn effectively.' This quote comes from the international Brain Gym® organisation. The ® tells you that this is a registered trade mark and designed to protect the commercial interests of Paul and Gail Dennison who started the Brain Gym® movement in the US. It grew rapidly and moved into both schools and commercial training institutions.

It was originally developed to help adults and children with learning difficulties such as dyslexia, dyspraxia and ADHD. It has now developed into a more generic action programme claiming to improve everyone's life. The benefit claims are fairly extensive, but are closely linked to the healthy schools programme in the UK. The Brain Gym® movements are claimed to help with:

• academic skills – reading, writing, spelling and mathematics;
• memory, concentration and focus;
• physical co-ordination and balance;
• communication skills and language development;
• self-development and personal stress management;
• the achievement of goals, both professional and personal.

I have to say that I don't personally subscribe to all these statements, but have a general feeling that enabling children to move in classrooms does improve learning. Over the years I have watched many children (and adults) atrophy when their experienced curriculum was too static. Indeed, in my own learning, I need to move around to wake myself up and refocus.

Paul Dennison describes human brain function in terms of three dimensions: laterality, focus and centring: 'Successful brain function requires efficient connections across the neural pathways located throughout the brain. Stress inhibits these connections, while Brain Gym® movements stimulate a flow of information across the networks.' The exercises suggested in the guidance for Brain Gym® participants and those seen in school are nearly always related to the laterality dimension of the brain. This is based on the traditional belief that the right side of our brain is programmed for creativity, whereas the left side is for logic. Exercises that force us to think across this laterality will therefore build up nerve net formations in the brain, across the two sides. A very popular one you may have seen, is known as cross crawl and involves touching your right knee with your left hand or elbow, and then changing to left knee and right hand. This is done quite quickly and is very much better to music! This and many exercises like it concentrate on the relationship between the two sides of the brain, in particular the 'midfield' where the two sides must integrate. The focus dimension describes the relationship between the back and the front areas of the brain and the centring dimension concerns the connection between the top and bottom structure of the brain. There is now much more doubt about this very tight distinction between left and right brain patterns, and certainly a lot of evidence to show a lot of cross laterality.

There are a very limited number of properly accredited Brain Gym® trainers as full accreditation takes several years. For this reason, it is very rare to see Brain Gym® being carried out in schools as it was originally intended with its PACE (positive, active, clear and energetic) ladder:

1   *Positive* is linked with drinking water at the start of the exercise to provide energy.
2   *Active* is the cross-crawl which we looked at earlier.
3   *Clear* is rubbing your stomach at the same time as rubbing two points just below your breast bone. This is known as Brain Buttons. And, finally,
4   *Energetic* involves sitting down, with your hands together and your tongue at the roof of your mouth. This is known as Hook-ups and the hands can have a number of different positions. It is a relaxation technique and has similarities with saying a prayer with your hands together.

More information can be found on the UK Brain Gym® site, together with a list of accredited trainers. The training sessions I have attended have been very useful and certainly provided plenty to bring back to the classroom in terms of short, manageable exercises to revitalise learners.

ALPS and brain breaks

Alistair Smith, mentioned in Chapters 6 and 7, calls these types of exercises brain breaks, forming part of the accelerated learning package, and suggests in the ALPS approach that these exercises to support learning can be broken down into six different categories:

1   *Laterality exercises.* Any exercise that involves crossing the mid-line of the body, e.g. the cross-crawl described above.
2   *Focus exercises.* For example, Nose 'n' ears. Children put their right hand on their nose and their left hand across the front of their face to hold the right ear lightly. They then swap round, so that the left hand is holding their nose and the right hand is across the front of the face and holding the left ear. Smith suggests that these types of activities require intense focus and this can be transferred to learning once the activity has been done. It is certainly fun.
3   *Relaxers exercises.* For example, ear rolls. With the finger and thumb massage ears slowly, starting at the top and roll round to the ear lobes.
4   *Learning numbers, letters and words.* Children clasp their hands together, with index fingers or thumbs pointing out. Then, in front of their faces, they move their hands in the shape of the numbers, letters or words.
5   *Handwriting.* As above.
6   *Chaining material.* Encourage children to remember information in sequence by linking it with a series of physical movements, e.g. miming.

Primary children, in particular, really seem to enjoy the physical activity involved with these movements and they certainly seem to provide much-needed breaks in schools where less physical education is taking place than ever before. It may also be because so many children have so much less exercise outside school. These exercises can be taught and used at home as well.

Critiques

Brain Gym® has not been without its critics. Both Ben Goldacre (Bad Science), a medic, and Phil Beadle, an advanced skills teacher, who both write regularly for the *Guardian* and have their own websites, have criticised Brain Gym® as pseudo science (www.badscience. net). This critique received a large number of negative responses; people praising Brain Gym® and disagreeing with him. Phil Beadle wrote a similar critique on Brain Gym® and this can be found on the badscience website as well as in the *Guardian* archives. It was written on 13 June 2006.

Activity/Thinking Task 3

What do you think? Visit the official Brain Gym® website for the UK and work out what you believe. Read around, including Alistair Smith's work and his Alite website. Review the Brain Gym® website (www.braingym.co.uk) and then outline three advantages that *you* think can come from involving children in more movement to enhance their 'experienced curriculum'.

---

14 Language

English as an additional language and modern foreign languages

QTS Standards

10, 15, 17, 18, 19, 20, 25

Learning objectives

- to know about the needs of children who are not yet fluent in English and investigate access to support for how they can best be helped in mainstream classrooms;
- to examine the growth of MFL in primary schools.

In this chapter we are looking at two language-related curriculum and planning issues. First, how we can support learners entering our schools whose first language is not English. This involves the emotional support through the curriculum, which has been already discussed, and also the challenge of helping these new arrivals to learn English, so that they can take full advantage of the education provided. Second, how we can help our mono-linguist learners to feel confident about learning other languages and becoming part of a much richer multi-lingual world. In this chapter we look at both these areas and also the relationship between the two. There is also a closely linked issue about partnership with the local community on both issues. This can be made much more challenging when political issues such as fear of terrorism are stirred up by the media and sometimes specific groups targeted.

Children who have English as an additional language

Overview

The terminology in this area has changed, initially these children were known as second language learners. Now they are increasingly known from central government literature as bilingual pupils. Bilingual in everyday speech usually refers to fluency in two languages. However, in this context, it often means the ability to communicate in two or more languages and does not necessarily mean fluency.

The growth of globalisation has meant that language teaching in primary schools has faced challenges that would have be unheard of fifty years ago. Far more is being demanded of teachers and colleagues in terms of language expertise and this can be particularly challenging for many of us, who have grown up in very mono-linguist environments. Today, in many areas, we have a rich mix of cultures and heritages from all over the world. This carries on a tradition that has always been present in England – the Celts, followed by the Romans, the Anglo-Saxons, the Vikings, etc. In recent times the rapid expansion of the European Community is bringing in new arrivals, and often their families, from regions that were previously behind the Iron Curtain. The year 2005 saw 49,000 arrivals from Poland, for example.

The data

The data for this can be easily accessed through the National Statistics website and provides a good picture of how the wider 'language' curriculum is important for all of us. In 2005, for example, 565,000 people came into the UK; 145,000 of these were European citizens and 64,000 more were citizens of the EU Accession countries. This 64,000 is a figure arrived at after you take off the numbers who left in the same year. If we look directly at the implications for schools, in 2003 there were 9.6 per cent of pupils with EAL, by 2007 this had risen to 12 per cent of all pupils. The largest increases have been in the north-west, Yorkshire, Humberside, East of England, Inner and Outer London. Over 50 per cent of pupils in Inner London are EAL.

In any one area, we can see migrants have moved into the country in response to a variety of situations; the economic, social and/or political circumstances of the country they have left, which may not have been their country of birth; the relatively booming UK economy with its pressing need for more labour; and finally, the political impetus behind global movement. New arrivals come with a variety of experiences. For example they may:

- have spent time in a refugee camp or asylum centre;
- have been involved in war as both participants and victims; seen their communities destroyed and those they loved killed and/or violated;
- had periods of interrupted schooling;
- had no schooling;
- have good oracy and literacy skills in their first language;
- have some experience of written English, but have few oral skills; and
- they may live in homes where English is not used, where it is not the only language used, or where it is used as a second language among the children.

Children coming into school with EAL have sometimes been identified under the 'special needs' banner. The Code of Practice is quite clear that this is not how they should be categorised, although it is acknowledged that some of these children may have special needs. There are huge variations of EAL between schools. In some schools and indeed in some LAs all children are monolingual. In other schools there may be fourteen or fifteen different languages being spoken. Schools qualify for additional funding if there are a significant number of children who have English as an additional language, but this has never been generous. Staffing is the most expensive resource and appropriately qualified EAL specialists for primary children are in very short supply.

EAL children present unique opportunities and unique challenges. The first challenge for the student teacher is to understand who these children are. Many, particularly at the start of KS1, have been born in the UK and their parents may also have been born in the UK. Make sure that you know which heritage languages are spoken at home and in the local community. Some children may already be skilled in speaking more than one language. Look at the histories of the local communities from which the children come. In some localities, the majority of the families may come from one area, but in another locality the families may come from a much wider range of regions and countries. Racial conflict migrates as well and can appear in schools, playgrounds and the local community. Reasons for the movements of peoples vary. There are many very settled communities, where children arrive at school with English as an additional language, but sadly, wars, environmental and family disasters can force reluctant movement. Particular cities, such as Liverpool, London and Manchester have traditionally attracted different heritage groups, but it is also true that towns such as Preston, Bolton and Bury have schools where a substantial number of children have EAL.

Understanding a little of the way in which the heritage languages are constructed helps to identify possible misconceptions in early reading and writing, although children are very quick to identify different ways in which a book works and can often tell you how they read differently in different languages.

Stages of language acquisition

For readers who are monolingual, it might be useful to think back to learning a foreign language if you did that in primary and/or secondary school; although I am aware that some student teachers may not have studied a foreign language at school.

1 *Pre-production.* Learners can start to understand the new language, but cannot engage in conversations or respond to questions. Appropriate activities include listening and pointing.
2 *Early production.* There is better understanding and learners respond to simple questions with one-word or two-word answers.
3 *Speech emergence.* Comprehensive starts to increase and learners can speak in simple sentences. There are plenty of errors, but children can be encouraged to retell, define, describe and explain.
4 *Intermediate fluency.* Comprehension is very good and the learner can construct complex sentences and engage in higher-order speaking skills in the new language.

The teacher's role in EAL

There is a delicate balance between giving children challenging opportunities to demonstrate their knowledge and skills and giving them frustrating tasks that they are not yet equipped to deal with. Ironically, when the NLS was first produced there was very little attention given to pupils with EAL. The emphasis was on all pupils, whatever their personalised needs, being taught together. EAL has been addressed since then and there are some government publications in this area from both the DfES, the National Primary Strategy and Ofsted. Sometimes, this material needs to be read with care. In 2003, for example, Ofsted produced materials on the raising of attainment of minority ethnic pupils. This looked at existing evidence and presented key issues for schools and LAs. It was, however, limited to four specific groups – Bangladeshi, black Caribbean, Pakistani and traveller pupils. This resulted in a rather 'deficit' model of the attainment of minority ethnic pupils and this contrasted with the experience of many schools where EAL pupils are achieving well above the national average, once their English is fluent.

In some schools there are teaching assistants who speak a common language with some of the children and this can be really useful, particularly if the bilingual assistant has had specific strategy training in EAL. However, very often support will be available only from an adult who, like the teacher, does not share a language with the child. In some cases there may be little or no support. Digital support is becoming more common, but the commercial potential has not been realised yet and appropriate and personalised software is difficult to find.

The primary strategy

The primary strategy consultants have emphasised the importance of positive relationships and ensuring that there is a whole-school commitment to raising achievement through:

1   educational inclusion;
2   effective use of target-setting, leading to greater equality of outcome;
3   focused support to secure full access to the curriculum; and
4   commitment of partnership approaches in the deployment of additional resources.

As this sounds exactly the same as what we would expect from any good practice statements, I am not entirely convinced that the challenge is recognised and supported through adequate resourcing in schools where there are children speaking a number of different languages. Nor am I convinced that the recommendations coming out of the DCSF can be adequately funded. Some of these recommendations arose from a DfES 2006 evaluation of a pilot project in twenty-seven LAs to raise achievement of bilingual learners in KS2. It found, not surprisingly, that it was the confidence and expertise of mainstream teachers that was crucial in meeting the needs of advanced bilingual learners and closing the attainment gap between these learners and those whose first language was English. Schools were encouraged to have:

*   appropriate welcome procedures;
*   preparation and planning that included administrative assessment, pedagogical awareness and an appropriate curriculum;
*   support systems that include class buddies, mentors, involvement of parents and carers and deployment of support staff;
*   intervention that should include cognitive challenge of lessons, identification of next steps and scaffolding the acquisition of English;
*   target setting, using the child's first language as a tool for learning, and making special arrangements for tests.

LAs are advised to have ethnic minority achievement staff, who can identify and share good practice within the authority, such as schools sharing bilingual teaching assistants and admission protocols. They are further advised to work alongside the strategy regional directors to provide professional development for teacher; time for the consultants to meet with schools to decide how best to meet the specific needs of the school. Many LAs have had good provision and support for teachers for many years and have built up expertise that is very freely shared. These are often authorities that have numerous ethnic groups coming into their area and so have built up good operational practice over the years. The provision for EAL support outside these areas is less good and may be practically non-existent; for both teacher and pupil.

Student teachers

Student teachers who are working with EAL children who do not receive additional help in the classroom could try some of the following strategies:

- seek out support in the school well before you start teaching;
- go round the neighbourhood, try to gain a sense of the local experience your pupils have and the local support available for ethnic minority groups;
- find out about where families have come from, for how long have they lived in this area, employment, etc.;
- provide a caring classroom environment that acknowledges the child's first language and culture;
- seat the child(ren) near the teacher, where directions and instructions can be given with fewer distractions;
- speak naturally, but slowly, to allow for comprehension;
- use clear, simple language – short sentences, simple concepts;
- support instruction with visual materials such as pictures, diagrams, etc.;
- provide manipulative materials to enable lessons and activities to be more meaningful
- do not call on the child for a lengthy response;
- avoid correcting pronunciation, structural or vocabulary errors – either accept the response or say it again correctly, without comment;
- do not expect the accuracy of a native English speaker;
- assign a friend to provide additional instruction;
- do not treat the child as if he or she is 'different'.

Lesson objectives

In Chapter 7 we looked at writing learning objectives for lessons and activities, and recommended that these involved six different levels of thinking – knowledge, comprehension, application, analysis, synthesis and evaluation. Each of these levels has its own vocabulary. Analysis, for example, would involve pupils in categorising, classifying, examining and deducing. These are all quite complex concepts and EAL learners may easily be able to do this in their first language, but may have linguistic challenges when presented with a learning objective that has a specialised verb in it in another language. Of course this is an issue for many children, who may be able to say the word 'classify', but then need help in the action because they do not really know what it means.

Questioning

The same is true for questioning, which is often a very different technique inside and outside school. Questions outside school tend to be linked with the need to gain information not known to the questioner. In school, teachers' questions tend to have answers known to the questioner. Questions, however, are seen as an important teaching strategy to challenge children and pace the lesson. The language of classroom questioning is therefore an important one for EAL pupils to learn – and indeed for other less confident English speakers. When the Leverhulme Primary Project analysed the findings of over 1,000 teacher questions they found that they could be sorted into three main categories. Each of these need to be understood by pupils, although the intonation and non-verbal messages will also need to be made clear to EAL learners in particular.

- *Managerial questions*, to do with running the classroom, e.g. 'Have you got your books?'
- *Informational*, involving the recall of information, e.g. 'How many legs does an insect have?'
- *Higher-order*, if a child had to do more than just remember facts, and analyse or make generalisations, e.g. 'Why is a bird not an insect?'

Most student teachers find it useful to write down the types of questions they want to ask. The advantage of doing this is that they can then analyse what sort of category the majority of their questions fall into. This can in turn help to make it clear to all children, not just those with EAL, exactly what activity is being requested.

If we return to questions linked to the six different levels of thinking, that may help to make it clearer. It also points to how teachers and teaching assistants can work with small groups of EAL learners (and others who may need the same experience) modelling questions and getting children to use the words themselves. Learning walks around school are one way of 'practising questions' and of course outdoor education is a wonderful opportunity.

Examples

1 Knowledge

These questions show how well children have remembered previously learnt material by recalling facts, terms, basic concepts and answers.

Key words: who, what, why, when, select, omit, where, which, choose, find, how, define, label, show, spell, list, match, name, relate, tell, recall.

Questions:

- What is . . .?
- Where is . . .?
- How did . . . happen?
- Why did . . .?
- When did . . .?
- Which one . . .?
- Can you list the three . . .?

2 Comprehension

These questions demonstrate understanding of facts and ideas by organising, comparing, translating, interpreting and giving descriptions.

Key words: compare, contrast, demonstrate, interpret, explain, extend, illustrate, infer, outline, relate, rephrase, translate, translate, summarise, show, classify.

Questions:

- How would you classify the type of . . .?
- What facts or ideas show . . .?
- What can you say about . . .?
- Which is the best answer . . .?
- Can you say that in your own words . . .?

3 Application

These questions solve problems in new situations by applying acquired knowledge, facts and rules in a different way.

Key words: Apply, build, choose, construct, develop, interview, make sure of, organise, experiment with, plan, select, solve, utilise, model, identify.

Questions:

- How would you use . . .?
- What examples can you find to . . .?
- How would you solve . . .?
- What would result if . . .?
- What questions would you ask in an interview with . . .?

4 Analysis

These questions examine and break down information into parts by identifying motives or causes. They make inference and find evidence to support generalisations.

Key words: analyse, categorise, classify, compare, contrast, discover, dissect, divide, examine, inspect, simplify, test for, function, conclusion, list, take part in.

Questions:

- What are the parts or features of . . .?
- Can you list the parts . . .?
- How would you categorise . . .?
- What ideas justify . . .?
- What is the theme . . .?

5 *Synthesis*

Bring information together in a different way by combining elements in a new pattern or proposing alternative solutions.

Key words: build, choose, combine, compile, compose, construct, design, develop, estimate, formulate, imagine, invent, make up, originate, plan, predict, propose, solve, solution, suppose, discuss, modify, elaborate, test, improve.

Questions:

- What changes would you make to solve . . .?
- What would happen if . . .?
- Can you invent . . .?
- How would you adapt . . .to create a different . . .?
- What way would you design . . .?
- Can you predict the outcome if . . .?

6 *Evaluation*

Questions that present and defend opinions by making judgements about information, validity of ideas or quality of work based on a set of criteria.

Key words: award, choose, conclude, justify, select, support, estimate, compare, judge, value, estimate, agree, mark, prove, disprove, explain.

Questions:

- Would it be better if . . .?
- What choice would you have made . . .?
- What information would you use to support the view . . .?
- How would you evaluate . . .?
- Why was it better that . . .?
- How would you justify . . .?

Several of these questions appear in the writing frames material set out in the NLS. These higher-order questions can be used with EAL as we tease out their ability to understand what is meant by instructions 'to evaluate, judge and make choices'.

In their book on *Questioning* (1993), George Brown and Ted Wragg work through six units. They look not only at the types of question we ask pupils, but also the tactics that are involved in effective questioning, the sorts of lesson we teach, the process of learning and key questions in relation to the objectives for learning. In relation to EAL children, it is worth remembering that there may be subtle cultural differences involved, which need identifying.

Explaining

Another key pedagogical skill for challenging children lies in the effectiveness of the explanations given by adults. For learners listening in another language this is key to making progress with their own English acquisition and understanding what is expected of them. A good explanation can help someone understand:

- *concepts* – including those that are new or unfamiliar to the learner, such as 'friction' (This is often linked to subject knowledge. A non-scientist is likely to define friction very differently from someone who has a good scientific background. Bobbie Neate's *Finding Out about Finding Out* also identifies some of the language involved in subject-specialist explanations (1999). She highlights those found in non-fiction texts, but oral explanations often use the same type of language, particularly when there is uncertainty about the content and the explanation is written down aloud and read to the children. Dictionaries and glossaries are both good examples of when explanations may confuse, rather than aid.);
- *cause and effect* – that darkness is caused by the absence of light;
- *procedures* – classroom rules;
- *purposes and objectives* – the purpose of the activity and what is expected to be learnt as a result of it;
- *relationships* – between people, things and events;
- *processes* – how people behave.

(Adapted from Wragg and Brown, 1993)

Children who speak English as an additional language have much to offer. Geography lessons, for example, come alive for all children when a classmate speaks about visiting a country and can show objects and evidence from the visit. Both questioning and giving explanations can be practised within a context. EAL children are often in a good position to identify bias and stereotyping in textbooks and provide valuable insights into ways knowledge is constructed by such books. It is humbling to ask a child of ten how many languages he or she speaks and be told of three languages in which they are fluent, then to ask about their favourite authors and be told about different authors in different languages. We must value this diversity and learn from it, particularly as all the background research for MFLs tells us how very poor the English are at learning languages. Pauline Gibbon's very practical book *Learning to Learn in a Second Language* (1996) has some very positive and practical teaching strategies and involves a very thoughtful examination of the challenges of learning in an additional language.

A child's view

The account shown on the next page describes one child's experience of her first days in school and the support she received from her friends.

Modern foreign languages

Most of you will have come across aspects of the government's framework for languages in primary schools. Although aimed at KS2 pupils, most schools are also working with KS1 and foundation stage children.

THE FIRST TIME I WENT TO SCHOOL

The day came when I had to go to school. The awkward thing was I couldn't speak any English. The nursery door stood right in front of me. I trembled and my legs were like jelly. I hid behind mom's coat. Mrs Renodon opened the door. My mom had to drag me in. I was so frightened that I almost cried, but Mrs Renodon smiled at me so I followed her dragging my mom behind me. I saw so many different faces. Mrs Renodon asked me a question but I couldn't understand, and to this day I've never known what she had asked me. My mom was going and I began to walk to the door with her but she was telling me I was staying there. She walked out of the door and I was crying until my brother Andrew came and explained to me that I was there to learn. When I went out to play I just stood out and watched how the other children played. A girl walked up to me and told me something. Her name was Danielle. Two other girls were behind her and their names were Sarah and Hortense. I also told them my name. After about four weeks I knew how to speak English, now I was able to join in with all the games with the other children. I wasn't perfect at English. Danielle, Sarah and Hortense tried to teach me more English. So I was able to show off to my sister and brother to say I knew more English than they did. By the end of the nursery I was able to speak English 100 per cent. This is how I remember the first time I came to school.

Background

MFL in primary schools has had a long and chequered history. Private schools, including preparatory schools, had taught a MFL (usually French) for a considerable period of time, before government support was offered in 1963 to a pilot scheme to start French from when children were eight years old. This covered 35 per cent of primary schools in thirteen pilot areas and covered 6,700 pupils. It lasted approximately ten years as the aim was to follow it up into secondary schools, to see if there was a significant difference between those who had learnt French in primary schools and those who had not. It is no coincidence that the early 1960s were also the time when British entry into the Common Market was discussed.

In 1974 the project was evaluated in terms of its added value. The political climate had changed; Britain was no longer thinking about becoming part of Europe. The evaluation criticised the project in terms of finding no evidence that there were any substantial differences between those pupils who had been taught French for three years in the primary school and those who had not. The report was met with a great deal of criticism over its methodology, but the net result was that the pilot was not expanded and central government funding stopped. At this stage, too, it was not compulsory for secondary pupils to study a language, and many of those educated in the 1970s and 1980s did not learn an additional language in either primary or secondary school. This still has some quite serious implications for professional development for some teachers and other adults over a particular age, who may never have studied an additional language.

The Education Reform Act of 1988 introduced MFLs as an entitlement for all pupils in secondary schools and laid the ground for introducing MFLs in primary schools at a future date. The movement for teaching MFLs in primary schools was revitalised and by 1994 interested parties organised an important landmark conference 'Primary Foreign Languages – A fresh impetus'. The National Association of Head Teachers was also strongly supportive and, in fact, wanted all potential student teachers to have a foreign language before they could be accepted on an ITT course. Sadly, this has still not happened; but the conference marked a turning point for PMFLs (primary modern foreign languages) with a government spokesperson saying that the government would encourage primary language teaching because 'now is the time'. This 'encouragement' was reinforced by the 2000 revised National Curriculum, which contained some guidance on teaching MFLs in KS2.

The current government policy goes much further than this and in its *Languages for All: Languages for Life. A Strategy for England* it was made quite clear that by September 2010:

> Every child should have the opportunity throughout Key Stage 2 to study a foreign language and develop their interest in the culture of other nations. They should have access to high quality teaching and learning opportunities making use of native speakers and e-learning. By age eleven they should have the opportunity to reach a recognised level of competence on the Common European Framework and for that achievement to be recognised through a national scheme. The Key Stage 2 language learning programme must include at least one of the working languages of the European Union and be delivered at least in part in class time.

I have quoted this in full, because:

1   this is an entitlement, it is not 'yet' statutory;
2   the statement makes very clear the relationship between the European Economic Union and the teaching of MFL – although within the 2005 framework (see below) there are guidelines about teaching Urdu, Japanese and Chinese;
3   learning an additional language is linked with developing an interest in the culture of other nations and this is linked with learning objectives;
4   learning should involve native speakers and e-learning;
5   success criteria are identified;
6   MFL teaching should not be seen solely as an extra-curricula activity.

Activity/Thinking Task 2

What issues will need to be addressed if the PMFL initiative is to succeed?

At the end of 2005, the *Key Stage 2 Framework for Languages* was published. This set out learning objectives and quite brief teaching activities for Y3 to Y6. Central government set up 'Pathfinder' LAs who would link in with local secondary language specialist schools.

These LAs have at least one advisory teacher in place and considerable progress is being made. Other support for schools has come from NACELL (National Advisory Centre for Early Language Learning), which has regional support groups, and there is a gradual growth in HE offering continuing professional development (CPD) for teachers. There are also a growing number of commercial packs coming on to the market (print and electronic). These are more likely to take account of the existing expertise, or lack of it, in schools at the moment. There is, I think, a parallel to be drawn between MFL and music. Some very successful music programmes exist for the non-musically inclined primary teacher. It will not be long before there are programmes like this for MFL, which recognise not only the lack of expertise, but also the lack of confidence of many primary teachers in this area.

The framework also identified learning objectives for oracy, literacy, intercultural understanding and KAL (knowledge about language), and QCA have published schemes and guidelines for KS2 and exemplification for both KS1 and 2.

EAL and MFL

The primary languages entitlement may not be statutory, but it is inclusive and the framework acknowledges that learners with EAL can build on their experience of using a number of languages in their daily life and contribute to the intercultural understanding of the framework. Schools will have to make some interesting decisions about which MFL they decide to teach; or whether they decide to teach more than one. They will need to make decisions about inclusion. This will involve principles of setting suitable learning challenges; responding to diverse learning needs; and overcoming potential barriers to learning for individuals or groups. There may be challenging issues about which language to teach when there are several different languages in use in the school community and/or teaching staff and colleagues may not feel confident in any of them.

What is certainly true, is that language teaching has a much wider remit than the literacy hour, although much of the KAL work can by linked very easily to work undertaken in literacy.

Activity/Thinking Task 3

Think of two areas in which learning a second language is the same as learning a first one and two where it is different.

Language and group learning

If you return to the chapters on children's learning, many psychologists have shown the importance of oral language as a means of cognitive development. This is not just true for children, but for adults as well. The onus on the primary teacher is to plan for genuine collaborative and co-operative work, where learners' ideas are enhanced through group work. Both EAL and MFL involve 'playing with language' in a distinctive way. The opportunity to use this language in context is a key feature in effective learning and it is to be hoped that in areas where MFL can utilise the local community, native speakers within the school will be able to contribute.

The importance of group learning

Catherine McFarlane, of the Development Education Centre in Birmingham, suggested six different reasons why group learning is important for children:

1 *Effective learning.* This is true where it encourages the creative sharing and generating of ideas. Of course, this must be linked to good group organisation, and group sizes should not be so large that children can slip into inactivity and not be missed by other group members.
2 *Working together.* Learning can be too individualised if children work through sheets – written or 'behind glass' on a screen – by themselves. Through well-organised group work children can develop self-confidence and maximise opportunities for building skills.
3 *Open-ended learning.* Group learning allows children to take more responsibility for control over their own learning.
4 *Confidence-building.* It takes confidence to share opinions and ideas in a class discussion, particularly if you are using your second or third language. Small-group work helps children test out their thoughts on others and clarifies their ideas. As we all know, talk is a valuable medium for sorting out our own ideas.
5 *Building on enthusiasm.* Group work involves children being active for a large proportion of the time.
6 *Learning to value their own experience.* All children come to school with a wealth of experience, and group work gives them the opportunity to talk about and share this with others.

Types of group

Groups may be self-selected, chosen by the teacher or teaching assistant, or random. It is best to start in pairs and then move into fours. Some children work well in groups of six, but effective participation is more strained and it becomes easier for a child – particularly a sole EAL speaker – to opt out if he or she is one of six. Some other points to think about to support challenging learning in groups are:

* *Make sure that the group task is clearly defined.* This probably works best with older children, when the group task is written down and a concrete learning outcome is expected, e.g. a poster, role-play, drama.
* *Roles.* When first starting to work in groups, it is easier to give each child a specific role so that they are clear what their purpose is in the group. For classes used to a very structured working environment, a task card with the roles on it helps.
* *Rules.* Small-group rules are much the same as class rules, e.g. only one person should talk at a time; but many children are tempted to see small-group work as family-type relationships where everyone talks at once and snatching someone else's property is part of being in a small group. As with whole-class management, set out the ground rules, practise, and keep the expectation that they will work. If possible, take photographs of rules in action and give them captions. This too will help the EAL learners in particular. For a child who has real problems working in a group, make sure that he or she has a task which covers the learning objectives, but avoids them becoming disruptive to other children.

- *Evaluation.* Children's evaluation of small-group work is important and should be valued. Several recording checklists are available for children to complete after they have worked in a group. The plenary session can also be used to look at the success of a group activity and ways in which it can be improved next time.

- *Use of circle-time activities.* These can be used to promote skills useful for group work. There are many publications, both old and new, on activities for learning skills in group work. These are useful for any class as they raise co-operation as a discussion point and establish a series of behaviours to encourage it. Older publications tend to come under the heading of development education; more recent ones can be found under social education, citizenships and personal and social education. There are an increasing number of posters about co-operative working and a glance through most current educational publishers' catalogues will show how publishers are responding to the demand for more materials in this area.

15 Thinking skills in the curriculum

QTS Standards

1, 8, 10, 15, 17, 22, 25

Learning objectives

- to evaluate what is meant by the term 'thinking skills' and its significance for teaching in today's primary schools;
- to examine the work of several researchers in the field including Edward de Bono, Robert Fisher and the Philosophy in Schools Movement.

Background

Five thinking skills

In 1999, David Blunkett, the then Education Secretary, added five 'thinking skills' into the National Curriculum for 2000. These were:

1 information processing
2 reasoning
3 enquiry
4 creative thinking
5 evaluation.

This re-started an interest in whether 'thinking' could be taught in schools. Philosophy teaching was seen as being linked to this and perhaps included in the primary curriculum. In this chapter we look at both of these themes; while recognising that we can only just touch the surface of what has been a long, long debate over thousands of years.

The DfES interest in thinking skills in 1999 was very probably a pragmatic response to trying to raise SATs results and little informed about the whole debate about thinking skills. However the DfES standards website on thinking skills did provide a good website aimed at primary teachers. This looked at the history of thinking skills development, some case studies and a short list of references. Unusually, for government websites, it also named the authors – Steve Higgins and Jennifer Miller. At the time of writing, the website still existed (www.dfes.gov.uk/thinkingskills), but some of the links are no longer there.

Thinking skills and cognition

Figure 15.1 is a Venn diagram that shows the link between the cognitive invention approaches and the philosophical approaches. Higgins and Miller would have also included the brain gym ideas, which I have not done as they seem to link more closely with healthy schools (Chapter 13). Feuerstein worked initially with troubled young Jewish migrants into Israel after the Second World War, whereas Lipman started from his experience as a university academic. He identified some of his undergraduate students as having poor thinking skills. As Figure 15.1. shows, they both shared a belief that change was possible; they both audited what learners could and could not do, then they set out to produce 'teaching' strategies to improve thinking. Feuerstein's strategies concentrated on direct teaching to improve cognitive functions he had identified as being deficient. Lipman used fiction as a starting point for philosophical discussion with children and through this to improve their thinking. Both these strategies can be seen in use in many of today's primary schools to improve thinking – oral and written. Edward de Bono's work, which we look at later in this chapter, looks at strategies to improve cognitive functions. Robert Fisher's work concentrates on the use of fiction and poetry to provide a contextual framework for developing thinking skills.

There is often nothing very new about so-called new ideas in education. The ancient philosophers such as Aristotle and Socrates taught – or tried to teach – thinking skills: basically, on a set question and answer basis to aristocratic boys. It would seem a very traditional teaching method today. Much later, Piaget and other psychologists looked at how children learnt to think. Piaget, in particular, had what we would now think was a very conservative view, where children went through different cognitive stages and could not be pushed through any particular stages. Later psychologists such as Vygotsky, Bruner, etc. recognised that specific strategies could develop children's thinking and learning. Words such as scaffolding, modelling and metacognition came to be used as ways of expanding children's cognitive experiences.

Edward de Bono

One of the best-known writers in the thinking skills field is Edward de Bono. I personally find his work quite hard to read. I am not quite sure why this is and so worry that it is because my thinking skills aren't in his league! This is why I recommend one of his books addressed to parents on teaching their child to think. A Google search for Edward de Bono, will give you about 44,000 different sites, so you would be well advised to go for his official website. Like many personal websites, it tends to be in the selling business, but it does give you a reasonable overview of the development of his thinking. Today he does a great deal of work in commercial organisations and his thinking programmes have been adapted and used with managers and executives worldwide – often without any credit.

De Bono's CoRT thinking programme was produced in 1973. In this he was looking at strategies for generating ideas for lateral thinking. He called these strategies 'attention-directing tools'. CoRT stands for Cognitive Research Trust, which de Bono established

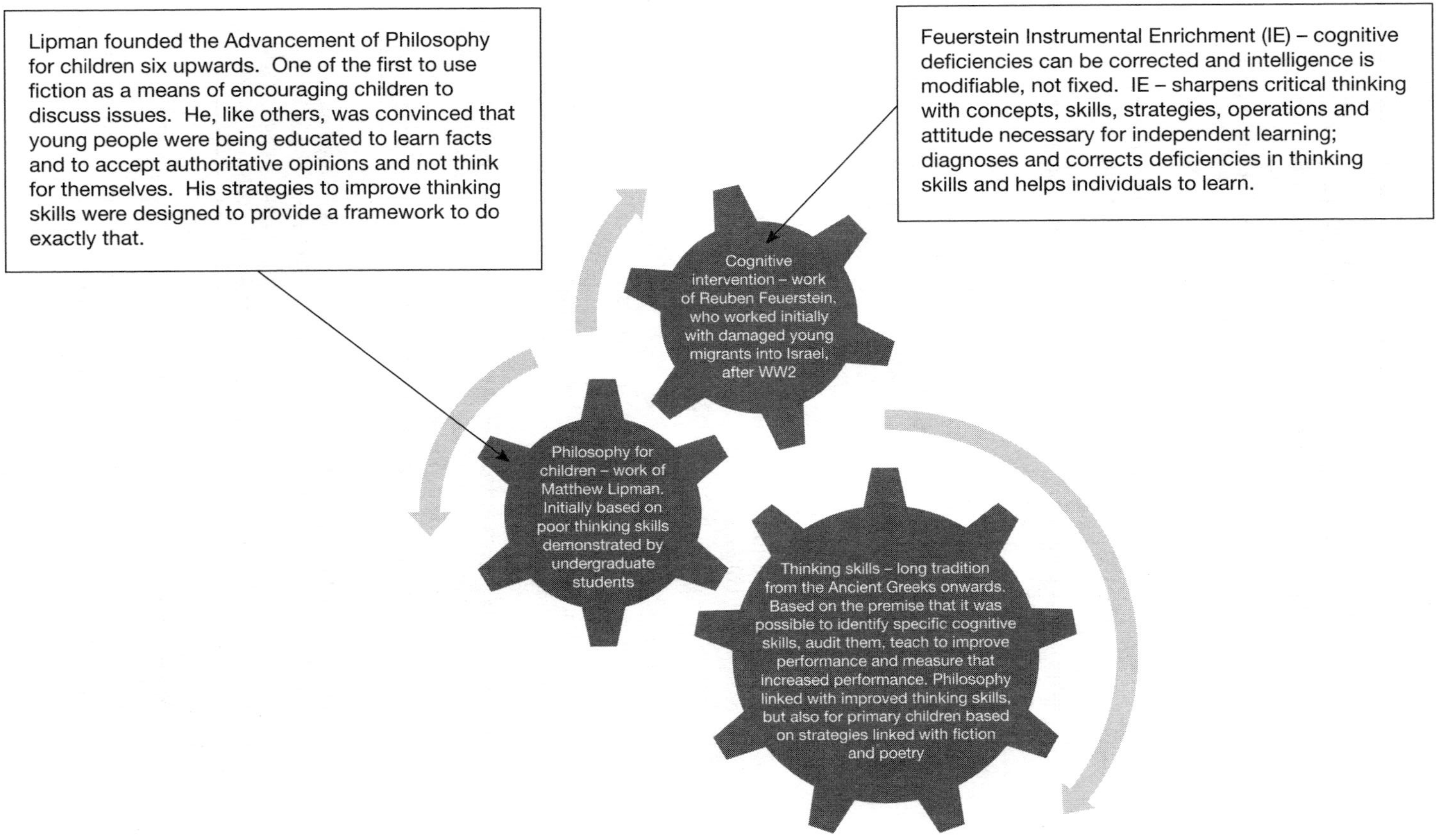

Feuerstein Instrumental Enrichment (IE) – cognitive deficiencies can be corrected and intelligence is modifiable, not fixed. IE – sharpens critical thinking with concepts, skills, strategies, operations and attitude necessary for independent learning; diagnoses and corrects deficiencies in thinking skills and helps individuals to learn.

Cognitive intervention – work of Reuben Feuerstein, who worked initially with damaged young migrants into Israel, after WW2

Thinking skills – long tradition from the Ancient Greeks onwards. Based on the premise that it was possible to identify specific cognitive skills, audit them, teach to improve performance and measure that increased performance. Philosophy linked with improved thinking skills, but also for primary children based on strategies linked with fiction and poetry

Philosophy for children – work of Matthew Lipman. Initially based on poor thinking skills demonstrated by undergraduate students

Lipman founded the Advancement of Philosophy for children six upwards. One of the first to use fiction as a means of encouraging children to discuss issues. He, like others, was convinced that young people were being educated to learn facts and to accept authoritative opinions and not think for themselves. His strategies to improve thinking skills were designed to provide a framework to do exactly that.

Figure 15.1 Thinking skills

Table 15.1 De Bono's CoRT programme

Thinking tool	Useful for
PMI	*Plus, minus, interesting* This is an explorative and evaluation tool. It provides children with an attention directing framework to widen thinking. Learners can put forward the things they like about something, those they don't like and those they find interesting. It frames the discussion and/or report. It is useful in reading as a scanning tool.
CAF	*Consider all facts* Look around, explore. We ask learners to identify what factors should be considered in their thinking? Have they left anything out? PMI is more concerned with judging good and bad. CAF notes all possible factors. This reflects real life thinking which is often messy. It should not of course be confused with another CAF!
OPV	*Other people's views* People are doing the thinking and others are going to be affected by this. Children are asked to broaden their perspectives. Some find this extremely difficult, even though many of our PSHE programmes require them to do this. Who are these other people? What views might they hold? Why do they think differently? Let us take as an example, a pupil who has been involved in a playground fight with another pupil and told to report the incident to his/her class teacher. What might be the point of view of the other child; the teacher/professional colleague on duty; their own friends; the other child's friends? This encourages long-term thinking.
APC	*Alternatives, possibilities and choices* It requires the learner to think and look at alternative courses of action. What can be done? You find a £10 on the pavement, what choices do you have?
AGO	*Aims, goals and objectives* What is the objective/focus of the thinking? What do we want to achieve? If we know exactly where we want to go we will have more chance of getting there. There may emerge some sub-objectives that provide steps towards the main objective.
FIP	*First important points* This tool looks to identify what really matters. Not everything is equally important. After generating a number of ideas, pupils need to decide which are the most important, e.g. in running a disco what are your priorities? Priorities may vary between individuals.
C&S	*Consequence and sequel* When you have chosen one alternative as a possible outcome of thinking, what would happen if we went ahead with the alternative. Will it work out? What are the benefits? What are the problems and dangers? What are the costs? You need to take into account time scale, risk, certainty. You also need to make a decision. We all know people who are frozen into indecision because they spend so long on looking at consequences and sequels.

in Cambridge, and the programme of sixty lessons was a product of his research. This has been widely adapted in both commercial and public sectors. Today, the most widely known de Bono strategy used in primary schools is that of the Six Thinking Hats which we will look at later. First, let us examine the CoRT thinking programme out of which the thinking hats grew.

CoRT thinking programme

There are seven different forms of thinking strategy. These are known for short by their initials – PMI, CAF, OPV, APC, AGO, FIP and C&S.

Obviously you need to chose your thinking tool or tools carefully and part of helping children to use these as effective thinking/speaking and writing frameworks, is to identify how best to use them.

Activity/Thinking Task 1

Use the PMI template (Table 15.2) to identify some positive and negative points about television use with young children.

This type of template is useful for helping children to review a book they have read. Generally, this is done as a group exercise and learners record what they enjoyed about the book, what they didn't enjoy so much and what they found interesting. This provides a very good way of representing the views of several children within a group who hold different opinions about the same book. It recognises that differences are acceptable and valid. I have worked with primary children at all ages doing this and found it most useful when using picture books, which provide quick access to often quite complex ideas at the top end of the primary schools and a much simpler interpretation with younger children. The older children used the template structure and younger children either had adult help or we used a note form. It also works well at adult level, when discussing the use of children's books.

Table 15.2 PMI template

The government thinks children are watching too much TV, so all parents must put a coin box on the television and children have to pay so much an hour for watching it. Record your comments in the box. Try to think of at least three plus points, three minus ones and two interesting ones.		
Plus	*Minus*	*Interesting*

Table 15.3 Some CoRT questions and issues

Response framework	Questions and issues	Responses
CAF	What factors come into choosing a holiday?	
OPV	All children should have their own laptop in school	
APC	Someone is walking down the street with a paper bag on his head. Why do you think he is doing it? Try five different possibilities	
AGO	What are your own immediate aims, goals and objectives?	
FIP	Four top priorities for a friend	
C&S	A new, but expensive medicine comes on to the market with a promise of healthy life until 100	

Table 15.3 provides some other questions and discussion points used with children to explore specific thinking tools. It is best to adapt them for your own particular class based on their current concerns. Those in Table 15.3 are more generic and can be used at adult level.

CoRT tools: a summary

- evaluation tools
- exploration tools
- value tools
- action tools.

This is just a summary of the thinking skills identified through the use of these tools. I actually think that they provide excellent scaffolds for promoting more informed discussion in schools at all levels (including the staff room!). I also think that they can and are easily adapted for very much younger children.

Claimed benefits of CoRT tools

- they avoid impulsive behaviour and snap decisions;
- it enables learners to see alternatives, when others only see difficulties, confusion and dilemmas;
- it improves decision making and generates new ideas and skills;
- it increases learners' abilities to consider consequences before taking action;
- it provides a framework to work more productively when working with others in a group/team;
- the tools can be transformed into writing frames for different forms of non-fiction writing. At adult level, it is easy to see how they could be transferred into assignment and dissertation writing to demonstrate good evaluative skills.

These are some of the benefits claimed for the CoRT programme. I think it makes the assumption that because we are taught these techniques we are always able to use them, i.e. transfer of skills directly. I would like to think that I avoid impulsive behaviour and don't make snap decisions, but sadly my friends tell me differently. However, perhaps it does help me sometimes.

Thinking Hats

Thinking Hats has been de Bono's most popular set of thinking tools for primary schools. The thinking tools (CoRT) we have just looked at can be used independently or as small groups of two or three. They are attention directing tools. The hats serve a slightly different purpose; although they can be seen as developments that have grown out of the CoRT research:

1 *The White Hat.* This signifies the gathering of information, data, facts and figures. It links with CAF, OPV and FIP.
2 *The Red Hat.* This represents intuition, hunches, feelings and emotions. It is linked most closely with OPV.
3 *The Black Hat.* This covers thinking linked with assessment and checking and is similar to PMI and C&S.
4 *The Yellow Hat.* This type of thinking looks at the benefits and advantages of what is proposed and is most closely associated with C&S and PMI.
5 *The Green Hat.* This represents creativity, action, proposals and suggestions. It utilizes constructive ideas and new ways of thinking. Links with APC.
6 *The Blue Hat.* This supports thinking which gives an overview and control of thinking process itself. What are we doing?

Figure 15.2 shows this in a more visual format.

The 'Thinking Hats' idea has taken off well in primary schools because the hats can be made visible and 'funny'. I have seen all sorts of hats in use – woolly ones, character ones, paper ones and imaginary ones. In some primary classrooms you can see them on display on the wall and they stand as a reminder of different ways of thinking. This is particularly useful for writing non-fiction texts.

And why hats? – Because you can physically put them on and take them off, i.e. you can think in one way and then in another. Something happens, my gut reaction is the

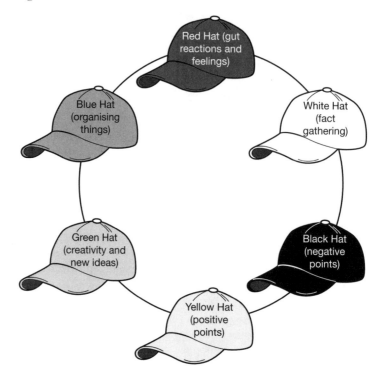

Figure 15.2 Thinking Hats

red-hat thinking; then I spend some time with some white-hat thinking, etc. They are particularly useful for role-play, drama and talking heads activities.

Activity/Thinking Task 2

For each of the following situations which hat would you use first of all:

- You are accused of being a liar;
- You break your right arm in an accident;
- Your mother/child/friend is very ill and has to go to hospital;
- You find an envelope with a lot of money in it;
- You discover your mate is a thief.

Before settling down to this task, think of specific problems you have to deal with at the moment – only those you are willing to share with others. Pick one and decide which hats you have already used. What hat could you add to the process?

Philosophy for schools within a thinking skills programme

We now turn to the work of Robert Fisher, whose website 'teachingthinking' is well worth visiting and his books for teachers read well. He identified five specific thinking skills – information-processing skills, enquiry skills, reasoning skills, creative thinking skills and communication skills. Each thinking skill involves learners in developing different cognitive strategies.

1 *Information-processing skills*

- locating, collecting and recalling relevant information;
- interpreting information to show they understand relevant concepts and ideas;
- analysing information e.g. sorting, classifying, sequencing, comparing and contrasting;
- understanding relationships e.g. part/whole relationships.

This information processing is very similar to the white hat data gathering and CAF, OPV and FIP.

2 *Enquiry skills.* This involves learners in:

- asking relevant questions;
- posing and defining problems;
- planning what to do and how to research;
- predicting outcomes, testing conclusions and improving ideas.

A key challenge is getting children – and indeed adults – to ask any questions, never mind relevant questions. Very young children do ask the most wonderful questions, but then seem to have it bullied out of them. I've done it myself as a parent, when the constant 'why' and 'what' can be very tiring. Keeping children asking questions about the world in which they live is a key task in early years settings, but learners of all ages need help in keeping awake the natural curiosity that the very young have.

3 *Reasoning skills.* Learners need to be taught to:

- Give reasons for opinions;
- Draw inferences and make deductions;
- Use precise language to explain what they think;
- Make judgements and decisions informed by reasons or evidence.

Again, we all know people who are not good at reasoning through issues. Racist and sexist comments are the most obvious ones to tackle – why do you think that? What is your evidence? Teaching reasoning skills is an attempt to move people on from a gut reaction, to a more reasoned response, in which they can give reasons for their opinions, make deductions, use appropriate language and make judgements informed by evidence. Many children and adults need to be taught the language in which to do this.

4 *Creative thinking skills.* This involves teachers working with learners to:

- generate and extend ideas;
- suggest possible hypothesis;
- be imaginative in their thinking;
- look for alternative innovation outcomes.

This is very much in the green-hat world, where APC thinking skills come into action.

5   *Communication*

Philosophy for children helps to develop communication skills through careful listening and constructive discussion. It gives them confidence to think for themselves. Listening and speaking is seen as key to learning for all of us, the thinking skills strategies provide a scaffold to extend this. Another rapidly growing form of communication is via mobile phones and the Internet. It is an area where perhaps the thinking skills ideas need to be introduced, to make such communications much more meaningful and productive.

Robert Fisher's website shows several examples of specially written or selected fiction, poetry and games that can provide starting points for discussion. There is also a philosophy website for children known as SAPERE (Society for the Advancement of Philosophical Enquiry and Reflection in Education). This also looks at issues such as questioning, reasoning, creative thinking and evaluative skills.

Thinking actively in a social context

Thinking actively in a social context (TASC) was originally a programme aimed at gifted and talented children and more often towards the upper primary and secondary school population. Now it is recognised that the strategies are supportive for all children (and adults). The TASC website is a useful resource (www.nace.co.uk/tasc/tasc_home.htm), but like the other websites in this field, is also about selling the website visitor its products. It needs to be reviewed with care.

TASC is about developing effective strategies so that teachers can use research, investigation and problem-solving skills across the curriculum. They identified eight different skills, each of which needed to be taught, modelled and demonstrated with children. These were:

1   gathering and organising existing knowledge;
2   identifying exactly what the task consists of;
3   generating ideas to carry out the task;
4   deciding which is the best idea;
5   implementing it;
6   evaluating it;
7   communicating your findings; and, finally,
8   learning from experience.

These ideas were developed into a TASC mind-map wheel that covered each skill. Like Bloom's taxonomy, these skills are all verbs – gather, identify, generate, decide, implement, evaluate, communicate and learn from experience. The wheel itself has clear relationships with the mind-friendly lesson planning framework that we looked at earlier.

The mind-map wheel was developed so that it covers key teaching principles, assessment of skills and a menu of activities to be used across multiple abilities. Here it makes explicit links with Gardner's multiple intelligences and covers: linguistic, mathematical, visual, movement, musical (and auditory), social, emotional, spiritual, scientific and mechanical. There are also assessment checklists that can be linked with the initial skills identified.

TASC also claims that the use of its strategies:

- enhances lesson planning so that objectives systematically develop pupils' thinking and personalises learning;
- provides effective planning for differentiation and extension;
- provides a holistic approach to incorporating full use of human abilities;
- assesses the processes of pupils' learning.

I find the hype rather off-putting. It seems to offer too much, but Belle Wallace's books are good and cover thinking skills for developing topics from the national curriculum framework for early years, primary and middle years.

16 Managing and leading a class teaching team

QTS Standards

3, 4, 5, 6, 9, 13, 20, 21, 30, 32, 33

Learning objectives

- to recognise the changing role of the teacher in terms of management and leadership for a class team;
- to be aware of four significant theories of change in education that can help to identify potential challenges and opportunities when managing others;
- to identify some of the practical skills and strategies needed:
  - to support a classroom leadership role;
  - to manage other adults to support children's learning;
  - to provide subject or phase leadership.

Rationale for choice of current issues

In these final three chapters, we look at a number of current issues and changing patterns in primary schools, all of which are part of political changes occurring at the same time in other public services. I have made the choice of these next three chapters – managing and leading a class teaching team; schools as learning communities; and extended schools and children's integrated services – for the following four key reasons.

1 Primary schools as part of the agenda for change in children's services

The agenda for ICS and a united children's workforce is in the process of being embedded in schools and is here to stay. This agenda, which rose out of the ECM legislation, will significantly change and broaden the role of schools and those who work in them.

As we have already noted, a major change over the past few years has been the growth of the support services within schools. This has resulted in many class teachers leading their own teams within the classroom and taking over unfamiliar whole school responsibilities. The role of the teacher as manager and leader is a key one, as well as a challenging one for student teachers and NQTs.

2 Primary schools with a broadening and more formalised educational remit for adult education

For some considerable time schools have been involved in the education of adults – both formally and informally. The formal side initially started with parental briefings about what went on in early learning centres and schools; later schools supported parents and carers in ways they could help children at home. Many of these courses developed into recognisable and accredited adult education classes and were often responsible for helping parents return to education themselves via access to HE courses and later through to foundation degrees. Primary teachers have often been involved in teaching on these courses because they were seen as 'trusted' by parents who would not normally have come forward for adult education.

3 Shared service centres

In many areas, developments in education and other public services, such as health, social care and leisure, have resulted in large community sites where there are several schools/ learning centres, clinics, sports centres, welfare centres situated alongside each other. The public funding initiative (PFI), which is responsible for building many of these developments – including primary schools – requires the buildings to be profitable. This means that they will be open at least fourteen or fifteen hours, and in some cases twenty-four hours. This concentration will require professionals to have a greater understanding of the work of other professionals serving the same geographical community.

4 Secondary-based BSF programme

'One of the only places operating largely as it did more than 50 years ago would be the local school'. These words from Dryden and Vos in their 2005 edition of *The New Learning Revolution* should soon sound very dated. Already in many LAs, the secondary-based BSF programme has changed the name of the proposed schools into 'learning centres' and the language is about transformational education to inspire learning. This has huge potential for primary schools, which will be working alongside the secondary and tertiary sector in their learning networks. It should make for more flexibility for primary-trained professionals, particularly enabling them to become more involved with adult education.

In this chapter we will look in more detail at the role of the student teacher and class teacher in managing and leading a class team of fellow educational professionals. For student teachers most of these professionals will be far more experienced and this may require some challenging skills learning.

The class team

As a team leader, the class teacher is ultimately responsible for:

1 ensuring that learning is enhanced by the addition of other educational professionals;
2 having a good knowledge and understanding of the roles of these educational professionals;
3 having a good understanding of their existing qualifications, expertise and experience and ways in which this can be developed;
4 having the skills to promote collaboration and co-operative working;
5 understanding and leading the ongoing change agenda within the classroom;
6 visioning, creating and maintaining a purposeful, safe and highly motivating learning environment for both adult and child learners.

Figure 16.1 provides an example of a potential team any primary class teacher may be managing. I have deliberately left out other allied professionals who may come in from outside to visit individual children, e.g. the educational psychologist, or to work with particular groups such as children who have opted for music sessions.

Figure 16.1 Possible leadership responsibilities within any one primary classroom

Activity/Thinking Task 1

In Chapter 2, we looked at how three major initiatives had been responsible for the growing number of allied educational professionals working in primary classrooms – inclusion, the primary strategy and growth of ICT. In what other areas may we see primary schools bringing in non-QTS staff to cover expertise and skills that QTS training does not provide? What implications would this have for the class teacher?

MFL is another area in which I can visualise more expert help being employed. At the moment, its development in primary schools is patchy, but once children start learning at least one MFL from nursery onwards, the subject knowledge and skill expertise required will be considerably more than a GCSE in the subject. Other areas may be a formalisation of the creativity element of the curriculum. Dancers, drama groups, writers and artists in residence are already being used to stimulate and motivate both pupils and teachers.

Class teachers may be acting as line managers to allied educational professionals who work in several different classrooms and/or in more than one role. Welfare assistants may often work as trained teaching assistants for example; an STA working with a child in one class three mornings a week, may be working with small groups in two different classrooms the other two mornings. Examples of work that class teachers may be acting as line managers for include:

- adults working semi-autonomously with pupils throughout the school and reporting to them as their line manager;
- giving generic learning support to pupils in classrooms or learning units with work or assessment tasks prepared by the class teacher;
- working with a specific child who has special needs;
- working and/or managing a unit or centre within the school;
- informal adviser about professional issues such as CPD, appointments, appeals, promotions, etc.;
- liaising with school-based mentors for work experience and student teachers as well as reporting to secondary school, FE and HE tutors.

This line management role varies a great deal from school to school and age group to age group. There tends to be more evidence of adult support the younger the children are.

Management training for class teachers

National Council for School Leadership

This has expanded its original remit considerably over the past few years and one very successful course 'Leading from the middle' looks at exactly this issue of leadership of a class team, as well as other more whole-school issues. Many teachers are encouraged to take this course quite early in their career and several LAs are running similar courses with accreditation from local HE institutions towards certificates and master's degrees. The course materials suggest that there are four essential characteristics for the teacher/manager:

1   a desire to make a difference to pupil learning;
2   a commitment to professional learning;
3   a belief in the abilities of colleagues;
4   a commitment to developing emotional intelligence.

Not only are these four characteristics unsurprising, but we would also expect most post-graduate student teachers to be demonstrating this prior to entry on their short training course. Much the same applies to the five key skills for management identified in the same publication:

1   establishing rapport and trust;
2   listening for meaning;
3   questioning for understanding;
4   prompting action, reflection, learning;
5   developing confidence and celebrating success.

Again, these sound a lot like the skills needed for teaching pupils, don't they? But in this case the skills are aimed at other adults – the need to establish trust; listen to what they are saying (or not saying sometimes); questioning their understanding of practices and processes, etc. Initially, you will do this in order to learn from them how the classroom is managed and what their role is in this. Later you will be managing them and may need to alter what they do in order to promote more effective support for children's learning.

Starting points for student teachers

*   Take note of current practice in relation to the use of adult support workers, if you are unsure ask the class teacher.
*   Ask to see job descriptions and 'tactfully' find out levels at which they are operating.
*   Ensure that your planning covers the work of all adult support workers.
*   Find time to plan collaboratively, discuss the teaching assessments and evaluate the activity.
*   Clarify where the activity will be carried out.
*   Clarify who is responsible for preparing materials and special resources, and make time for this before the lesson.
*   Share IEPs with appropriate support workers and develop programmes of work to achieve targets set.

(Adapted from Wood, 2006)

The first two are very obvious starting points. (1) Making sure you understand exactly what these adult support workers are doing at the moment, and if you are unsure, asking the teacher. If you are working in more than one classroom, it is useful to see differences between the use of adult support and the reasons for it. (2) You also need to know exactly what role individuals have, and the level they are at in terms of professional support. Find out tactfully!

The NCSL also use the term 'the shadow side' to describe some of the challenges of management and leadership. If you manage effectively, you will inevitably find a shadow side. This may hinder progress or undermine performance. Seddon (2007) speaking at a conference on subject leadership and management in primary schools suggested the following were some ways in which to manage the 'shadow side' effectively:

- raise awareness of shadow-side activity – identify trouble spots;
- assess impact on teaching;
- know what to bring into the light and what to leave in the shadows;
- build strategies at every stage of the change management process;
- use your interpersonal skills to maintain awareness;
- listen, negotiate.

Listening skills

Management courses suggest particular strategies to improve our listening skills:

1 Maintain eye contact.
2 Face the speaker and lean slightly forward.
3 Ignore distractions.
4 Make non-interrupting acknowledgements – nods and smiles.
5 When the speaker pauses, allow them to continue without interrupting – only add your comments when the person has finished.
6 Be alert for non-verbal cues: body language speaks volumes.
7 Don't ignore offhand comments – they often give insight into personalities and family situations.
8 Ask for clarification when necessary.
9 Check your understanding of what the person has said by summarising the essential points and reaching some agreement on them.
10 Find out what parents know about what goes on in school and what expectations they have for their child.

It is also important to remember there are cultural differences, e.g. relating to eye contact.

Understanding and managing change

In this section we look at several models of change. One of the reasons for this is that the TDA, in a statement about workforce remodelling in 2005, made it quite clear that schools needed to draw on the research literature on change in order for individuals to develop as effective managers. These change models tend to be multi-disciplinary because management and leadership is seen as generic and the skills a manager has can be used anywhere. That is just one reason why you need to be critical about the different models, because although they can be useful they need to be used sensitively.

Comfort/discomfort/panic zones model

We looked at a slight variation of the model shown in Figure 16.2 in Chapters 8 and 9 when we explored it in terms of behaviour management and emotional health. This particular version is adapted from Peter Senge's (2000) work on change. Senge's models and ideas are used quite a lot in educational management, as well as in other areas. This particular model is simple and applies so easily to everyday life.

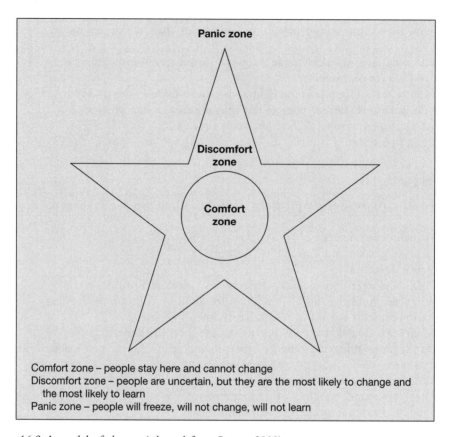

Figure 16.2 A model of change (adapted from Senge, 2000)

Management change is often stressing and a new team manager, albeit a student teacher, represents change. This model acknowledges that. Some individuals are more susceptible to change than others and sometimes seemingly very confident and experienced teaching assistants may be worried about changes in their and the children's routines.

In the centre, we are in our comfort zone. This doesn't mean to say we like it, but it does mean we feel comfortable with the status quo. Things feel familiar and certain; work is controllable and predictable; people feel comfortable and competent; there is no threat to self-esteem and there is a sense of belonging.

Change means we have to move out of that comfort zone; for example if you are asking a teaching assistant to provide some form of written assessment on the work a small group of children are doing and they have not done this before. This moves them into a discomfort zone. I actually prefer the term 'challenge zone' as I think it represents more than discomfort, change challenges us. If the challenge is too much, we are in what this model calls the panic zone. It is often called the stress zone. And we've all been there. When there, people are most likely to feel stress, worry and fear; anger, irritation and annoyance; sadness, hopelessness and apathy; guilt and shame; inadequacy and frustration. As a team manager you need first to avoid moving into this zone yourself and second to keep members of your team out of it. You are aiming for discomfort, not stress.

So according to this model, how do people change, or rather how do you as manager of a class team help to change practice through challenging a particular practice? First of all you need to help move people from their comfort zone to discomfort/challenge zone, where they are most likely to change and learn how to do things differently.

How does this change take place?

It takes place by using the following:

- creating the right learning environment and culture;
- creating a vision of how things could be;
- providing access to appropriate training and positive role models;
- providing feedback and support groups;
- ensuring systems and structures are consistent.

This requires considerable sensitivity as a student teacher; but it actually is challenging for very experienced leaders. You can probably think of many times when someone has been urging change and gone through many of these processes with different levels of success. What these change models do is provide us with a knowledge-base about change and through that a means of devising our own personal models, depending on circumstances.

Stereotypes

The second change model is one linked to stereotypes. I do not actually agree with this change model, but have included it so that you can see whether you recognise yourself and perhaps members of your team within it. It looks at understanding different stereotypes in relation to change.

1 *Advocates.* These are team members who are open to change and with significant experience of change.
2 *Willing followers.* These are members who are open to change, but with little experience of change.
3 *Resistants.* These are colleagues who are resistant to change, but with little experience of change.
4 *Blockers.* These represent those who are resistant to change and with significant experience of it. They are often extremely accomplished at invisible blocking. They do not challenge the change, they simply do not follow it!

I think change is more complex than this because the context of change varies and in one situation you may be an advocate and in another a blocker. Blockers are most easy to recognise when they are blocking something you are advocating. However, it is important to recognise that change is not always 'a good thing' and that blocking may sometimes be the moral/correct thing to do.

A research programme on teaching assistants reported in the *TES* (22.9.06) said that some of them felt like 'Pond Life'. Your task is to prevent anyone working with you feeling that low about their work. Their rate of pay, certainly, is very poor and does not reflect the wonderful work they do and commitment that many of them have.

Activity/Thinking Task 2

Can you remember a particular change in which you have been: an advocate; another in which you have been a willing follower; a third in which you have been a resistant; and, finally, one in which you have been a blocker?

Table 16.1 provides one way of recording this. Be honest, it helps to understand others as well as yourself in relation to change. It is also important to remember that there are many outside factors that influence change in schools. A teaching assistant caring for an elderly parent with dementia may be under appalling strain and your wonderful new idea about formal monitoring of behaviour in his/her literacy group is just the last thing with which s/he can cope.

Table 16.1 Understanding stereotypes in relation to change

Stereotype	Situation	Rationale
Advocate		
Willing follower		
Resistant		
Blocker		

Grief and loss model

Another model of change has likened it to change brought about by bereavement, particularly if work-related changed is very dynamic. Figure 16.3 shows this visually. It covers seven stages – denial, anger, loss, despair, understanding, learning and acceptance.

1   Starts with an emotional event, upset or shock. This can include changes in the work place.
2   Cannot flight, flock, freeze or fight (as in Smith's ALPS of fear in the classroom) so initially deny what has happened.
3   Evidence says it has happened and we believe it and this causes anger, stress, often physical illness.
4   'Emotional fog' – you don't know where you are, feel uncertain, lost.
5   Despair thinking you won't get through it.
6   Understanding, learning and acceptance – often comes with the help of others and with space and time.

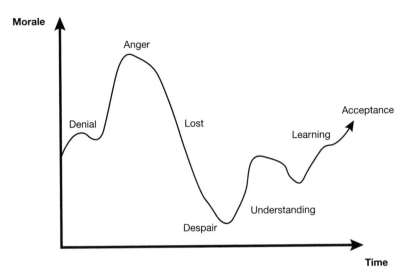

Figure 16.3 Model of change: grief and loss

Activity/Thinking Task 3

How might changes a student teacher brings into a classroom produce something akin to this grief and loss model – for children and staff?

Michael Fullen

Michael Fullen is one of the great gurus of change. He visits the UK quite often to deliver extremely popular courses on change. His change model is based on five key dimensions of change that individuals and schools go through. This is looking at change on a school basis, rather than a classroom basis. You might feel that this is out of your league because when you are classroom based, that is what concerns you. But it is useful, because student teachers are often placed in schools that are looking seriously at change. This is sometimes because the LA or Ofsted has determined that they should do, but increasingly often, because they see themselves as learning organisations who want to be pro-active about advancing good practice. Fullen, who is a regular speaker at the NCSL, has national influence. He is one of the very few academic researchers who can bridge that communications gap between their strategic research and operational practice. Fullen suggested that change involves – or *should* involve:

1   *Moral purpose* – underpinned by values and vision with understandings that the change will make a positive difference to the lives of staff, pupils, parents, governors and the community. Does it in your experience?
2   *Understanding change* – developing the capacity to problem solve; encouraging others to buy into the change; building the capacity for change through collaborative team building; listening to the concerns of those who may have some reservations about the change. Again, does it in your experience?

3 Relationship-building – developing emotional intelligence.
4 Knowledge creation and sharing – defining the learning community, raising awareness, developing skills, creating and sharing new knowledge.
5 Coherence-making – some creativity encouraged to prevent stagnation, but not too much, which could lead to initiative fatigue and overload.

The NHS Institute for Innovation and Improvement have produced some useful Improvement Leaders' Guides.

Changing leadership patterns in primary schools

Subject leaders

Just as the role of the teacher is changing in primary schools, so is that of the leadership and staffing structures. The old Victorian staffing structure of a head teacher and perhaps an assistant teacher changed as schools grew larger and employed more staff. Deputy head teachers were appointed, for example. But it was not really until 1978 that formal management posts were given to mainstream teachers. This was as a result of a piece of DES research which showed that in primary schools where there were subject co-ordinators teaching was better. Co-ordinators were appointed and by the mid 1980s specific subject and generic co-ordinator courses were funded by central government. This expanded rapidly with the introduction of the national curriculum in 1988. In 1998, the TTA produced a set of National Standards for Subject Leaders and by this time all mainstream teachers after their NQT year were responsible for co-ordinating at least one subject. Most did not get paid for doing this co-ordination.

Such standards no longer exist, and the role of the subject co-ordinator/manager/leader has significantly changed over the past few years. The main reason for this has been workforce remodelling in schools, where teaching and learning has been given the priority. Many primary schools do still have staff who hold a specific overview of one or more subject areas, and this section looks at some of the specific areas of management and leadership this involves for teachers after they have finished their induction year. It is worth noting that in some schools, other professionals such as learning mentors and HLTAs may have responsibility for subject co-ordination. It is also worth noting that most subject co-ordinators only became specialists in their subject area after they were appointed as manager. They do not necessarily have any degree or even an A-level in the subject. This is a direct result of appointing primary teaching staff on the basis of their ability to teach effectively across the curriculum, rather than to be a subject specialist in one area.

Activity/Thinking Task 4

Choose a specific subject area and make a list of what you could look at to see if the subject is being effectively taught and resourced. You might find that you want to draw up an audit of aspects such as classroom-based resources, school-based resources, displays, relevant ICT, policy documents, including schemes of work, questionnaires for children about what they enjoy/don't enjoy about the subject, lists of related visits out and visitors in, budget, etc. It might also be useful for foundation subjects to audit curriculum time and how the subject is permeated through core subjects.

A whole school perspective

Subject managers need to have a whole school perspective. Over thirty years ago Eric Hoyle in his work on the role of the teacher made a distinction between the 'restricted' and 'extended' professional. The restricted professional just kept to classroom issues, whereas the 'extended' professional took a full part in the life of the school and had good understandings about its strategic and operational management. There was no room then, or now, for the restricted professional. As a starting point the subject leader would need to consider:

1 the overall school aims and values;
2 long-term strategic plan;
3 school development plan (written every year);
4 SEF (written every year);
5 school approach to subject leadership;
6 ways in which policies are formulated, implemented and reviewed;
7 assessment, recording and reporting procedures;
8 raising standards initiatives;
9 whole-school monitoring procedures.

The extended professional also needs to keep their eyes on what is happening at both central and local government level in relation to schooling.

Teaching and learning responsibility

One of the key staffing features that came out of the workforce reform agenda in schools, was the establishment of management posts with teaching and learning responsibility (TLR). Initially, this has resulted in probably the same members of staff as members of the school SMT, but with post responsibilities that are more generic than subject responsibility. There is also a very obvious emphasis on teaching and learning.

Table 16.2 provides a comparison between the post of subject leader and TLR, and Figure 16.4 shows how this fits in with an overall staffing structure. Staffing Structure School A looks at the whole staff of a primary school, Staffing Structure School B shows a different form of structure – the relationship between subject manager and TLR. Staffing Structure C provides a breakdown of the subject co-ordination from part of School B. There are many differences between schools, but understanding the structure helps those working in it – including student teachers.

Learning to relax

Stress

Learning to relax and helping others to avoid stress is an essential element in maintaining a mentally healthy and purposeful working environment in the classroom. In Britain at least 40 million working days are lost each year owing to the effects of stress. Stress can affect health, performance and relationships. Most of us can benefit from developing personal strategies to help us become more healthy, relaxed and effective. There are a number of publications for teachers about stress as well as helplines. It often helps just to recognise what is happening at an early stage and take remedial action quickly. If you don't feel you have got time – then you are seriously stressed.

Table 16.2 Sample post responsibilities

Subject leader responsibilities might include:	*TLR working with other relevant teacher in phase to:*
• Produce a policy statement for the subject	• Identify school improvement issues
• Produce written guidelines – schemes of work/long-term plans for the subject	• Define and agree improvement targets
• Assess resource implications/requirements	• Co-ordinate CPD needs
• Monitor the success of schemes in terms of teaching and learning	• Evaluate impact of improvement activities
• Evaluate long-, medium- and short-term plans	• Identify pupil achievement targets
• Utilise expertise of the staff, LA and outside agencies	• Monitor pupil standards and achievement
• Produce a progress report once a year	• Monitor planning and learning outcomes
• Purchase resources using a delegated budget	• Monitor standards of behaviour
• Keep a record of co-ordinator activities in file	• Maintain personal expertise and share with other teachers
• Develop manageable systems of recording children's progress	• Monitor and evaluate standards of teaching
• Presentation to the Curriculum Committee of the Governing Board	• Induct, monitor and support new staff
• Provide CPD or organise provision for colleagues	• Act as a performance management team leader. Member of SMT

Table 16.3 gives two checklists of physical and mental symptoms of stress. It is worth looking at children in your class who may exhibit a number of these symptoms. This is particularly relevant after the 2007 Unicef report placed British children last in their international league table examining the physical and emotional well-being of children in the world's twenty wealthiest nations.

Teachers are not alone in feeling stress, although if you are the stressed individual, it does feel lonely. As Jack Dunham (1992) notes in *Stress in Teaching,* stress has important implications for teachers themselves, those with whom they work, the children they teach and their own families. He notes that stress has different definitions because the stressed person has different perspectives. What stresses one individual will not stress another. One definition sees stress as external pressures, e.g. new central government initiatives. Another definition sees stress as emotional reactions, such as anger, and physical reactions, such as tension headaches. Dunham defines it as a significant excess of pressures over coping resources, which leads to the development of positive and negative reactions. His work looks at:

- the pressures in teaching
- children's behaviour and attitudes
- the pressures of poor working conditions

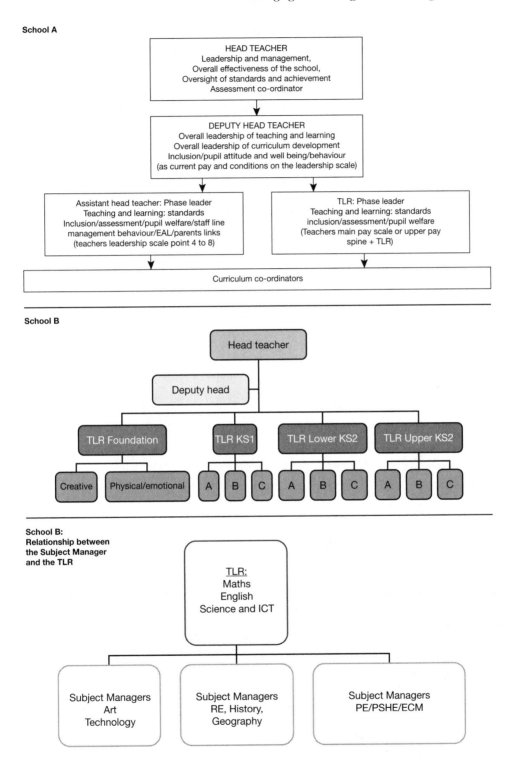

Figure 16.4 Staffing structures

Table 16.3 Symptoms of stress

Physical symptoms	Mental symptoms
• Lack of appetite	• Constant irritability with people
• Craving for food when under pressure	• Feeling unable to cope
• Frequent indigestion or heartburn	• Lack of interest in life
• Constipation or diarrhoea	• Constant fear of illness
• Insomnia	• A feeling of being a failure
• Constant tiredness	• A feeling of being bad or self-hatred
• A tendency to sweat for no good reason	• Loss of interest in other people
• Nervous twitches	• Awareness of suppressed anger
• Nail-biting	• Inability to show true feelings
• Headaches	• Loss of sense of humour
• Cramps and muscle spasms	• Feeling of neglect
• Nausea	• Dread of the future
• Breathlessness without exertion	• A feeling of having no one to confide in
• Fainting spells	• Difficulty in concentrating
• Frequent crying or desire to cry	• The inability to finish one task before rushing on to the next one
• Impotence or frigidity	
• Inability to sit still without fidgeting	• An intense fear of open or enclosed spaces, or of being alone
• High blood pressure	• A feeling of ugliness

- role conflict
- staff reactions to pressure
- the identification of teachers' coping resources.

Relaxation

The literature identifies several different techniques for dealing with stress and many tapes, DVDs and courses on the subject are available. Robb and Letts in their *Creating Kids Who Can*, devote an appendix to 'Turning can't do into can do through relaxation'. They explain why and how relaxation works. For children they explain that relaxation means:

- they learn faster
- they realise they are loved
- they become able to control how they feel
- they can enjoy other people
- they can make sense of their world
- they can use their imagination
- they become more likeable people.

Time management

Time management and stress are closely linked. How often do you feel 'I have to . . . or else . . .' and 'I can't . . . because . . .'. Stress prevents the individual from organising his or her time rationally. Sadly, stressed managers create stress by being poorly organised and a climate of stress then permeates the workplace.

Activity/Thinking Task 5

Write down ten statements that start with the words 'I have to' and finish with the phrase 'or else . . .'. How often do you feel 'I have to . . . or else . . .', for example, 'I have to finish this marking or else I will not be able to return the work tomorrow' and other expressions such as 'I can't . . . because . . .'?

The 'I have to . . .' statements represent some demand on your time or energy at work or elsewhere. The 'or else . . .' statements represent a threat. If you work on this with someone else, you could ask them to challenge the statement 'I have to . . .'. Does it really mean 'I want to'?

---

17 Schools as learning communities

QTS Standards

3a, b, 7, 29, 32, 33

Learning objectives

- to identify how primary schools are developing to become critical parts of a much wider learning community;
- to look at this in relation to the changing role of parental involvement in school and expectations within school inspection;
- to explore some ideas from Claxton's model for building learning power (BLP), implications for lifelong learning and relating this to work in schools and early years settings;
- to investigate evidence on the work of primary schools in networked learning communities.

In this chapter we look at some of the initiatives that have drawn in primary schools to be part of schools as 'learning communities'. This involves looking at programmes that involve primary schools in community and adult education. Programmes such as city learning centres (CLCs), network learning communities (NLCs), adult education, early invention, and generally preparing children, within their mainstream teaching, for lifelong learning. The chapter looks at the work of Guy Claxton for this final section.

City learning centres

These were established under the Excellence in Cities (EiC) initiative and were very much about sharing facilities with partner schools, colleges and the wider community. Their original brief was to 'exploit and test new and innovative ways of teaching and learning' and to promote community and lifelong learning. About ten years ago, I was involved with Liverpool EiC as part of a national writing and training programme for learning mentors in secondary and primary schools across the country. The broad remit and funding enabled the two project leaders to produce something that was truly transformational at the time, and much of the material developed is still in use today.

CLCs were established under the EiC programme and were generally based in secondary schools with primary school satellites. It was acknowledged that reluctant learners would be more likely to be tempted by a course at their child's school, than by a more traditional and formal adult setting. Primary schools were seen as particularly important because so many parents/carers physically dropped their children off at school. Primary school newsletters contained details of the courses available and the timings were closely linked to parents being able to leave their children in school while they did the course. Crèches and toddler groups have also been an important feature of this form of adult education. If you remember, the computer tutor in my tour of the primary school in Chapter 1 was paid for her work in the primary school by the local EiC, although her contract of employment was with the local FE college. Funding was free for those who were not in employment and fairly minimal for those others.

The computer teacher I had was an excellent teacher, but I am not so sure that the vision of 'exploiting and testing new and innovative ways of teaching and learning' is always one of the main priorities of learning centres today. Certainly they have been strongly pressured to provide vocational courses, rather than non-vocational. This is a direct result of central government policies, which are keen to promote adult classes that will enable unemployed adults to build up marketable skills. This rather goes against the experience of those working in FE, who argue that reluctant adult learners may come in for an interesting non-vocational course – belly dancing, car maintenance, reiku for example, and then gain confidence to do a more vocational course. All the attendees at the computer class I followed were, like me, associated with the school and if the centre had not been so convenient would have been most unlikely to undertake the courses offered.

Network learning communities

Many student teachers go into schools that are part of NLCs. These were established in order to improve achievement through collaboration. This was for both pupils and educational professionals working in schools. Worrall and Noden (2006) provided a summary of evidence about the NLC to the NCSL. The researchers found:

1 There were 132 NLCs across England in 2005.
2 These involved 1,500 schools, 690,000 children and 43,000 teachers.
3 The average size of a network was eleven schools.
4 30 per cent of the networks were in the North-west, making it the region with the largest number of networks.
5 The networks all comprised secondary and primary schools.
6 Initially, the networks focused on raising standards of pupil achievement in language and literacy.
7 They also covered CPD for teachers. This included subject knowledge, curriculum knowledge, pedagogical knowledge, knowledge of learners, educational contexts, educational outcomes and self-knowledge.

Action-based research from some of the schools involved has been very positive about what has been achieved so far and provided case studies for 'adding value; closing the gap;

leadership and management learning in the networks and continuing professional development, including research'. Research was very much 'action based' and involved primary teachers looking at practice in their own classrooms or early years settings. Many of these researchers were able to bid for monies through a 'Best Practice' scheme. Unfortunately, this proved rather too popular and expensive to become a central government long-term commitment to funding school-based research. But, for a short time, it did enable classroom teachers to 'buy' a little bit of research time to enhance what they were already doing and inform their network schools about new developments.

Adult education

The CLCs and the NLCs really built on what many good schools had already been doing for a number of years. Both the initiatives gave schools a much greater profile and awareness of themselves as 'self learning communities'. Another aspect of schools as learning communities is linked with a much broader approach to adult education that had also grown out of what schools had already been doing.

In Chapter 1, when I made a tour of a primary school and met two adult tutors, one was my ECDL tutor, who took the weekly adult computer class at the primary school, and the other was a parent mentor, working with parents on a children's literacy project. Both tutors were employed by the LA and funded through a variety of different central government initiatives. The ECDL tutor was employed via the local CLC and FE college and the parent mentor by the FACE service. You will find differences in all authorities about the names of these adult education initiatives, but a visit to your LA website will give you a picture of where alternative education is taking place in our schools.

Activity/Thinking Task 1

Visit your LA website and identify adult education programmes that are taking place in local schools. During the summer term and early autumn term, local newspapers run advertisements for adult education courses and many FE colleges provide prospectus. This will give you an idea of the huge variety of courses that are taking place in schools, early learning centres, etc.

My own LA provides (among others):

- Family learning programmes in 80 per cent of its schools (involving 500+ parents last year).
- Twelve parent mentors in its northern NLC, which supports community involvement, parental involvement, family learning and adult education.
- Five foundation mentors who work across the LA in all schools to support parental involvement in the foundation.
- Home learning programmes, supporting parental involvement in schools.
- Community education classes in six secondary schools (all in the process of being rebuilt into learning centres), CLCs, libraries and outreach. (This is managed through the extended schools programme and provides IT, MFL, Arts and Craft, personal and

creative development. This covers approximately 2,500 learners each year, usually at night school. The courses are both accredited and non-accredited.)

- The voluntary sector is also involved and often uses schools as its base for activities such as skills for life, food hygiene, mentor training, floor laying and childcare.

Early invention programmes involving adult education

Sure Start

There are a number of early invention programmes for very young children. At the time of writing Sure Start is one of the best known. Claxton's research findings (see below) are linked with the need to support very young children with early experiences that will have a positive and sustained effect on their development as lifelong learners.

The Sure Start programme was a major, if sometimes controversial, central government initiative. It involved both children and their parents and was specifically aimed at those in extreme socially and economically deprived areas. This was backed by an ideology about raising aspirations and achievement in order to eradicate poverty. This was really ambitious and whatever criticism has been laid at the Sure Start door, its underlying principles to get children and their families out of the poverty trap, is inspirational and potentially life changing.

The aims for Sure Start outlined on the government website when it was first introduced, were more prosaic and linked with:

1 *providing increased availability of childcare for all children*: initially this was to be in socially and economically deprived areas at a subsidised rate, later to be at an economic rate (in areas not covered by Sure Start, the market was to determine the availability and cost of childcare);
2 *improving health and emotional development for all children*: through practice modelled in pre-school settings and in taught inputs to parents and carers;
3 *supporting parents*: as parents, and in their aspirations towards employment.

This intervention looked heavily weighted towards childcare as a means to getting people into employment, rather than creating lifelong learners for the children themselves. One key challenge was that in many of the targeted areas, employment prospects for unskilled parents and carers were usually very poorly paid and made little economic sense for those on welfare benefits. Indeed, the wages of a number of school-based employees, paid only in term times, would not cover the economic cost of childcare. Fortunately, good Sure Start centres and other early learning settings do provide some very exciting learning programmes for adults, which enhance the rather more utilitarian government programme of getting people back into the workforce. There has also been a real attempt to persuade fathers and male carers to take part, and some LAs specially employed male workers with a remit to do this.

Children's centres

These cover about 20 per cent of the most disadvantaged wards in England and incorporate similar early intervention programmes. They are aimed at providing integrated education care, family support and health services for children and their parents/carers. They are closely linked to Sure Start, since they cover much the same disadvantaged areas; but rather interestingly the government has committed itself to ensuring that there must be qualified teacher support in any children's centres. This does not necessarily mean an early years QTS practitioner must be employed by the children's centre, but these should also be able to draw on such expertise from local nursery and primary schools. The government also introduced a new qualification, the Early Years Professional (EYP). The aim is that by 2015 every early years setting, including full day care, will have one of these EYPs. They are expected to provide the following services to children under five and their families:

1   early education integrated with full daycare, including identification of those with SEN and disabilities;
2   parental outreach;
3   family support, including support for parents with SEN;
4   health services;
5   a base for childminders and a 'service hub' with the community for parents and providers of childcare services;
6   effective links with Jobcentre Plus, local training providers and further and higher education institutions;
7   effective links with Children's Information Services, neigbourhood nurseries, out-of-school clubs and extended schools;
8   management and workforce training.

Two children's centres I visited recently had cafés, both with Internet access. One was based within a brand new primary school, the other next door to a primary school. The cafés in both were working extremely effectively in attracting school staff, parents, carers and childminders involved with the primary schools and the centre. Also, the ability to be able to provide cheap, nutritious and healthy hot and cold food, was attracting members of the local community.

Home–school connections

This is the much more traditional link with parents that schools have had for many years. However, it has changed considerably over the past ten years and the changing role of the primary school in the community means that it will continue to change. The Internet cafes mentioned above involved some school staff and parents meeting on a very regular basis, and the use of e-mail has changed relationships in many schools.

Good relationships between the class teacher and parents do not just happen, they have to be worked on, and this is often harder if you have not had the experience of being a parent yourself. I was a great expert on parenting, until I became one myself!

It is useful to remember:

• Parents are the first and primary educators. They are also children's most important teachers. Research and common sense have shown that intelligence is heavily influenced by the experiences a child has in his or her first years, i.e. well before they enter school. Teachers can encourage parents to continue playing a critical role by reading to their children, taking them on visits, talking and listening with them, giving them opportunities to engage in creative activities and modelling self-discipline and task commitment.

- Parents need to feel their time is well spent, valued and useful. Formal contracts will never replace the friendly encouragement and support of a class teacher.
- Parents have important insights and understandings about their children and most really care about them.
- Schools and homes have shared goals. Parents and teachers are partners.
- All families have strengths, however oddly they may be constructed. Many family forms exist and are legitimate.
- Cultural differences are nearly always valid and valuable.
- Parents (and grandparents) have a wealth of talent, information, ideas, skills and hobbies to share. Parent instructors not only supplement the curriculum but also act as role models.
- Parents can learn new techniques.
- Communicate respect – through your tone of voice, choice of words, facial expressions and general courtesy. Keep to appointment times, however fascinating another discussion may be. Parents who are kept waiting feel under valued. This can also be dangerous. In my first year of teaching, a child climbed over a balcony and fell to his death because his parents had been delayed at a school open-evening for over an hour. This is also true at the end of the day, when children are going home. As a parent, nothing is more frustrating than dashing to school to find that the teacher delays the children coming out because the room is not tidy.

Parents as volunteers

Figure 17.1 sets out some of the types of work that parents are often asked, or volunteer to do. It is often through this process that parents become involved in looking at

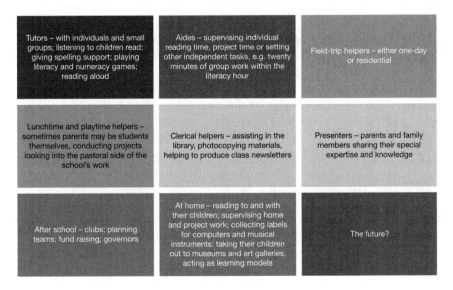

Figure 17.1 Parents as volunteers

educational opportunities for themselves and it certainly provides a wonderful opportunity for the proactive class teacher to encourage parents into further or higher education. It is personally deeply rewarding to persuade a parent who felt a school failure that they are bright and can do successfully what they could not do at school. A surprising number of mature student teachers come through this way.

A number of primary schools have a member of staff who is responsible for parental involvement in the school, and an increasing number of schools have special rooms for parents.

Parents evenings/days/conferences

1   Know the school policy and if possible track an experienced member of staff through an open event with parents.
2   Know the school policy and practice.
3   Be clear about the purpose of the meeting/open event/conference. It is much easier when you have the written report to discuss. It helps if you have a form to complete with the name of the child, the child's strengths and areas for development and suggestions for action at home and at school. The latter can then be agreed at the meeting.
4   Make a note of what parents/carers say to you with their permission. It shows that you value their views and wish to make a record of them.
5   Be sensitive – for the vast majority of parents, their children are the most precious people in the world. If you criticise or withhold praise, their own self-worth is questioned. Self-esteem for a parent can be closely linked to the child's progress and attainment in school.
6   Do not compare one family member with another and try to avoid agreeing with parents who do, or who have different gender-related models for their children.
7   Defuse a difficult situation by remaining calm yourself and asking parents to be seated. Let them talk first, so you can find out exactly what is the matter. If you are in the least worried, make sure another adult is present. Let the head teacher know what has happened and if you have been unable to resolve the problem record it on paper as soon as you can.
8   Do not surprise parents with a big problem. Make sure they are kept up-to-date with the progress the child is making. Ideally, regular reports and homework support this, but some children may withhold information from their parents – often for quite good reasons. Let parents know you have an open-door policy and a regular time for seeing parents.

Building multicultural partnerships

Cultural, class and language barriers can inhibit partnerships and interactions between home and school. Often this affects the children who would most benefit from closer understandings. Some schools work extremely hard at involving the whole community in the life of the school and have community rooms and support workers to ensure that the communities are truly welcomed. If this is not true of the school you are working in, here are a few pointers:

- Learn more about the children's cultures and backgrounds.
- Be aware of the inter-racial conflicts often present when families have fled from a war zone.
- Watch for hidden cultural differences – relationships between parent and teacher; male and female; time seen as a simultaneous process rather than linear; ambiguous statements made rather than a clear, explicit complaint; different forms of eye contact, looking down, rather than directly into another's face; a smile used to express confusion rather than pleasure.
- Make a checklist for parental involvement – this can include a place for people to meet informally within the building; an open, friendly reception area; somewhere to make a drink; defined policies regarding parental involvement in the school; policies regarding homework; communications between home and school, clear attractively presented and in the heritage languages represented by the school population; good communications between parents and teachers; local businesses and communities involved in the school; parents' opinions asked for and respected; all staff aware of cultural and language differences; parents in evidence in the school.

Ofsted has long taken an interest in parental involvement and Figure 17.2 shows some of the areas that have been noted, either formally in reports or informally in Ofsted feedbacks.

Figure 17.2 Ofsted and parental involvement

Activity/Thinking Task 2

What sort of provision is made for parental involvement in a primary school known to you? The most useful rule of thumb for parental involvement is whether you would feel comfortable as a parent volunteer in this school.

- Are parents planned for?
- Are their roles clear?
- Is there somewhere to put their coats and bags safely?
- Can they make a drink or heat up food for themselves?
- Does the school or one of its neighbouring learning communities run an in-service programme with regard to parental involvement?
- Do parents have a genuine role in decision making?
- Do class teachers make time to speak with parents?

Many of the factors involved with being a student visitor to a classroom are in evidence with parental and community involvement.

Preparing for lifelong learning

We have to be lifelong learners ourselves, but we also have to prepare our pupils (and their parents) for lifelong learning. In this chapter, we have already looked at just a few of the school-based initiatives linked with lifelong learning. In this section, we examine the work of Guy Claxton who has been involved with teaching strategies of learning how to learn – learning to learn, or L2L. Of course this also means for student teachers, that we need to explore how to teach effective learning skills to our pupils. Originally, Claxton worked with adults, but more recently he has piloted his materials successfully in schools. The Bibliography provides useful supportive reading.

BLP

Claxton's work on building learning power, is as important for those employed in schools and learning centres as it is for those who are the 'formal' learners – adults or children. The point is made several times in Claxton's book, that teachers are simply the 'lead learners' in primary schools and this carries through to the idea that schools are learning communities for a much wider catchment than those of statutory school age.

L2L

Claxton's work on building learning power is very much about the importance of identifying what makes an effective learner and how this can be developed. Much of his earlier work was linked with adult education and lifelong learning; often among those who had learnt failure from their own schooling.

Like many other actionbased researchers, Claxton and his co-workers audited what learners needed in order to L2L and then developed strategies to help them achieve these characteristics. This is all part of a programme about building up learning power for lifelong learning.

In order to L2L, the effective learner should have:

1   resilience
2   resourcefulness
3   reflectiveness
4   reciprocity.

Claxton calls these the four Rs of learning power and makes it quite clear that in order to develop learning power, educational professionals need to work on these four aspects of learners' learning. When we look at this in relation to schools as learning communities, the learners are of all ages and have very different learning experiences. As this book has made very obvious, even pupils are not a homogenous mass.

Table 17.1 identifies specific characteristics from each key skill.

1   *Resilience.* The first R of learning power involves learners learning to be resilient. The effective learner gets caught up in the pleasure of learning. Watch a four-year-old carefully absorbed in moving sand in small spoonfuls from one container to another, not being distracted by others coming to the sand tray or building blocks on the floor by them; watch them noticing and really getting a sense of the relative size of the containers, the quality of the sand, the tiny grains and the colour; note their ability to stick with a task. This makes a nonsense of the 'rule of thumb' concentration equation, which says you should only expect a child to have the concentration span in minutes of their age. So we should only expect a four-year-old to have a concentration span of four minutes. What sad and rather dangerous nonsense. How many of us have watched two-, three- and four-month-old babies spend fifteen or thirty minutes, trying over and over again to roll over and then, when they succeed in doing that, working at trying to roll back.

2   *Resourcefulness.* Let's take examples of resourcefulness with a slightly older child, remembering that none of these 4 Rs are age related and apply in different ways to all of us.

Table 17.1 The effective learner has . . .

Resilience	*Resourcefulness*	*Reflectiveness*	*Reciprocity*
Absorption	Reasoning and capitalising	Planning	Interdependence
Managing distractions	Questioning	Revising	Collaboration
Noticing	Making links	Distilling	Empathy and listening
Perseverance	Imagining	Meta-learning	Imitation

Questioning in the classroom situation is always rather a mute point, but there are often times when curriculum tasks in class do build on areas children are already interested in. The eight-year-old, who is about to embark on a history topic about the Ancient Egyptians, may already know a little bit about mummies and pyramids. Although, of course, the very word 'mummy' is deeply contextual when used in this sense. We would want the child to ask questions about what they are reading or being told; they may link to other learning they have done – for example making square pyramids in mathematics and finding Egypt on a map; they may imagine what it would be like to live in a warm, dry climate; be able to reason out why particular clothes were worn and lifestyles lived; they would be keen to look at resources such as books, pictures, CDs and DVDs on Ancient Egyptians.

3   *Reflectiveness.* This involves the learner in being able to work out their learning in advance. Obviously many learners need to be taught how to do this, and much of the work of the educational professional involves looking at how to teach children to plan their work in advance, monitor and adapt it along the way; draw out the lessons from experience and, finally, be able to understand the learning and yourself as the learner. The NNF and the NLS have shown particularly good models of this meta-learning, by encouraging teachers to think out their thoughts as they complete – for example – a piece of writing on the board, 'Shall I use this word or do I need a longer sentence?' or 'What sort of words would go best here?', and in mathematics requiring children to explain how they came to a particular answer. This meta-learning is particularly important in helping both the educational professional and the pupil to work out how misconceptions develop.

4   *Reciprocity.* This is linked very closely to Vygotsky's work on learning in social and cultural contexts. It involves pupils in being ready, willing and able to learn both alone and with others. It involves the delicate balance of being self-reliant and sociable; learning the complex skills of learning with others; getting inside others' minds and picking up others' habits and values – hopefully the positive ones.

Building up learning power

Claxton found that teachers can build up learning power, i.e. teach children to learn through a series of different professional skills; many of which we have already examined. His emphasis is very much on the lifelong aspects of these skills, not short-term strategies for raising SATs levels (see Table 17.2).

First, *explaining* – which as we all know from day-to-day living, is not as easy as it sounds. Remembering the mind-friendly framework from Chapter 7, we know that learners need to be in a positive state of mind before being able to even start on the type of learning that takes place through the formal curriculum. Here Claxton outlines how explaining involves telling students directly and explicitly about learning power. It involves making clear the overall purpose of the classroom; offering ongoing reminders and prompts about learning power; inviting students' own ideas and opinions on learning and giving direct information and practice about learning.

Orchestrating – involves selecting activities and arranging the learning environment. As we select curriculum-related tasks for pupils to do, so teachers need to choose activities that will help to develop the four learning Rs. These need to be built into the curriculum

Table 17.2 Building up learning power for lifelong learning

Explaining	Orchestrating	Commentating	Modelling
Informing	Selecting	Nudging	Reacting
Reminding	Framing	Replying	Learning aloud
Discussing	Target Setting	Evaluating	Demonstrating
Training	Arranging	Tracking	Sharing

tasks and not be seen as an additional extra. This is not always easy, although student teachers should be able to identify through detailed lesson-planning links with specific Rs. They certainly aid target setting for children with behavioural difficulties that are hindering their learning. Framing clarifies the intended learning behind specific activities and again links closely to much of the good practice seen in schools, where teachers set out child-speak objectives and ensure that pupils understand the purpose of the activity.

Target setting is also a familiar area to most of those working in schools. It is important that pupils, however young, are involved in their own target setting. As discussed earlier in this book, how many of us are happy about targets set for us without consultation. Setting targets also involves monitoring and the less confident the learner, the more important is the way in which targets are set and monitored. I tend to set targets for myself with fairly generous timeframes, so that I reach them, tick them off, and have time to move on to the next one before time. Then if anything happens, I have a bit of time to spare and feel less stressed. This does not of course always work, but when it does, it makes me feel better. Of course, perhaps if I had been good at ambitious target setting, I might be making mega bucks running a company! Claxton sees arranging as making use of displays and physical arrangements to encourage independent learning. The best examples of this are often found in the nursery, with picture and word labels on trays and great encouragement for independence. Ironically, this 'arranging' may fade as pupils work through school.

Commenting – involves conveying messages about learning power through informal talk and formal and informal evaluation. Nudging does not mean prodding pupils, but simply drawing an individual's attention towards his or her own learning; responding to his or her comments and questions in ways that encourage learning to learn; evaluating on difficulties and achievements in learning-positive ways and finally tracking learning by recording the development of students' learning power.

Finally, *modelling* – involves showing what it means to be an effective learner. As we saw earlier, learners need to see teachers modelling this 'commenting' behaviour. They need to see what it means. This is why successful teachers and other adult colleagues are genuinely learners and model this. This covers how they react to things they did not expect, such as questions that come out of the blue or when a fixed routine needs to be changed. Teachers have to show they can model good learning – not rushing around like a three-year-old, when a wasp flies in at the window, balking when a child is physically sick or has soiled themselves. Such modelling is often difficult, but it is essential.

Before trying to put some of these strategies into place, Claxton suggested that learners' current strengths and weaknesses as learners needed to be identified.

Activity/Thinking Task 4

Table 17.3 is a checklist adapted from Claxton's (2004) *Building 101 Ways to Learning Power*. It looks at indicators for resilience in adults and children. Decide where you fit on the resilience line – do you like a challenge? Of course it varies doesn't it, on how you feel, the time of day or night, the context in which the learning is taking place, the subject matter to be learnt and a lot of other variables? But these are some generic skills that involve us supporting our pupils to learn.

Table 17.3 Checklist for indicators for resilience for lifelong learning

Indicator	Yes	No	Comment
I like a challenge			
I'm not afraid of finding things hard			
I get really interested in learning and sometimes do not know what is going on around me			
I can make accurate descriptions and observations			
I am able to minimise negative distractions			
I can stick at things, even when they get difficult			

Pedagogic approaches

Table 17.4 comes from a free DfES (2004) publication for secondary teachers on *Pedagogy and Practice*. There are also three particularly good booklets, written for KS3, to extend your teaching repertoire – one on questioning, one on modelling and one on explaining. They may be aimed at secondary teachers, but in actual fact provide good (and free) support for teachers and other allied professionals at any stage. These all fit with Claxton's work and actually demonstrate how to do it.

Table 17.4 Pedagogic approaches

Direct	Inductive	Exploratory
Purpose To acquire new knowledge or skills	To develop a concept or process	To use, consolidate or refine skills and understanding
Key features A structured sequence, often beginning with whole-class work with modelling, demonstration or illustration. Typically this is followed by individual or group work. The sequence often ends with whole-class review	A structured set of directed steps. Pupils collect and sift information, then examine data. They construct categories, and generate and test hypotheses	Testing a prediction or hypothesis based on the understanding of a concept. Pupils decide what information to collect, obtain the data and analyse it
Examples Developing communications skills, such as using different writing text types; listening to argument; constructing sentences orally in French; in mathematics, drawing to scale; using a spreadsheet to model the impact of light intensity on plant growth	Generating spelling rules, e.g. when to use *-sion* rather than *-tion*; collecting visual and other information in order to understand the use of materials and processes to make a sculpture; assessing the usefulness of portraits as sources of historical information	Exploring the best method of making a light crispy batter; exploring the likely causes of flooding in a particular area; exploring the best method of removing grease from clothes
Key questions • How could you . . .? • Why am I doing this?	• Can you group these? • Can you see any pattern?	• What might affect . . .? • What possible reasons are there for . . .?

18 Integrated children's services, extended schools and other agencies

QTS Standards

1, 2, 3, 5, 6, 8, 9, 10, 15, 20, 21a and b, 30, 32, 33

Learning objectives

- to explore some of the current initiatives of extended schools;
- to examine and critique the government's policy on extended schools as part of the ECM agenda and the ECM agenda itself;
- to identify 'inclusion', 'equality' and funding issues within the extended schools strategy;
- to use PMI technique to evaluate the policy;
- to predict some of the possible implications for primary schools.

Chapter overview

This chapter looks at the changing role of schools in the context of integrated children's services. This is part of a much larger vision and programme to address social inequalities and provide a much better deal for children. This was partly triggered by the appalling life and death of Victoria Climbie in 2003. Out of this came the ECM agenda, followed by the 2004 Education Act. The chapter looks first at the extended schools provision and provides some activities for you to explore to gain some understanding of one of the most obviously school-related outcomes of the ECM agenda; it then looks in more detail at some other aspects of the ECM agenda that will have specific implications for primary teachers.

Extended schools

At the time of writing, the concept of the 'extended school' in the second half of the first decade of the twenty-first century is still uncertain. The government has been setting the agenda, with – in my view – some very traditional views about what is appropriate for young people, who have already spent over six hours in school. What is certainly true is that the government is expecting all schools to provide access to a 'core offer' of services, which includes wrap-around childcare provision for 364 days from 8 a.m. to 6 p.m. for school-age children. Initially, this was on a school-by-school basis, but this was quickly found to be impractical and it is developing into more of a cluster and specialist provision.

The teachernet website covers this topic well and provides some interesting background information about current provision from commissioned work on new extended schools. In 2005 researchers from BMRB Social Research found that one in ten schools provided the core offer of childcare or activities for school-age children during the school term time. Only two per cent of primary schools and less than one per cent of secondary schools provided the core offer all year round. By 2007, Beverley Hughes, the Minister for Children, Young People and Families was announcing that 5,700 schools were providing access to the core offer for extended schools. This accounted for almost one in four schools – a massive growth in provision.

The teaching unions made it very clear from the beginning that they supported the concept of extended schools as long as it does not 'place additional burdens on schools'. Hopefully, by the end of this chapter, you will be in a position to predict some of the possible implications for teachers as well as other allied educational professionals. In particular, the likelihood of new opportunities for educational professionals.

Activity/Thinking Task 1

Before reading or researching further write down what you think is meant by the term 'extended school'. Remember there is no right answer to this question.

Compare notes with:

1   a colleague;
2   someone employed in a school (if not the same as 1);
3   someone who is not in education.

What are the differences – if any – in their definitions, compared to yours?

Provision prior to the 2004 Education Act

- *Breakfast and after-school clubs.* These were variously run by different people including a surprising number of head teachers, who recognised it as a means of improving attendance. Many had done it for years. Also, schools ran breakfast clubs using learning mentors, teachers and other allied professionals employed by the school.
- *Mid-day clubs.* Teachers, other allied professionals employed by the school ran these and in some areas teacher-training students were used as part of their service learning commitment.
- *Bussing children/young people.* A school would provide transport to another school when post-school childcare was not available at their own school. Charities such as Save the Children, for example, had funded this sort of provision for ten or fifteen years in areas of high economic deprivation.
- *Holiday provision.* This provision was funded by LAs and charities and often held using school halls and grounds.
- *Adult provision.* This included parenting classes, basic skills provision.
- *Study support.* Booster classes and homework clubs for primary and secondary pupils were provided, run by schools themselves and often unfunded. Some LAs provided funded support in schools and libraries.

- *ICT facilities.* These were linked with several initiatives including *Success for All* and *Heading for Success* run by educational sections of football clubs.
- *Community sports programmes.* These were funded by schools, LAs and charities. They provided trained coaches for enhancing sports skills.
- *Pilot extended schools.* There was LA funding with some limited government support for these. One of our local, small church primary schools, for example, has provided extended services for several years. This has included adult education, study support ICT facilities and a community sports programme. The school had a community outreach worker and a social inclusion manager, who worked together. The school website (Our Lady Star of the Sea) is well worth a visit.

These initiatives provided the vision and framework for the extended schools programme.

Government vision for extended schools

As we saw in the previous chapter, effective change needs to be heralded with a vision, which the target change agents can 'buy into'. Extended schools are part of the government's vision for 'schools for the future' as well as a series of practical strategies to reduce/eradicate poverty. The three statements below represent different elements of this vision from senior government officials in post at the time.

> Each pupil should see him or herself as a member, not just of a specific school community, but of a wider learning community committed to his or her success.
>
> (Michael Barber, Chief Advisor on Delivery to the Prime Minister)

> In disadvantaged areas in particular, extended schools have the potential to transform lives. Our aim is to see more schools at the heart of their local community, providing learning and cultural experiences for all and offering help and support where it can be easily accessed.
>
> (Baroness Catherine Ashton, Minister for Sure Start,
> Early Years and Childcare, 2005)

> I want parents to shape how extended services develop in their child's school and I want schools to ask for their ideas . . . Extended schools will not only help children in their education, but also support hard working families to manage their home and work life.
>
> (Ruth Kelly, Education Secretary, 2005)

Barber states that children see themselves as part of a school community. You might like to question that in relation to the apparent difficulties that many secondary schools in urban areas are experiencing. It may be that those young people most at risk may be the most difficult to attract into extended schools. And there is nothing exceptionally new about seeing schools 'at the heart of the community'. In rural areas, schools have long been at the heart of the local community. The continuing existence of a 'village school' has often been identified as evidence that a particular village is in fact thriving. Closure of small rural schools has been seen as the death knell for a community. At the time of writing, there are planned closures and amalgamations of schools (primary and secondary) in many north-west LAs. Many of these are in heavily urban areas, where the child population has fallen. Nearly every proposed school closure and amalgamation is met with opposition from members of the 'local community' concerned about their 'community' school. So when the government states that it sees schools at the heart of the community, this is not a new idea. It is really only stating what is already the case. What perhaps is different is that not only will schools extend their role in childcare, but will have to draw on outside agencies to fulfil the requirements of the 'core offer'.

Baroness Ashton's statement has huge resource implications, as well as being a fairly deficit model for areas such as the one in which I live, where there are large inequalities in health and education. However, it is not all about money. One of the best definitions I have heard on poverty is that 'poverty is poverty of experience, poverty of opportunity and poverty of aspirations'. Replace the word poverty by disadvantage and the meaning is clear. So it is important that extended schools do something to widen children's and young people's experiences, opportunities and aspirations. On a sceptical day, I might ask myself why we seem to be failing to do that with some children between the hours of 9 a.m. and 3.30 p.m., when they attend compulsory schooling. Does 'extending' the time they spend in school necessarily 'extend' their experiences, opportunities and aspirations.

Ruth Kelly's point is an interesting one because it seems to miss out consultation with children. I recently went to listen to an input about a book project in an early excellence centre. The manager explained how they had consulted the under fours widely about what was wanted. New initiatives need to listen to children and young people, who after all are the ones for whom the initiative is aimed. Parents may be very keen on homework clubs, but young people may prefer some light relief from study.

Activity/Thinking Task 2

Visit the ECM website, which shows how the initiative for extended schools is linked with the overall strategy plan for childcare. Again, think about the implications for teachers and other educational professionals working in schools. Extended schools in one area will need to make different provision from those in another area, but you also need to question exactly what is meant by the term 'community' – geographical, cultural, social stratification. We all belong to a number of different communities. This 'community' element is complicated further because many of the public services have different catchment areas for their fieldworkers. Funding is also a key issue. It varies considerably and in the end 'extended schools' will have to be self-funding. It is difficult to see how high quality provision can be cheaply and economically bought in.

The core offer for the extended schools programme

- Wrap-round childcare provision from eight in the morning until six at night for all school-aged children. From 2008, provision is made for 'disadvantaged' children to have free access to these activities.
- Activities linked to the school curriculum and supportive of increased academic achievement.
- Menu of activities – sports, arts and crafts, drama, volunteering, music, business and enterprise.
- Parenting support opportunities, including family learning.

- Signposting services to enable swift and easy referral to specialised support services.
- Use of school facilities to support community involvement, e.g. adult learning.
- Quick access to community-based health and social care services – such as speech therapy, intensive behaviour support, sexual health, etc.
- Wider parental and community involvement with access to ICT, sports, mental health, adult learning and family support.

Note: The first three of these services have to be offered throughout the whole year, not just during term time.

Food for thought

An extended school is one that provides a range of services and activities often beyond the school day to help meet the needs of its pupils, their families and the wider community.

(DfES, 2005)

Looking at this very exciting initiative raises four major questions:

1 Who are the target groups?
2 Who will provide the operational services?
3 Who will provide the staffing and administration?
4 From where will come the long-term funding?

Activity/Thinking Task 3

Scan through the DfES booklet on *Extended Schools,* which is available online as well as being a free publication from the DCSF, and see if you can find the answers to the above questions.

My views are that the target group is very clear, but how the service will be funded, administered and served is unclear. Schools may for a short time put on activities, but in the end, if they are not cost effective they will be forced to take them off. I've certainly seen that with some breakfast clubs and also questioned the low cost value of a rather unhealthy breakfast of white toast with a bit of margarine. Qualified and experienced staff are also needed and should not come cheaply. The commercial sector is certainly becoming interested and small businesses, such as 'Kids Club' and 'High Hopes', have moved into offering to supply schools with a dedicated service tailored to their needs. I suspect that in the end the private sector will be running much of the extended schools provision. This will mean some interesting openings for allied educational professionals with a range of skills. It may in the longer term mean some imaginative opportunities for trained teachers who prefer to work with children and young people in other settings.

Case study: Knowsley LA

This is my own authority and is in the Merseyside conurbation. It has a very clear vision about extended schools and services that it shared with its school governors at their 2005 conference, namely that extended schools should:

1   ensure higher achievement for all its pupils;
2   increase the number of adult learners;
3   make more use of community schools and the development of full-service schools;
4   be effective, self-managing, learning organisations;
5   make schools the heart of the community;
6   join up services that work for local people.

A key factor in vision making is a charismatic speaker – ideally more than one. This conference had several, including the then Director of Education and several national names. Very little of the change literature (see Chapter 16) makes this point, but it is important. Visions have to be sold. Health and social care are already well integrated at the strategic level in the Borough and are increasingly integrated at the operational level. Joint appointments have been made over several years, budgets pooled and several new health and social care centres built and planned for school sites. But for me, it was (and continues to be) the goodwill and belief that this particular aspect of the integration of children's services was possible, as well as being needed, that was the most encouraging aspect of the vision. This too is likely to impact on the type of extended schools and services that will become available.

Visioning into action

1   The authority built on existing provision in schools.
2   It made further links between all those working with children and their families and carers.
3   It continued with its programme of full integration of health, social care and education services, including shared buildings and sites.
4   It reformed and revitalised the area partnerships.
5   It increased the number of schools working together.
6   It increased community awareness and involvement.

So the borough has already moved quite far towards provision. Ironically, this has been helped by its very disadvantaged population profile. This has attracted government funding to build up networks and services to iron out inequalities. Recently, for example, I visited a young carers unit, which gives support to children and young people with caring responsibilities. Many carers are in primary and secondary school, often with horrendous hidden responsibilities that affect their health and education. Close links with learning mentors in schools has helped schools to become aware of these invisible responsibilities, and young carers have an opportunity to meet with others, in a similar position to themselves, to socialise, have fun and have an opportunity to regain some of their childhood.

Again, there is no right answer to these questions. If you speak with head teachers, they are often unsure of the benefits of having children in school for ten hours. In particular, if they are expected to take the overall responsibility for them. Some heads see it as a good

Activity/Thinking Task 4

- What provision does your local primary school, or a primary school in which you work, make for pre- and post-school provision? What does it cost parents? How else is it funded? This may be on-site, but it may also be at another local school, sports or community facility. How close is the provision to the promise of 'wrap-around care'? Is it needed or wanted, by the school community? The numbers of pupils taking it up are a good indication of this. What sort of pre- and post-school childcare is available to the children in your class? How important is it for class teachers and their colleagues to know this?

- Use the PMI template to evaluate the whole initiative. Record all the positive, negative and interesting things about the extended schools initiative, taking into account equality and inclusion issues. Try for at least three separate points under each heading. Chapter 15, on thinking skills, provides the methodology of this means of evaluation and Table 18.1 provides the template.

Table 18.1 Evaluating the extended schools initiative using the PMI framework

Plus	Minus	Interesting
1		
2		
3		
Overall comment		

Try for at least three points under each heading.

way of attracting pupils to their school. For example, a head of a primary school with falling rolls told me that her main reason for running the pre- and post-school clubs was to ensure that pupils were not taken to other primary schools where they could have that service. For the moment, she was content to run the extended school provision at a loss, but could not continue this indefinitely.

Workforce remodelling and reform

Figure 18.1 provides an example of the staffing structure in one extended primary school provision that I visit. A charity is running it and provides a full daycare nursery from nought to four years; after-school clubs for children aged five to eleven and a holiday club, also for children aged five to eleven. All these are costed for parents and carers at well below economic cost. Their brochure claims that their staff are 'highly trained and have extensive experience in childcare'. I am not sure that this staffing structure reflects this because of its heavy dependence on students. What other issues come out of this surprisingly common way of staffing such provision? The ECM agenda has several provisions about improving staffing in the children's workforce by recruiting more high-quality staff into it; retaining high-quality personnel by offering better development and career progression; strengthening inter-agency and multi-disciplinary working and promoting stronger leadership and management.

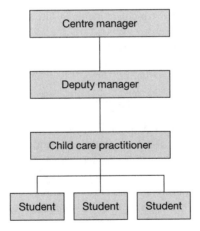

Figure 18.1 Staffing structure

Extended schools agenda within the 2004 Education Act

I am making the assumption in this section of the chapter that you are familiar with the 2004 Education Act, which followed up from the Laming Inquiry Report into Victoria Climbie's death and the ECM publications. If you go to the publications section of the everychildmatters website you will find all of these publications – plus many more – under the publications section. The website is run by the DCSF, but the publications are from a partnership of education, health and the Home Office. They are all free. If you prefer to have hard copies, these can be obtained from the DCSF publications unit.

We will review the Children's Act of 2004 and identify some of the key features of this and the ECM agenda directly. This area is changing rapidly. It is perhaps useful to think of it all as a massive pilot scheme, although central government and the LAs would probably not be too happy about it being described in this way.

The Laming Report

The Education Act and the ECM agenda comes from the horrific account of the death of one small, helpless child. For those of you who have not read Lord Laming's Report, Victoria was left by her parents with an aunt and uncle to have a better life in England. The report is an appalling read, noting that public services such as health, education and social care failed to do anything to help this child effectively. When I entered teaching in 1975, a similar case was in the papers. In this case the child was called Maria Colwell. Again, the subsequent inquiry showed that a significant number of public services, including education, health and social work were involved with Maria's family and many of them were unaware of what others were doing. During the twenty-seven years between Maria's and Victoria's deaths, many other children have been identified formally as being 'at risk' and like them have been failed by the very services set up to prevent the repeated occurrence of such neglect and abuse.

Local impetus

The Laming Report looked at the tip of the iceberg. The social deprivation figures, health, housing, etc. will be available for your own LA via the government statistics website. Here are a few figures from my own authority:

- total population 40,609;
- 254 looked-after children;
- 145 on child protection register (CPR);
- 430 children enduring mental illness;
- 2,699 reported incidents of domestic abuse (although these may not involve children directly, they may be party to watching a parent being abused);
- 63 per cent of under five-year-olds with dental decay (most caused by neglect);
- 18.3 per cent of girls and 8.8 per cent of boys aged eleven upwards smoke;
- just under 25 per cent of pregnant mothers smoke.

Note how virtually none of this data comes from the education section and how unlikely it would be that educational professionals such as teachers and teaching assistants would be aware of these sort of statistics. One of the intentions of the ECM agenda is to ensure that data is more widely shared and strategies co-ordinated. Just look at that appalling figure for dental decay in the under fives for example.

The ECM vision

This vision encompasses:

- a radical improvement in the opportunities and outcomes for all children from nought to nineteen;

- bringing about systematic change in order to:

  - build services around the child, young person and family;
  - support parents and carers;
  - develop the workforce, changing culture and practice;

- and to integrate:

  - universal and targeted services;
  - services across the age range nought to nineteen.

As you know, a vision needs to be actionable, the initial responses have been built up at strategic and operational level since 2003. This is not just about avoiding another Victoria Climbie tragedy, it is about improving life chances for all children. For the first time, the ECM has defined childhood as being from birth to nineteen, i.e. well over the age of majority.

Variable strategic progress to date

Table 18.2 shows the progress so far of the legislative foundation created through the 2004 Education Act. This happened at an extremely fast pace and testifies to the determination to change and improve effectiveness of existing practice. Most LAs had already instigated changes well before the 2004 Act was in place.

My experience is that the school's inspectorate, Ofsted, has been very successful in making ECM an important issue for inspection. Certainly, schools documentation at the time of writing is full of evidence about how each area is addressed and the formal Ofsted report – at the moment – has a section for reporting back on this. My only proviso is that in short inspections I am not sure how much an inspecting team can actually see. Their evidence has to draw heavily on what the school has already provided in its documentation; in particular the SEF.

Operational progress

The strategic aims of the ECM agenda have to be made effective through change at operational level. This was visioned through six different strategies. It is really these six strategies that, in varying degrees, affect those working in schools. And none of them can be effectively achieved overnight. This process will take time, funding and political continuity and will.

1   *Increased multi-agency* – working through panels, teams and services. This requires strong local and effective networks, where meetings are well run and seen as effective by those who attend them. It also requires the work release of those who really know the children, rather than a written report handled by the regular 'meeting attender'.

2   *CAF* – pre-assessment checklist shared by all those involved, a process for undertaking a common assessment and use of a standard form to record this.

3   *Common core of skills and knowledge* – this will take time. The framework, which was set up in 2005 and revised in 2007, has some useful materials that can be found on the everychildmatters website. They involve skilling-up those working in the children's workforce in effective communication; knowledge of children and young person

Table 18.2 ECM agenda – progress so far

Legislative requirement	Progress so far
Children's Commissioner	Appointed and independent on central government, i.e. not a political appointee
All involved with children have a duty to co-operate	No choice, LA and other public and private services have very effectively briefed staff. Staff and students in training also briefed. Issues with amount of time given on courses and updating of information
LA have duty to safeguard and promote welfare of children	As above
Duty to set up Local Safeguarding Children's Board	Established
Provision for indexes or databases to enable better sharing of information	Moving slowly for both IT and ethical reasons. Easier within an area than nationally. Yet some of the most vulnerable children need the national profile
Single Statutory Children and Young People's Plan	All authorities have this in some format, should be available on website
Director and Lead Member for Children's Services	Nearly all LA's have appointed an Executive Officer at a very senior level as Director for ICS. In many cases this would have been the former Director of Education, but many are from other related professions. The lead member is a Councillor and this is a political appointment from the leading political party in power
Joint Inspection Framework/Joint Area Reviews (JARs)	In place
Provisions on foster care and private fostering	In place – but concern in this very private area is challenging to turn into action
Duty to promote educational achievement of looked after children	Stated objective by all LAs and educational institutions, but outcomes are still poor. Made worse by numbers of looked after children steadily rising
An Outcomes Framework – covering outcomes for being healthy, staying safe, enjoying and achieving, making a positive contribution and achieving economic well-being	Very effective and simple chart produced, covering all five areas, well distributed and good initial briefings. These will need to continue as changes are made in practice and in relation to variations of circumstances in different areas. Heavily dependent on the effectiveness of communications in authorities
Cross-government change programme	Established formally, this will take several years to be operationally effective; particularly with database issues
National framework for local change programmes	As above

development; safeguarding and promoting welfare of the child; supporting transitions; multi-agency working and sharing information.

4   *Information sharing* – supported by the will to share information; central government provision of sharing good practice, toolkits, protocols, staff training, forms, etc. The sharing of really effective and useful information via ICT is likely to be slow. Just look at the controversy that the proposal to have identity cards has produced. In addition, individual data about children and their families is vulnerable to issues such as national IT capability, Freedom of Information Act and ethical considerations.

5   *Creation of a lead professional* – for children and young people with multiple needs to ensure professional involvement is rationalised, co-ordinated and communicated and guidance provided. The pattern for this seems unclear at the moment, in the past a very senior social worker took on this responsibility for all children as '*guardian ad litem*'. This raises issues about how personal the service can be and the general access that vulnerable children have to trained practitioners.

6   *Workforce changes in schools* – this is essential and has been taking place for many years. Schools are recognised as an essential part of the wider agenda in achieving the outcomes for the ECM agenda. There are more people working in schools than ever before, including well over half a million support staff.

Implications for student teachers

1   Be aware of the changing relationships between professionals in health, social care and education.

2   If possible track the work of another professional working with children and families outside the school setting.

3   Enjoy and learn from the available CPD implications of having greater understanding of the work of those directly involved in integrated services.

4   Develop an awareness of the relevance of the growing legislation concerning the development and well-being of children.

Activity/Thinking Task 5

Visit the everychildmatters website and examine the CAF form. Download it and fill one in for a child you know. What sort of issues might arise as a result of another professional filling in this form. For example, as a primary teacher I may feel fairly confident about looking at the straightforward educational needs such as basic reading skills, motivation to learn, ability to concentrate, but I would need training to make assessments linked with mental health and specialist learning needs. Hopefully, the common core of skills and knowledge for the children's workforce will support this sort of extended professional knowledge.

The future

Learning objectives

- to draw up a career plan;
- to market yourself.

Career plan

This involves investing in yourself. Most professional educators invest in their careers and this helps both the children they teach as well as themselves.

Activity/Thinking Task 1

Career evaluation life-line: Imagine your life is a line. Draw it on a piece of plain paper. It can be any line you like – straight, curved or diagonal. Mark where you think you are. Make a list of some of the things you want to do before you reach the end of your lifeline. This can include paid work, non-paid work and personal aims.

Simple action plan. Table F1 provides a simple action plan for you to reflect on strategies you could use to reach three of your key goals. It is designed to help you identify the goals you wish to reach, or changes you may want to make, at work and/or in your personal life. Make sure:

- that you start with a verb for your own goals/targets;
- that the action starts with a verb;
- that the goal is posed in a positive way.

It is useful to do this sort of activity with a colleague, so you can discuss action points, achievable goals and realistic timescales. A personal action plan is different from the formalised plan that you complete after you have finished your course. Unlike the induction plan it is private and can be related to your own needs and aspirations. It is also

Table F1 Simple action plan

Goals/targets (at least 4)	Action	Challenges	Time scale

useful to research what is available to you by looking at the TDA website. Opportunities in teaching are expanding all the time and this site will keep you updated.

In order to reach your goals – indeed any goals – you will require some skills. Many of these skills you will have already developed in terms of being an effective class teacher, but may need to be extended into other areas of your life.

Assertiveness

The implementation of a career plan requires assertiveness – at home as well as at work. There are many situations, when we 'swallow' our own feelings and stay silent, even when we feel very angry inside. Being assertive is one way to stop this inner anger, which is destructive. It is destructive to ourselves, our families, our work colleagues and the children in our classrooms who watch and learn. One way of looking positively at assertiveness is to compare it with being aggressive and being passive.

- *Being aggressive*. This means getting your own way at the expense of other people, putting them down, making them feel small, incompetent, foolish, worthless or tricked. Humour can, and often is, used in an aggressive way. Can you think of someone who has treated you in this way? Aggressive behaviour by a line manager is now recognised for being what it is – bullying. Several of the teaching unions as well as the Trades Union Congress, have identified bullying as a key problem and have set up helplines. Increased stress on managers can make them bully their staff. Through assertive behaviour you can avoid being bullied in most cases.

Table F2 The language of action

	Passive	*Assertive*	*Aggressive*
Verbal	'I'm sorry'	'I believe . . .'	Interrupting
			'You're only . . .'
Non-verbal – body language	Covering mouth with hands	Physically at ease	Infringing others' body space
			Finger-pointing

- *Being passive*. This means ignoring your own and your children's interests, needs and goals. It often means putting up with a situation that makes you very angry and burns you up inwardly.
- *Being assertive*. This means being honest with yourself and with others. It means being able to say what you want, need or feel, but not at the expense of other people. It means being self-confident, positive and understanding of other people's points of view and being able to behave in a rational, adult way.

Table F2 above provides some verbal and non-verbal examples.

Marketing yourself to find your first appointment

As a governor of two primary schools I have worked through hundreds of application forms for posts and these are just some of the points I think are important. All panels are different and panellists often disagree with each other, particularly after going through 120 applications as I have done on more than one occasion.

This involves knowing yourself. The best way of doing this is to write a profile of yourself, for yourself to give you a clear picture of your strengths and areas for development. If you are applying for a teaching post, make sure that you cover all the key QTS standards that a school governing body will look for, and if you are applying for a specific post ensure that you make your profile fit the school's requirements. Try to identify what you have that other candidates do not have. Scour every corner of your life for examples of teamwork, the use of persuasive skills, leadership, verbal and written communication skills, technological capability and general teaching awareness.

Golden rules of job hunting

Round 1: The paperwork

- *Do your research*. Find out about the school, LA and current issues in primary education. There is plenty of information on LA and school websites that give a real flavour of school philosophy, values, organisation, inspection reports and test results.

- *Spend time on the paperwork.* Each application needs to be distinctive. As a governor I've been on the receiving end of applications with the school wrongly named and no links made with what we're looking for. This is also true for LA pools, make sure that you make your application specific to the LA. Their website will help as will a visit to the government statistics site.
- *Take care about the bureaucracy.* Follow it to the letter. I have been at shortlisting sessions where forms that were sent to the school instead of the LA were dismissed because the candidate had not read the instructions.
- *Check completed paperwork.* Do this with at least one other person. Spelling and grammar mistakes are unforgivable and put the application straight into the 'No' pile. Avoid too many 'I's' at the start of paragraphs and try to cut up the text, for example with a couple of bullet points. Some schools are happy with a good handwritten form. But today many interview panellists would interpret it as someone who was computer illiterate. The overall presentation needs to demonstrate good computer skills.
- *Notify your referees.* Ensure your referees are aware that they have been named as referees and know enough about you to provide an enthusiastic and appropriate report. Referees appreciate an up to date CV and some may even ask you to draft your own reference. Ideally, one should be a head teacher of a school you have worked in.

Letter of application/personal statement

- Don't repeat the information that appears on your form.
- Provide an opening gambit that attracts attention. 'My aim as a teacher is to draw on my own enthusiasm for primary education in order to engage pupils in learning about the world around them.' 'Since being in school I have thrived on the day-to-day challenge of working with young learners and am committed not only to pupils but to the corporate life of the school.' Don't just repeat the details of the job you're applying for.
- Be positive and unconditional. 'I am sure that I will be an effective teacher' – this sounds as if you are not at the moment.
- Avoid meaningless statements such as 'I feel . . .', 'I believe . . .', 'I like working with children'. No good saying 'I am enthusiastic and lively' if your paperwork doesn't reflect it. Match the person specification that comes with the application form and post details.
- Avoid being negative about any school or course. As governors we want positive people in our school.
- Ensure the final paragraph – like the opening gambit – provides the flavour of who you are and why we would be mad not to interview you.

The CV

There are many different CV templates and you are probably best to pick out the one that best suits you. It needs to include:

- *Name and address.*
- *Telephone numbers.* Mobile and home. This is extremely important as a school may phone you at short notice.

- *E-mail address.* Avoid providing one that may offend or show indication of immaturity, e.g. 'camel'; 'sexy blonde'; (both true).
- *Date of birth.* The 2006 anti-discrimination legislation stated that forms should no longer contain a date of birth. However, it is still very easy to work out age by the rest of the career history.
- *Nationality and marital status.* Your choice, if you think you are offering something the school may want.
- *Education.* Start from current education and work backwards. You can also save space if you need to by including the qualifications alongside the education establishment:

    - 2008–9 Greenfields University – PGCE/BA/QTS expected June 2009.
    - 2000–3 Urban City College – BA in English Language and Literature (First class).

- *Qualifications.* If you have really fantastic qualifications from GCSE onwards, I would have them in a special qualifications section with all the As. They will stand out more.
- *Teaching experience.* Make this brief. Put in your main school attachments and block experiences in terms of age range taught, type of school, etc. Again, work backwards, most recent experience comes first.
- *Other relevant experience.* Include other experience in school and also if you have worked with children in other formal settings such as health or social care. This provides useful experience for the integrated children's agenda. If you have had experience of work in other situations that has provided you with specific skills, say this with the skills:

    - 1995–2000 BT Clerk of Works – good understanding of practical applications of technology; working with the public and in co-ordinating a small team.

- *Interests and activities.* Include anything that might be useful in school or as an after-school club. Avoid 'socialising' as a leisure activity!
- *Referees.*

Round 2: The interview process

Preparation

Many primary schools now have a very rigorous 'interview' process. This is particularly true in areas where there are far more candidates than jobs. You may be invited to see around the school before/after you have applied. If not, you need to invite yourself. It looks good, even if the response is negative. Most schools do this in groups, some of which can be quite large, e.g. thirty on Monday. This is a pre-interview and you need to be dressed appropriately and demonstrate a few of those skills that you have stated you have, without dominating the group. Note and acknowledge the children and other adults working in the school. The woman sitting in a corridor with a child may turn up on the interviewing panel as a parent governor. Before going on the school tour, do a placement analysis as you would do for a school practice. Look round the local neighbourhood, identify where local services are – clinics, shops, leisure facilities, libraries, etc. An increasing number of schools are on multi-agency sites, so make sure you know their purpose. This of course makes good sense to do prior to filling in an application form.

Nature of interview

The following are just some of the tasks interview candidates have been asked to undertake:

- Visit the school prior to interview with a prepared lesson and then teach it and evaluate it.
- Prepare a short presentation on a named current issue, e.g. the ECM agenda.
- Read a story to a sub-group of governors and then explain how it would be used with children.
- Provide a portfolio to evidence the width and breadth of their expertise – photographs of work, fieldtrips, residential, displays, example of a lesson plan with related assessment, evaluation and annotated children's work. Ideally, the lesson needs to have a formal positive evaluation by someone else attached as well.
- Out-tray exercise – now that all class teachers are expected to be team leaders, this exercise is seen as a means of exemplifying how individuals deal with prioritising and time management.
- Role-play.
- Formal interview – this includes the 'informal talk' used by many heads, when they wish to fill a short-term gap such as that caused by sudden sickness. Make no mistake, it *is* a proper interview.

Before the interview

Read the job description fully and convince yourself that you fulfil just what is needed. Look at how you could evidence this in the formal interview. Do not assume that because you have had a school placement in the school, that the job is yours. Some schools interview students as a matter of courtesy to give them interview experience. Ask yourself potential questions in front of the mirror. If possible ask someone who sits on an appointment panel in school to interview you. Decide what you are going to wear. Be safe and traditional – suit for men and something even an ancient granny would approve of for women. Avoid showing too much flesh – it is not a night out. Dress to look the part and make sure you try the outfit on before the interview, so you feel comfortable.

All student teachers should be a member of at least one teaching union or association. Membership is free and provides you with the opportunity for free legal advice. Employment issues are changing constantly and you need to be quite sure that you understand what is being offered – fixed-term contract, temporary contact, permanent contract, job share, part-time. Consult the professional associations and unions if you are in any doubt.

If you are failing to get as far as the interview stage in a number of posts, get some other people to read your application who know how schools work. If you are unsuccessful at interview you are usually provided with some feedback. If this is not forthcoming – ask. You have nothing to lose.

During the interview

Opinions are divided on whether you walk in and shake hands. Usually you are shown in and introduced to each of the panel. Their role often indicates the types of question they are likely to ask. A teacher governor may well ask about curriculum interests and expertise. A parent might ask about homework, discipline and control. Teacher trainers on the interview panel may ask you about your course. So avoid saying you learnt everything in the classroom. Value all the questions and answer them with respect. Establish eye contact, it is usually best to answer mainly to the person who has asked the question, but to try to include the rest of the panel as well. Don't just relate to the person on the panel who you think is the most important.

The questions

A school interview panel will include the head teacher, governors (e.g. parent, foundation, LA, community, teacher, allied professional) and possibly a representative from the LA. A LA pool panel is likely to be subdivided into a number of smaller panels and contain a head teacher, governor and LA representative. The opening remarks will probably be ice-breakers to put you at ease, e.g. 'Tell us about your course'. You can't tell them everything so be selective. Choose the relevant areas. Interviewers almost always want to know 'why' (e.g. 'Why did you take that course?'; 'What were you doing between 2004 and 2007?'; 'Why did you re-take your A-levels?'; 'Why did you decide to quit being a senior nursing manager to go into teaching?'; 'Why have you applied to our school/this LA?'). Be sincere, indicate you know something about the authority/school. Faith schools will ask about your own faith and about RE.

Some examples of questions you may get include:

1   Tell us about your experience in school (ages taught, where, kind of area, some aspect you think was particularly successful).
2   What kinds of learning experiences do you think are important for foundation/KS1/KS2 children?
3   How would you organise your classroom/nursery? (give examples).
4   How do you know the children are learning and developing through these provisions (AfL).
5   How would you promote good discipline in the classroom? (link first with motivation, before moving on to following school procedures and your own personal strategies).
6   What is your experience of SEN/EAL within mainstream?
7   How can parents be involved in their children's learning?
8   What experience have you had of leading a class/nursery team?
9   Give examples of records you have kept?
10 What current issues in education do you feel are most significant for primary learners today?

At the end

To mark the end of the interview you should be given a chance to ask any questions you have. You could say (and as an interviewer I welcome this response) 'All the questions I had, have now been answered', but this may be the opportunity to clear things up. Avoid asking questions at this stage about pensions, school holidays or other conditions of employment that do not relate directly to the responsibilities you have applied for. The teaching unions will have the information on this. However, now that the range of schools is widening, you do need to check up on contractual issues before accepting the post. Some schools do not pay the union agreed rates.

Sometimes, you may be asked if there was any question that the panel had not asked for which you had a wonderful reply. This gives you a 'quick' opportunity to include some key aspect you had not been asked about. You may want to ask about induction in the school and arrangements to support you through your first year in teaching. Take care, recently we interviewed someone who sounded as if she needed so much support we could not cope.

Finally, you are likely to be asked if you are still interested in the post. If you realise at some stage during the day that the post is not what you want, this is your chance to withdraw tactfully.

Acceptance

Once you have accepted a post a legal contract immediately exists on both sides, even if there is nothing in writing. It is quite unacceptable and unforgivable to decline the post later. You must also withdraw all other applications that you have made.

And now the future is yours.

Bibliography

1 Understanding primary schools today

Campbell, A. and Fairbairn, G. (2005) *Working with Support in the Classroom*. London: Paul Chapman.
DfES (1999) *Excellence in Cities* (EiC), London: HMSO.
DfES (2003) *Every Child Matters*. London: HMSO.
Hayward, A. (2001) *Good Practice Guidelines for Learning Mentors*. Notttingham: DfES.
Hughes, P. (2005) 'Learning Mentors in Primary Classrooms and Schools' Chapter 4 in Campbell, A. and Fairbairn, G. (eds) *Working with Support in the Classroom*. London: Paul Chapman.
TDA (2003) 'Raising Standards and Tackling Workload'. Available online at www.tda.gov.uk/support.aspx.

2 Teachers in a changing role

Hughes, M. (2006) *And the Main Thing is Learning*. Cheltenham: ETS.
TDA (2007) *Standards for Qualified Teacher Status*. London: TDA. Available online at www.tda.gov.uk/partners/ittstandards/guidance_08/qts.aspx.

3 Learning from children

Blakemore, S. and Frith, U. (2006) *The Learning Brain: Lessons for Education*. Oxford: Blackwell.
Central Advisory Council for Education (1967) *Children and their Primary Schools*. London: HMSO (commonly known as the Plowden Report). Also available online at www.dg.dial.pipex.com/documents/plowden.shtm.
Claxton, G. (2005) *Building Learning Power*. Bristol: TLO.
DfES (2007) *Making Great Progress*. Nottingham: DfES.
Farrell, M. (2003) *Understanding Special Educational Needs*. London: Routledge Falmer.
Gardner, H. (1993) *Multiple Intelligences: The Theory in Practice*. New York: Basic Books.
Hughes, P. (1991) *Gender Issues in the Primary School*. Leamington: Scholastic.
Jones, P., Moss, D., Tomlinson, P. and Welch, S. (2008) *Childhood: Services and Provision for Children*. London: Pearson.
National Research Council US (2000) *How People Learn*. Washington: National Academy Press.
Palmer, S. (2006) *Toxic Childhood*. London: Orion.
Pritchard, A. (2005) *Ways of Learning: Learning Theories and Learning Styles in the Classroom*. London: Fulton.
Robb, J. and Letts, H. (1997) *Creating Kids Who Can Concentrate*. London: Hodder & Stoughton.
Robb, J. and Letts, H. (2003) *Creating Motivated Kids*. London: Help Yourself.
Sebba, J., Brown, N., Galton, M., James, M. and Steward, S. (2007) *An Investigation of Personalised Learning: Approaches Used by Schools*. Nottingham: DfES.

Smith, A. and Call, N. (2000) *The Alps Approach*. Stafford: NEP.
Smith, M.K. (2002) '"Howard Gardner and Multiple Intelligences": The Encyclopedia of Informal Education'. Available online at www.infed.org/thinkers/gardner.htm.

4 Establishing a safe and purposeful learning environment

Education Department Western Australia (1997) *First Steps Writing Programme: Writing Resources Programme*. Perth: EDWA.
Rose, S., Lewontin, R. and Kamin, L. (1987) *Not in Our Genes: Biology, Ideology and Human Nature*. London: Penguin.
Rosenthal, R. and Jacobsen, L. (1968) *Learning to Teach in a Primary Classroom*, Chapter 2. London: Routledge.
Smith, A, and Call, N. (2001) *The Alps Approach Resource Book*. Stafford: NEP.
Thornton, L. and Brunton, P. (2005) *Understanding the Reggio Approach*. London: Fulton.

www.teachernet.gov.uk/wholeschool/healthandsafety/.
www.rospa.com/news/index.htm.
www.bsf.gov.uk/.

5 Approaches to learning

Arnold, C. and Yeomans, J. (2005) *Psychology for Teaching Assistants*. Stoke on Trent: Trentham Books.
Bandura, A. (1977) *Social Learning Theory*. New Jersey: Prentice Hall.
Child, D. (2007) *Psychology and the Teacher*. London: Continuum International Publishing Group.
DfES (2007) *Statutory Framework for the Early Years Foundation Stage*. Nottingham: DfES.
Dunn, R. and Dunn, K. (1972) *Practical Approaches to Individualising Instruction*. New Jersey: Prentice Hall.
Fetsco, T. and McClure, J. (2004) *Educational Psychology: An Integrated Approach to Classroom Decision*. Boston, MA: Allyn & Bacon.
Kolb, D. (1984) *Experimental Learning: Experience as a Source of Learning and Development*. New Jersey: Prentice Hall.
LEP (2003) *Learning Mentor Training: Module 4*. Liverpool: DfES.
Nottingham Andragogy Group (1983) *Towards a Developmental Theory of Andragogy*. Nottingham: Nottingham Department of Adult Education.
Pound, L. (2005) *How Children Learn*. Wiltshire: Step Forward Publishing.
Robb, J. and Letts, H. (2003) *Creating Motivated Kids*. London: Help Yourself.
Smith, A. and Call, N. (2001) *The Alps Approach Resource Book*. Stafford: NEP.
Tracy, B. with Rose, C. (1995) *Accelerated Learning*. London: Simon & Schuster Audio.
Wood, D. (2004) *How Children Think and Learn*. Oxford: Blackwell Publishing.

6 Personalised learning, motivation and implications for planning

Beadle, P. (2007) 'Fiddle Around, Win Nothing' in *Guardian* 17 July 2007.
Becta (2007) *Learning Platforms and Personalised Learning: An Essential Guide*. Coventry: Becta.
Clare, John D. (2004) 'Differentiation'. Available online at www.greenfield.durham.sch.uk/differentiation.htm.
DfES (2004a) *A National Conversation About Personalised Learning*. Nottingham: DfES.
DfES (2004b) *The Five Year Strategy for Children and Learners*. Nottingham: DfES.
DfES (2007c) *Statutory Framework for the Early Years Foundation Stage*. Nottingham: DfES.

Kohn, A. (2001) 'Reasons to Stop Saying "Good Job!"' in *Young Children* 56(5): 24–8.

LEP (2000) *The Nature of Children's Learning – Module 4, Learning Mentor Training Pack*. Liverpool: DfES.

NLP Comprehensive (1993) *NLP The New Technology of Achievement*. London: Simon & Schuster Audio.

Prochaska, J., Norcross, J. and Diclemente, C. (1994) *Changing for Good*. London: Morrow.

Raveaud, M. (2005) 'Hares, Tortoises and the Social Construction of the Pupil: Differentiated Learning in French and English Primary Schools' in *British Educational Research Journal* 31(4): 459–79.

Robinson, P. and Dakers, J. (2004) *Personal Learning Plan Programme 2002–4 Evaluation*. London: National Literacy Trust Research Database.

www.gifted.uconn.edu/siegle/epsy373/Tomlinson.htm.

www.fctel.uncc.edu/pedagogy/basicscoursedevelop/Bloom.html.

7 Planning for mind-friendly learning

Caviglioli, O. and Harris, I. (2001) *Mapwise*. Stafford: Network Continuum Press.

Finn, G. (2007) *The Heart of the Dales*. London: Michael Joseph.

Greenhalgh, P. (2002) *Reaching Out to All Learners*. Stafford: Network Continuum Education.

Pollard, A. (2002) *Reflective Teaching*. London: Network Continuum Press.

Pollard, A. and Tann, S. (2004) *Reflective Teaching in the Primary School*. Cassell.

Smith, A. and Call, N. (2001) *The Alps Approach Resource Book*. Stafford: Network Continuum Press.

Tracy, B. with Rose, C. (1995) *Accelerated Learning*. London: Simon & Schuster Audio.

8 Emotional health and learning

Call, N. (2003) *The Thinking Child*. Stafford: Network Continuum Education Press.

Corrie, C. (2003) *Becoming Emotionally Intelligent*. Stafford: Network Continuum Press.

Dann, J. (2002) *Emotional Intelligence in a Week*. London: Hodder Arnold.

DfES (2007) *Social and Emotional Aspects of Learning*. Nottingham: DfES.

DfES, DH (2004) *Every Child Matters*. Nottingham: DfES.

Fox, G. (1998) *A Handbook for Learning Support Assistants*. London: Fulton.

Goleman, D. (1996) *Emotional Intelligence*. London: Bloomsbury.

Greenhalgh, P. (2001) *Reaching Out to All Learners*. Stafford: Network Continuum Education Press.

LEP (2003) *Learning Mentor Training: Module 4: Booklet Two – Promoting Personal Growth and Change*. Liverpool: EIC and DfES.

Maslow, A. (2000) 'Hierarchy of Basic Needs' in Carlson, N., Buskits, W. and Martin, N. (eds) *Psychology: The Science of Behaviour*. London: Pearson.

Mosley, J. (2006) *Step-by-Step Guide to Successful Circle Time for SEAL*. Wiltshire: Positive Press.

Smith, A. (2002) *The Brain's Behind It*. Stafford: NCE

Smith, A. and Call, N. (2000) *The Alps Approach*. Stafford: NEP.

9 Behaviour management and discipline

Ayers, H. and Gray, F. (1998) *Classroom Management*. London: Fulton.

Bandura, A. (2001) 'Social Cognitive Theory' in *Annual Review of Psychology* 52(1): 1–26.

Brophy. J. and Evertson, C. (1976) *Learning from Teaching*. Boston, MA: Allyn & Bacon.

Canter, L. and Canter, M. (1992) *Assertive Discipline* (updated 1996, 2001, 2002, 2007). Santa Monica, CA: Lee Canter Associates.

Cowley, S. (2006) *Getting the Buggers to Behave*. London: Continuum International Publishing Group.

Hoskyn, M. and Swanson, L. (2000) 'Cognitive Processing of Low Achievers and Children with Reading Disabilities' in *School Psychology Review* 29: 102–19.

Kounin, J. (1970) *Discipline and Group Management in Classrooms*. New York: Holt, Rinehart & Winston.

Lee-Corbin, H. and Denicolo, P. (1998) *Able Children in Primary Schools*. London: Fulton.

Palmer, S. (2006) *Toxic Childhood*. London: Orion.

Purkey, W. and Schmidt, J. (1990) *Invitational Learning for Development*. Ann Arbor, MI: University of Michigan.

Robb, J. and Letts, H. (2003) *Creating Motivated Kids*. London: Hodder & Stoughton.

Rogers, B. (2006) *Classroom Behaviour*. London: Paul Chapman.

Rudolf, D. (1989) *Children: The Challenge*. Boston, MA: Dutton Books.

www.criminology.fsu.edu/crimtheory/bandura.htm.

10 Special children and inclusion

DfEE, QCA (1999) *The National Curriculum*. London: DfEE, QCA.

DfES (2001) *Special Needs Code of Practice*. Nottingham: DfES.

DfES (2007) *The Early Years Foundation Stage*. Nottingham: DfES.

Hall, W. (2004) 'Inclusion – Special Needs' in Bold, C. (ed.) *Supporting Teaching and Learning*. London: Fulton.

Hall, W. (2005) 'Making the Most of the Teaching Assistant for Special Educational Needs' in Campbell, A. and Fairbairn, G. (eds) *Working with Support in the Classroom*. London: Paul Chapman.

Hall, W. (2007) 'Special Needs' in Hughes, P. (ed.) *Study Guide CD-ROM*. Liverpool: Liverpool Hope University.

Lee-Corbin, H. and Denicolo, P. *Recognising and Supporting Able Children in Primary Schools*. London: Fulton.

Ofsted (2002) *Evaluating Educational Inclusion: Guidance for Inspection & Schools*. London: Ofsted.

www.devon.gov.uk

11 Planning

DfES (2002) *Special Needs Code of Practice*. Nottingham: DfES.

DfES (2003) *Excellence and Enjoyment: A Strategy for Primary Schools*. Nottingham: DfES.

DfES (2004) *Excellence and Enjoyment: Learning and Teaching in the Primary Years*. Nottingham: DfES.

DfES (2004) *Primary National Strategy: Planning and Assessment for Learning*. Nottingham: DfES.

DfES (2007) *Excellence and Enjoyment: Learning and Teaching for Bilingual Children in the Primary Years*. Nottingham: DfES.

DfES (2007) *Making Great Progress. Schools with Outstanding Rates of Progression in Key Stage 2*. Nottingham: DfES.

DfES (2007) *Statutory Framework for the Early Years Foundation Stage*. Nottingham: DfES.

Quigley, C. (2004) *Key Skills for an Excellent and Enjoyable Curriculum*. Saddleworth: Focus Education.

12 Assessment for learning

ARG (2002) *Assessment for Learning: 10 Principles*. London: QCA.

DfES (2007) *Making Great Progress. Schools with Outstanding Rates of Progression in Key Stage 2*. Nottingham: DfES.

www.becta.org.uk.

13 Brain breaks and healthy schools

Blakemore, S. and Frith, U. (2007) *The Learning Brain: Lessons for Education*. Oxford: Blackwell.

Dennison, P. and G. (undated) *Brain Gym*. Edu-Kinesthetics, Inc. Available online at www. braingym.co.uk.

Naidooo, J. and Wills, J. *Health Promotion*. London: Bailliere Tindall.

NRC (2000) *How People Learn: Brain, Mind, Experience and School*. Washington, DC: National Academies Press. Available online at www.nap.edu/catalog.php?record_id=9853.

Smith, A. (2002) *The Brain's Behind it*. Stafford: NEP.

Smith, A. and Call, N. (2000) *The Alps Approach*. Stafford: NEP.

www.everychildmatters.gov.uk/health/healthyschools.
www.hull.ac.uk/ces/researchandconsultancy/FreeHealthySchoolMeals.html.
www.schoolfoodtrust.org.uk.
www.standards.dfes.gov.uk/sie/si/SfCC/goodpractice/nhss.

14 Language: English as an additional language and modern foreign languages

Brown, G. and Wragg, E.C. (1993) *Questioning*. London: Routledge.

DfES (2002) *Languages for All: Languages for Life*. Nottingham: DfES.

DfES (2005) *The Key Stage 2 Framework for Languages*. Nottingham: DfES.

DfES (2006) *Raising the Achievement of Bilingual Learners in Primary Schools*. Nottingham: DfES.

Dunne, R. and Wragg, E.C. (1993) *Effective Teaching (Leverhulme Primary Project)*. London: Routledge.

Gibbons, P. (1996) *Learning to Learn in a Second Language*. New School Wales: Primary English Teaching Association.

McFarlane, C. (1991) *Theme Work: A Global Perspective in the Primary Curriculum in the '90s*. Birmingham: Development Education Centre.

Neate, B. (1999) *Finding Out About Finding Out*. London: Hodder & Stoughton.

Wragg, E.C. and Brown, G. (1993) *Explaining*. London: Routledge.

15 Thinking skills in the curriculum

De Bono, E. (1993) *Teach Your Child How to Think*. London: Penguin.

De Bono, E. (2000) *Six Thinking Hats*. London: Penguin.

Feuerstein, R., Rand, Y., Hoffman, M.B. and Miller, R. (1980) *Instrumental Enrichment: An Intervention Programme for Cognitive Modifiability*. Baltimore, MA: University Park Press.

Fisher, R. (2005) *Teaching Children to Think*. London: Nelson.

Lipman, M., Sharp, A. and Oscanyan, F. (1980) *Philosophy in the Classroom*. Princeton, NJ: Temple University Press.

Wallace, B., Maker, J., Cave, D. and Chandler, S. (2004) *Thinking Skills and Problem Solving*. London: Fulton, NACE.

www.nace.co.uk.tasc/.
www.sapere.net.

16 Managing and leading a class teaching team

Dryden, G. and Vos, J. (2005) *The New Learning Revolution*. Staffordshire: Network Continuum Press.

Dunham, J. (1992) *Stress in Teaching*. London: Routledge.

Hoyle, E. (1980) 'Professionalization and Deprofessionalization in Education' in Hoyle, E. and Hegarty, J. (eds) *World Yearbook of Education: Professional Development of Teacher*. London: Kogan Page.

Institute for Innovation and Improvement (2005) *Leading Improvement in Improvement Leaders' Guide*. Warwick: NHS.

NCSL (2004) *Leading from the Middle*. Nottingham: NCSL.

Robb, J. and Letts, H. (1996) *Creating Kids Who Can*. London Hodder & Stoughton.

Seddon, L. (2007) *The Subject Leader, A Changing Role*. Presentation at Liverpool Hope University, February 2007.

Senge, P. (2000) *The Dance of Change*. London: Bearley.

Wood, E. (2006) '*Managing Other Adults in the Classroom*' in Arthur, J., Grainger, T. and Wray, D. (eds) *Learning to Teach in the Primary School*. London: RoutledgeFalmer.

www.innovation-unit.co.uk.

17 Schools as learning communities

Chambers, M., Powell, G. and Claxton, G. (2004) *Building 101 Ways to Learning Power*. Bristol: TLO.

Claxton, G. (2000) *Wise-Up*. London: Bloomsbury.

Claxton, G. (2005) *Building Learning Power*. Bristol: TLO.

DfES (2004) *Pedagogy and Practice*. Nottingham: DfES.

Worrall, N. and Noden, C. (2006) *Pupils Experience of Learning in NLC*. Nottingham: NCSL.

18 Integrated children's services, extended schools and other agencies

Clemens, S., Gilby, N., Mackey, T., Mason, J. and Ullman, A. (2005) 'Extended Services in Schools: Baseline Survey of Maintained Schools' BMRB Social Research from the teachernet website. Available online at www.teachernet.gv.uk./wholeschool/extendedschools/research.

DCSF (2007) *Extended Schools: Building on Experience*. Nottingham: DfES.

DfES, HO, DH (2003) *Every Child Matters*. London: HMSO.

DfES, HO, DH (2004) *ECM Next Steps*. London: HMSO.

DfES, HO, DH (2004) *ECM: Change for Children in Health Services*. London: HMSO.

DfES, HO, DH (2005) *Common Core of Skills and Knowledge for the Children's Workforce* (updated 2007). London: HMSO.

DfES (2005) *Extended Schools: Providing Opportunities and Services for All*.

Hughes, P. (2006) 'Education and Integrating Children's Services' in Sharp, J., Ward, S. and Hankin, L. (eds) *Education Studies: An Issues-based Approach*. Exeter: Learning Matters.

Knowsley MBC (2005) *Shaping the Future: Knowsley Governors' Conference Papers*. Liverpool: Knowsley MBC.

Laming, A. (2003) *Victoria Climbie Inquiry Report*. Nottingham: DfES.

www.continyou.org.uk (Building Learning Communities).

Index

Note: numbers in italics indicate figures and tables.